Effective Multi-Unit Leadership

*To Sheenagh, Maxim, Mum and Dad
and all my students (past and present) on the
Multi-Unit Leadership and Strategy Programme at BCBS.*

Effective Multi-Unit Leadership

Local Leadership in Multi-Site Situations

CHRIS EDGER
Birmingham City University, UK

Routledge
Taylor & Francis Group

LONDON AND NEW YORK

First published 2012 by Gower Publishing

Published 2016 by Routledge
2 Park Square, Milton Park, Abingdon, Oxfordshire OX14 4RN
711 Third Avenue, New York, NY 10017, USA

First issued in paperback 2016

Routledge is an imprint of the Taylor & Francis Group, an informa business

Gower Applied Business Research
Our programme provides leaders, practitioners, scholars and researchers with thought provoking, cutting edge books that combine conceptual insights, interdisciplinary rigour and practical relevance in key areas of business and management.

British Library Cataloguing in Publication Data
Edger, Chris.
  Effective multi-unit leadership : local leadership in
  multi-site situations.
  1. Complex organizations--Management. 2. Span of control.
  3. Retail trade--Management. 4. Service industries--
  Management. 5. Hospitality industry--Management.
  I. Title
    658.4'02-dc23

Library of Congress Cataloging-in-Publication Data
Edger, Chris.
  Effective multi-unit leadership : local leadership in multi-site
  situations / by Chris Edger.
    p. cm.
  Includes bibliographical references and index.
  ISBN 978-1-4094-2432-1 (hardback)
  1. Leadership. 2. Management. I. Title.
  HD57.7.E32 2012
  658.4'092--dc23
                                                            2012011076

ISBN 13:978-1-138-25778-8 (pbk)
ISBN 13:978-1-4094-2432-1 (hbk)

Effective MUL Model
3Es ⟶ 3Cs ⟶ 3Ss

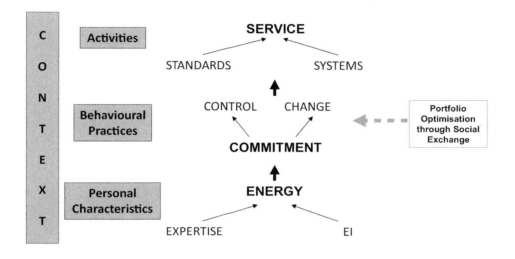

Contents

CONTEXT OF THE MULTI-UNIT ENTERPRISE

ACTIVITIES

CHARACTERISTICS

List of Figures

Abbreviations

AM	Assistant Manager
BCBS	Birmingham City Business School
BRC	British Retail Consortium
BHI	Bartrus Hollweg International
BOGOF	Buy One Get One Free`
BRAG	Black, Red, Amber and Green report
CCTV	Closed Circuit Television
CEO	Chief Executive Officer
CIPD	Chartered Institute of Personnel and Development
CRB	Criminal Records Bureau
CVP	Customer Value Package
DCF	Discounted Cash Flow
DGCS	Delivering Great Customer Service
DMS	Diploma of Management Studies
3 Es	Energy, EI and Expertise
EBITDA	Earnings Before Interest Tax Depreciation and Amortisation
EDLP	Every Day Low Price
EFQM	European Framework for Quality Management
EI	Emotional Intelligence
EMEA	Europe, Middle East and Asia
Epos	Electronic Point of Sale
EPS	Earnings per Share
ER	Employee Relations
ERP	Enterprise Resource Planning
ESRC	Economic and Social Research Council
EVP	Executive Vice President
F&B	Food and Beverages
FMCG	Fast Moving Consumer Goods
FT	*Financial Times*
FTE	Full Time Equivalent

GM	General Manager
HBR	Harvard Business Review
HIPO	High Potential
HRD	Human Resource Director
HR	Human Resources
HRM	Human Resource Management
F&B	Food and Beverage
IBM	International Business Machines
ILM	Institute of Leadership and Management
KPI	Key Performance Indicator
KM	Kitchen Manager
M&A	Merger and Acquisition
LL	Local Leaders
MD	Managing Director
MNC	Multi-National Corporation
MTQ	Mental Toughness Questionnaire
MUL	Multi-Unit Leader
MUM	Multi-Unit Manager
NED	Non-Executive Director
NPS	Net Promoter Score
NSBA	National Schools Board Association
OECD	Organisation for Economic and Commercial Development
OSM	Operational Services Manager
P&L	Profit and Loss
POS	Point of Sale
POSE	Portfolio Optimisation through Social Exchange
POV	Point of View
PRP	Profit Related Pay
Q&A	Question and Answer
RBM	Retail Business Manager
R&T	Recruitment and Training
ROM	Regional Operations Manager
RM	Regional Manager
ROI	Return on Investment
3 Ss	Service, Systems and Standards
SE	Senior Executive
SET	Social Exchange Theory
SEP	Service Excellence Programme
SKU	Stock Keeping Unit
SMC	Service Management Concept

SOM	Service Operations Manager
SPF	Service Personality Framework
SVP	Senior Vice President
TGROW	Topic, Goal, Reality, Opportunity, Will
TQM	Total Quality Management
UK	United Kingdom
UM	Unit Manager
US	United States
VAT	Value Added Tax
VP	Vice President

About the Author

Professor Chris Edger holds the chair of Multi-Unit Leadership at Birmingham City Business School (BCBS), Birmingham City University, UK. He also teaches at Warwick Business School, UK, where he is the winner of several teaching excellence awards on the Warwick MBA Programme.

Chris has over 20 years of senior leisure and retail multi-unit operations, sales and support expertise working for domestic and internationally-owned multi-site companies. During his career he has held Area Management, Operations Director (400+ units) and Sales MD positions. In addition he has also worked in support function capacities as a New Concepts Executive (conceiving, refining and rolling out new brands) and Commercial Director (covering Purchasing, Franchising, Property and M&A integration). Most recently he and his team won the 2010 Personnel Today 'HR Impact of the Year' Award in his capacity as the Executive Director of HR, Service and Productivity at one of the UK's largest leisure companies (22 brands and 2,041 units).

His specialist teaching areas on the Multi-Unit Leadership and Strategy Programme at BCBS www.bcu.ac.uk/mul (shortlisted for the CIPD 'Learning and Development' Award in 2011) are Service Leadership and Operational Improvement and Innovation within multi-site service contexts. Chris also provides specialist coaching, training and consultancy advice to a range of multi-unit organisations relating to MUL development and performance. He can be contacted at chris@localleaders.co.uk.

Chris has a PhD in International HRM and Cross-Border Mergers and Acquisitions (ESRC Award, Warwick Business School), MBA and DMS (Nottingham Business School), MSc(Econ) with distinction (London School of Economics and Political Science) and BSc (Hons) with University Prize for academic performance (Brunel University).

Acknowledgements

This book has benefitted from the academic contributions, insights and advice of many colleagues/students over the past few years; not least Professor Gerald Noone O.B.E (Newcastle and Leuven), Professor Chris Prince, Dr Clinton Bantock, Stephen Willson (BCBS), Professor Duncan Angwin (Oxford Brookes), Emeritus Professor Mike Terry (Warwick), Dr Amanda Goodall (Bonn and Cass), Dr Taman Powell (Cardiff), Dr Nollaig Heffernan (Ecole Hotelier Lausanne) and all the Unit Managers and MULs on the Multi-Unit Leadership and Strategy Programme at BCBS.

From a commercial perspective I would especially like to thank Helen Webb (Retail and Logistics HRD, Sainsbury's), Ian Burke (Executive Chairman and CEO, Rank), Reg Sindall (EVP Group Resources, Burberry), Simon Longbottom (MD, Greene King), Kevin Todd (President and CEO, Rosinter Restaurants, Russia) Sara Weller (ex-MD, Argos and NED Lloyds Bank and United Utilities) and Professor Martin Reynolds (BCBS) for reviewing various draught chapters of the book, making invaluable comments over the duration of its writing.

Thanks also to the following multi-unit practitioners/experts for their various insights and contributions since 2007; Liz Phillips (Retail HRD, Mitchells and Butlers), Sue Waldock (Group HRD, Rank), Paul Daynes (HRD, St Gobain Building Distribution), Caroline Hollings (HRD, Greene King), Mike Balfour (founder, Fitness First), David Jones (CEO, Lanner), John Woodward (CEO, Busy Bees UK), Kadisha Lewis-Roberts, (Director of L&D, Mitchells and Butlers), Kevin Allcock (Operations Director, Mecca), Steve Cash (Brand Operations Director, Harvester), Mark Taylor (Chief People Officer, Burberry), Michelle Wilkinson (Global Head of Talent, Burberry), Nick Rowe (Chairman, POD), Clive Clinton (ex-Greggs), John Holberry (ex-MD C&C), Fiona Holberry (Marketing Director, Wilkinsons), Peter Blakemore (CEO, Spar Blakemore), Nick Andrews (ex-Operations Director, Lloyds Bank), Peter Martin (Owner, Peach Factory), James Hyde (Korn Ferry WHM), Nick Wylde (Stanton Chase),

Adam Fowle (ex-CEO Mitchells and Butlers), Adam Martin (ex-Marketing Director, Mitchells and Butlers), Saudagar Singh (Group HRD, Mitchells and Butlers), Roger Moxham (CEO, Barracuda), Richard Cave (Operations Director, Gala Coral), Paul Willcock (MD, Genting Casinos), Andy Vaughan (Strategy Director, Sodexo), Lee Wooley (Head of L&D, Stonegate), Mark Stobert (DRHG), Paul Clowes (Group Display Manager, Signet), Kevin Gill (Head Coach, GB Olympic Shooting), Vicky Quin (Learning and Development Manager, Nandos), John Hegarty (founder, BPA), Deborah Kemp (CEO, De Vere), Bronagh Kennedy (Company Secretary, Severn Trent), Alasdair Murdoch (CEO, Gourmet Burger Company), Piers Tilbury (Art Director, Severn House), Lee Clarke (CEO, Landscape), Hamish Roberton (BDA), Tom Doherty (MD, Retail Solutions), Bryn Thomas (Strategy Director, Peugeot Franchise), Simon Hale (Operations Director, Waste Recycling Group), Jeremy Townsend (CFO, Rentokil), Chief Constable Simon Cole (Leicestershire Constabulary), Gary Harris (Deputy Chairman, British Rowing), Robin Young (ex-COO, Bradford and Bingley), Gary John (ex-SVP, Burger King) and Andrew Kitching (HRD, Booker).

Finally, I wish to acknowledge the profound influence of the idiosyncratic multi-unit branding genius Tony Hughes (founder TGI UK, ex-Director B&Q and M&B, currently NED Restaurant Group) upon my multi-site commercial career. Thank you for the MVP (Most Valuable Player) Award in 1995. From an academic standpoint I would like to pay tribute to Professor David Guest (Kings College, University of London), Professor Anthony Glees (University of Buckingham), Professor Michael Pinto-Duschinsky (Brunel University) and Professor Tony Watson (Nottingham University) – all great teachers and mentors during my earlier academic 'forays'. *Rerum cognoscere causas.*

'Unto whomsoever much is given, of him shall be much expected'
Luke 12:48

Context of the Multi-Unit Enterprise

1

Introduction

According to OECD data, the *service sector* represents at least 70 per cent of employment and gross value added (GVA) in developed economies; in the UK and US it accounts for approximately 75 per cent GVA (OECD 2005, Tily 2006 and Monaghan 2012). Multi-Unit enterprises (otherwise known as retail, leisure, hospitality or service 'chains' or 'multiples') dominate every aspect of the *service sector* landscape and are one of the most common organisational types in developed economies. Today, their highly geared, capital intensive land-based models face disruption from emerging technologies, changing consumer preferences and challenging economic conditions but, surprisingly, there is little research relating to both their organisational form and, alarmingly, their *key* managerial cohort; the Multi-Unit Leader (otherwise known as area or regional operations managers).

With regard to structure and operational configuration, a seminal HBR (Harvard Business Review) article by Garvin and Levesque on multi-unit enterprises states that; 'despite its prevalence, the multi-unit enterprise has received little attention from academics and consultants over the years' (2008: 2). More pertinently, given the subject of this book, Multi-Unit Leaders (MULs) have been equally overlooked with Mutch noting that they 'have been neglected in the historical record' (2006: 354) and DiPietro et al observing that there has been 'limited research done in the area of multi-unit management' (2007: 525).

Sitting between the Centre and the local Unit this *key* cohort of employees occupies a complex and ambiguous position in the organisational hierarchy. On the one hand they are expected by the Centre to seamlessly implement strategy and policies within their districts or regions whilst delivering outstanding brand standards and sales-led service, but, in doing so, are faced by a myriad of challenges and counter-forces at Unit level. How do they optimise performance in this classic middle-management space bedevilled with competing (and sometimes contradictory) interests, claims and demands?

This book, based on extensive research during the economic crisis that unfolded in developed economies during the period 2007–2012, is an attempt to address this question by asking; what are the key activities of MULs, how do they discharge their responsibilities effectively and what are their most important personal characteristics? It is aimed at both academics and practitioners. From an academic perspective this book should make a contribution in an area that has been largely overlooked, hopefully opening further avenues for debate and research. For practitioners the book offers a best-practice approach to Multi-Unit Leadership that should provide insights which lead to increased individual *capacity* for action and/or accelerated performance amongst this vital cohort of employees.

1.1 Why Multi-Unit Leaders?

The question that arises from the title of this book is, first, why the term 'leader' rather than 'manager' is applied to this middle management cohort and, second, why the preface 'effective' is used. Previous texts apply the generic nomenclature of 'multi-unit manager' (Umbreit 1989, Ryan 1992, Goss-Turner 1999, Di Pietro et al 2007); why are they classified differently in this book? It is the contention of this text that they merit such a term because of what they do and how they are perceived.

Research for this book established that – in addition to fulfilling normal managerial activities of planning and implementing – effective area managers practiced what might be termed *'portfolio optimization through social exchange'* (POSE) whereby they motivated their followers to implement operational systems, enforce brand standards and execute high levels of service resulting in superior sales, through means of the *law of reciprocity* (Gouldner 1960, Blau 1963, 1964, Cohen and Bradford 1989, Cropanzano and Mitchell 2005). With a high level of interdependence with their followers and limitations being placed upon their formal authority – due to the Centre's strategic policy making capability – they gained legitimacy and consent through fostering indebtedness and mutual collaboration. That is to say, rather than being passive conduits for their company's strategic and procedural frameworks and objectives, successful area managers exercised a high degree of tacit skill in firstly, interpreting, filtering and prioritising these objectives and frameworks, and, secondly, ensuring implementation through a judicious use of *locally applied exchange-based mechanisms*. Effective MULS transacted with their followers through *commitment, control and change-based* behavioural practices which were moulded around the types of inspiration, personal, task, relationship and position-related *currencies* of social exchange described by Cohen and Bradford (1989). Furthermore these *exchange currencies* could be sub-divided into four transmission mechanisms; *mutual goal attainment, free market exchange, compensated costs* and *uncovering hidden value.*

To this extent, in line with contemporary definitions of 'leaders' – managers displaying positive behavioural and cognitive attributes that *transcend* narrow technical abilities (Zaleznick 1977, Yukl 2006) – they can legitimately be described as MULs rather than multi-unit managers. Indeed, the perception of other actors within the multi-unit enterprise continually validated this perspective; one Regional Director commenting that he saw high performing area managers as 'superb tacticians, negotiators and psychologists ... who are highly versed in the complex skills of local leadership'.

The notion of *effective* MULs is also significant. Within all multi-unit enterprises researched for this book, there was a bell-curve of area management performance, with the most effective operators delivering consistently high performance (in *relative* comparison with their peers) with regard to employee, customer and operating metrics. Why? Some clues are given at unit-level where employees were apt to differentiate between those MULs who provided clarity, motivation, protection, direction, 'possibilities and potential solutions' rather than those didn't; particularly, as subsequent chapters will elucidate, during times of great uncertainty and change. Hence, the denomination effective MUL: *a high performing cohort of local leaders who, whatever the circumstances, optimize their portfolios through the imaginative application of exchange-based behavioural practices.*

1.2 What is the Multi-Unit Enterprise?

The multi-unit enterprise is defined as a geographically dispersed organisation built up from *standard* units such as branches, service centres, hotels, restaurants and stores (franchised or managed) which are aggregated into larger geographic groupings such as districts, regions and divisions. These organisations cross many industrial sectors such as retail banking, clothing, grocery and food retail, hospitality and leisure. Olsen et al provide a useful definition of multi-unit enterprises as organisations that 'compete in an industry with more than one unit of like concept or theme' (1992: 3). Their economic importance is signified by the fact that prior to the credit crunch in 2007 it was estimated that multi-unit firms constituted 10 out of 25 of the largest employers globally; in the US multi-unit organisations generated \$717bn in sales (Garvin and Levesque 2008).

1.3 History of the Multi-Unit Enterprise

In the late nineteenth century the growth of multi-unit businesses, which offered scale and product consistency, disrupted 'independents'. Previously, in the case of UK retail grocery, food and provisions had come from small independent grocers; skilled craftspeople (usually members of a guild) who, having served an apprenticeship, chopped and ground sugar, blended tea and mixed spices for their customers. Other vital necessities such as eggs, milk and bacon were provided by farmers at open air markets, and specialist shops such as cheesemongers, oil and colourmen (household goods) and tallow-chandlers serviced demand for other basic goods. Inevitably, the main issue with this supply chain was its variability and dependability, with product adulteration and short measures being a common problem. Another complaint was the feeling that traders and merchants could not be wholly exempt from the charge, in an unregulated market with a lack of strong competition, of fixing prices, leading Adam Smith to observe that 'people of the same trade seldom meet together, even for merriment and diversion, but the conversation ends in a conspiracy against the public, or in some contrivance to raise prices' (Benson and Ugolini 2003: 9).

There were four inter-related factors that led to the growth of the multi-unit enterprise in Europe and the US. First, industrialisation based upon mass production techniques, derived from inventions such as steam powered machinery, led to a growing urban population which concentrated demand in tight geographical areas. Second, the mass production of cheaply priced goods such as food, shoes and clothing opened up broader consumer channels. Third, the economic buying power of the new industrialised working classes and urban middle classes (whose real income per head doubled in the late nineteenth century) gave rise to high demand for consumer goods. Fourth, the development of a railway infrastructure revolutionised the supply chain, enabling mass produced goods to be transported in bulk to growing urban centres to service this growing demand.

The earliest multi-unit retailers in the UK were newsagents, such as WH Smith and J Menzies, which had established a large network of outlets within and beside railway stations by the 1860s. There then followed two distinct phases in the development of multi-unit enterprises (Jeffreys 1954). Between 1870 and 1890 multiples selling footwear, groceries, meat and household goods spread throughout the UK. From 1890 until 1914, menswear, chemists and variety store chains followed. These chains adopted strategies which are familiar in the present time, deploying 'economies of scale in buying, economies of specialisation in administration and economies of standardisation in selling' (Jeffreys 1954: 27). By 1900 multiples had 12 per cent of total sales of food and household stores, growing to 20 per cent by 1920.

In tandem with this spread in multiple chains, manufacturers began to develop national brands in order to generate a return on their capital investment. Confectionary firms such as Fry's and soap manufacturers like Pears began to brand their products, communicating directly to consumers in order generate 'must stock' status with retailers. Emphasising both the functional and emotional attributes of their products, branded goods producers conducted sophisticated advertising campaigns in newspapers, billboards and, in the early twentieth century, emergent forms of broadcast media. They also deployed large 'travelling' sales forces that, in addition to selling product into multiple and independent channels, visited outlets to check availability and monitor displays.

The major innovation in grocery retailing occurred in the US in 1916 when Clarence Saunders, announcing that his aim was to 'slay the demon of high prices', opened the world's first self-service grocery shop in Memphis, Tennessee (Seth and Randall 1999). In 1930 the first supermarket, King Kullen, opened in Queens, New York, positioning itself as 'the World's Greatest Price Wrecker'. Getting customers to select their own goods from the shelves proved popular with customers who appreciated both increased speed of service and the lower prices associated with a format that carried less labour overhead. In the inter-war years in the UK, although food retail stores had become larger and more hygienic with service innovation such as home delivery becoming a key differentiator for some operators, multiples failed to mimic their US counterparts.

It was not until 1947 that the self-serve market concept arrived in the UK, proving just as successful with consumers, spreading quickly through chains such as Sainsbury's and Fine Fare. As the growth of motor transport ownership increased and the suburbs extended out from major conurbations, the next innovation, firstly in the US and then in Europe (especially France and the UK), involved large scale unit development with the introduction of superstores (25,000 square feet) in the 1970s and then hypermarkets (50,000 square feet) in the 1980s. Size enabled further economies of scale to drive down pricing (helped by the scrapping of retail price maintenance, and bar code innovation in the late 1960s and 1970s), with the added benefit of extra space for non-food products (principally clothing, electrical and white goods) which had the dual benefit of extending the range for consumers whilst bolstering operator margins.

This trend towards scale was copied by other multi-unit retail firms. From the 1960s in the US (1970s in the UK) out-of-town malls and retail parks anchored by food retail, bulky goods and fashion began spreading next to arterial routes near major conurbations. These schemes were funded by developers and then sold on to pension funds or major property companies, attracted by the prospect of attractive covenants and high long-term financial yields. Such developments proved extremely successful in the 1990s and early twenty-first century as consumers, backed by cheap credit and rising incomes, sated their desire for cheap appliances, furniture and clothing. A parallel development, the rise in cheap imports from China and Asia, also fuelled consumption at this time as some product categories deflated in price over the period.

With regard to the leisure and hospitality sector, format standardisation came later than retail, its emergence being connected to the growth of air and motor transport, increasing amount of leisure time and rising levels of discretionary spend. Until the mid twentieth century the sector was dominated by a high level of owner-managers and self-employed entrepreneurs. In the case of hotels, innovators such as Conrad Hilton in the US began the distribution of upscale standard units with high levels of cleanliness, amenity and service. Mid-scale operators such as Holiday Inn followed, seizing competitive advantage against the variable and fragmented motel sector in the US. In the case of fast food and casual dining, entrepreneurs such as Ray Kroc who, having bought the McDonald's concept from the founder in 1952, designed a standard offer (mimicking extant chains such as White Castle) that could be duplicated and rolled out in both managed and franchised formats – which outsourced capital risk – in the US. Throughout the 1960s and 1970s standardised chains such as Burger King, Taco Bell, Bonanza Steakhouse and Wendy's proliferated next to interstate highways and in burgeoning suburbs. These branded operations benefitted from adopting many of the 'lean' principles of mass production and modern retailing (Levitt 1972, Schmenner 1986). Through standardising operations, consolidating the supply chain with bulk ordering and prescribed production/service delivery systems, these formats, offering consistency and cheap prices, created demand for out-of-home dining which by the late 1990s accounted for over one third of food consumption in the US (Jones 1999).

As with retail, the UK followed US trends in hospitality and leisure chain growth. The 1980s saw the swift roll-out of US chains such as McDonalds and Pizza Hut, allied to urban casual dining inventions such as Pizza Express. One of the main mitigating factors in the emergence of earlier chain scale, however, related to the unique leisure industry structure in the UK. The tied-trade pub sector, where brewing companies owned licensed properties which they let to tenants who had to purchase the brewer's beers, dominated the leisure landscape from the mid nineteenth century where, through a number of mergers and acquisitions, by the late 1970s seven major companies dominated licensed retailing in the UK, owning 35,000 tied outlets (Mutch 2006). Although these companies also had company managed units within their portfolio, they were fundamentally production (ie driven by the need to market and distribute beer) rather than retail orientated. Early chains such as Berni Inns in the 1960s, which offered consistency and affordability, made some impact on the brewers' estate positioning but it was the 1991 Beer Orders, which resulted in the split of brewing and retail assets, that accelerated casual dining chain scale in the UK. In the early twenty-first century the old brewers have been transformed into retailers; most notably Mitchells and Butlers (formerly owned by Bass Plc) which acquired and developed a number of food-led brands such as Browns, Vintage Inns, Toby Carvery and Harvester.

1.4 Disruptive Forces

In recent times the multi-enterprise model, with vast levels of sunk capital in physical assets, has faced considerable disruption from technology ('click versus brick'), consumer expectations (requirement for quality, service AND value) and severe economic conditions (the banking and sovereign debt crises squeezing consumer discretionary spend).

1.4.1 ON-LINE; THREAT OR OPPORTUNITY?

The switch in consumer behaviour from buying goods and services from land-based channels to the web is becoming increasingly pronounced. In 2010 UK on-line retail spend was estimated to have reached £44bn, in the US $263bn. By 2011 it was estimated that there were 80m visits to on-line services per day, with a total of 1,000 purchases per second (Pagano 2011b). For instance, over the period 2006–2010, UK internet clothes sales rose by 152 per cent (Wallop 2011). The web has offered consumers greater visibility of product and price, facilitating instant transactions for 'time poor' consumers. Its utility as an informational space where instant price comparisons can be made has been game-changing. Consumers can now identify what they want and make instant price comparisons as to when and where the cheapest option can be purchased. In 2011 the BRC (in conjunction with Google) estimated that in the UK 'retail searches' on mobile phones were up 168 per cent on the previous year (BRC 2011b). Price comparison apps have been launched by companies such as Amazon in order to enable customers to make mobile price comparisons, turning some multi-unit enterprises into showrooms, whilst other organisations such as New Look in the UK have launched new apps to enable their customers to scan their barcodes in store and then buy on-line. Verdict Research estimates that, by 2014, 79 per cent of UK consumers will use their mobile 'smart phones' for shopping, overtaking 'PC access purchasing' (Butler 2011).

A consequence of these changes is that certain categories of goods have been commoditised to such a degree that price is their only differentiating factor. Outlets selling books, cards, video games, music, value clothing, electrical and white goods have been most affected by the on-line revolution with consumers, aided by price comparison sites, increasingly opting to transact on-line. Partly in response to this trend, many retailers have set up on-line 'order and deliver' services but in doing so have cannibalised sales from their core channels, further threatening the relevance and viability of their physical estate (Felsted 2011). Supermarket retail firms that had significantly increased their 'non-food' space in the 1990s and 2000s in order to sell these product categories have reviewed their 'race for scale and space' approach (Wallop and Ruddick 2012). Indeed, some retailers (such as Littlewoods in the UK) have opted to vacate the High Street and move to a totally web-based model, whilst others such as House of Fraser have created 'virtual' stores – High Street spaces where consumers can search for and order products on-line, choosing their method of delivery – trends which are certain to accelerate over time (Pagano 2011b).

Many firms have optimised the opportunities presented by the web, enabling them to adopt a *ubiquitous* 'multi-' or 'omni-channel' strategy (Pagano 2011b, Terazano 2011). Why? First, the medium has enabled providers to showcase their service proposition. Using the web as a 'virtual i-Street' shop window, certain organisations have invested heavily in search engine applications to route browsers to higher margin product areas and/or additional product and service amenities in a 'market place' format that goes beyond what they offer within store (Wallop 2012). Second, it has helped companies utilise their assets more effectively through driving volume via 'click and collect', promotions and direct marketing. 'Click and collect', a growing sales channel, allows customers to collect goods from store at their convenience rather than relying on 'timeslot deliveries' (Pagano 2011a). For instance in 2011, whilst overall on-line sales were up 25 per cent at John Lewis; 'click and collect' services were up 75 per cent. As Andy Street, the MD of this chain reflected;

> ... businesses that do not have a multi-channel capability will be challenged and those that are simply commoditised online and cannot add any complimentary services on the high street will disappear ... (Cave 2011: B5).

In the leisure sector, in particular, firms have been able to increase demand in non-peak periods through a combination of revised product formulation (offsetting margin erosion) and aggressive price promotion through couponing sites (such as vouchercloud.com). This has been a particularly effective weapon during the recent recession where, for instance, 'fast casual' dining operators in the UK have aggressively marketed cheap on-line voucher deals to attract diners, and hotel firms have bundled up all-inclusive offers during off-season. To this extent the web has proved extremely successful in smoothing demand, decreasing operator reliance on peak sales to recover lost overhead; although it has had consequences for overall margins (Goodman 2011). It is notable that the performance of fast food and casual dining, providing 'small treat' occasions, has been more 'sales resilient' during the recent downturn than the retail sector, leading some commentators to describe it as 'future proofed' against economic vicissitudes (Steiner 2012b). For instance, it is estimated by the Local Data Company and Allegra Strategies that, given the latent capacity in the 'food-on-the-go' sector in the UK (compared to densities in the US), branded coffee, fast food and bakery chains (such as Costa, Starbucks, Subway and Greggs) have continuing growth potential until 2018 (Wood 2012).

Third, the emergence of cloud-enabled 'wallet apps' and pre-payment capabilities on 'smart' mobile or tablet devices offers firms the opportunity to reduce their transaction costs, principally through decreased labour. Indeed, innovation relating to means and speed of payment through contactless 'wave and pay' transactions (Weyer 2012) could herald the third major speed of transaction revolution (behind self-service and barcode scanning) in little under a century, rendering many till-based operatives redundant. One company surveyed during the course of this research was already in final stage simulation testing of a new in-store app-based smartphone customer transaction system which, potentially, could lead to reductions of 20–30 per cent in staffing costs. Remaining staff would fulfil a more knowledge-based function, advising customers on transactions rather than policing their payment.

1.4.2 CHANGING CONSUMER EXPECTATIONS

In developed countries the increasing sophistication of consumers, due to education and greater access to information, has empowered them to make more informed retail choices. They are capable, either intuitively or through rational analysis, to understand the proposition on offer; they then expect their experience to match or exceed their expectations. This has created a major conundrum for firms that operate low cost strategies. If their offer can be matched or exceeded by other providers how do they maintain a degree of competitive advantage? Some multi-unit businesses have addressed this through constant improvements in efficiency (through technology and supply chain enhancements) and productivity (increasing staff contribution per hour through better deployment and labour management systems). However, as Philip Clarke, CEO of Tesco, the UK's largest food multiple acknowledged after announcing his company's first profit warning in 20 years – Tesco had run the UK business 'too hot' with regard to a lack of investment in amenity, product and labour and, consequently, a £400m investment was required to ensure, in addition to price, 'quality, range and service is ramped up … as consumers are becoming more discriminating in their discretionary spend' (Walsh 2012: B7).

This has profound implications for many businesses. The added on-cost of bolting quality and service attributes to a low-cost product go against the grain of many multi-unit enterprises' business model dynamic (Pagano 2012). In order to pursue this route companies need to invest far more in the cost infrastructure of the business and, if they pass these costs on to the customer, move their businesses into dangerous mid-market terrains. In order to leverage their space more effectively retailers have resorted to two main strategies. First, many have engaged in 'format blurring' (Berman 2011; 8), enlarging their range and in-store *service provision* beyond their core offering (ie Walgreens in the US), in order to increase relevance, frequency and total spend per visit. For instance supermarkets have now included doctors' surgeries, hairdressers, opticians and dentists among their on-site offering. Second, many retailers (such as Best Buy) have reviewed their 'scale versus efficiency' models, opting to develop smaller, but higher margin, formats (Blackden 2012, Wallop 2012).

For instance, in the case of food retailing over the past decade, firms such as Tesco and Sainsbury's have successfully driven both sales and margin through the acquisition and organic development of convenience estates. Such a move ameliorates a trend towards smaller basket size purchases in large stores with a grocery store network that captures 'top up' occasionality. In the US. the giant behemoth Walmart has signalled its intention to enter the convenience sector, whilst in the UK its Asda subsidiary bought the Netto chain in 2011 to advance its convenience-led ambitions, reducing the average size of its stores from an average of 50,000 to 40,000 square feet (Craven 2012a).

1.4.3 ECONOMIC CONDITIONS

Completing this set of disruptive forces for multi-unit enterprises has been the economic crisis precipitated by the banking collapse in 2008, sovereign debt debacle in 2011 and euro currency crisis in 2012. Up to this point cheap credit underpinned by low interest rates and increased access to capital, through instruments such as property equity release schemes and attractively low introductory credit card rates (leading onto extortionate rates of interest), had fuelled an unprecedented retail consumer boom in developed economies. However, bad lending decisions and the subsequent collapse of the complex structured financial product 'system' within the banking supply chain meant that access to easy capital for consumers dried up. Consumption dropped off, with the GDPs of many leading economies seeing falls unprecedented in modern times. Unemployment rates rose, real incomes (due to wage freezes) dropped and levels of discretionary spend fell dramatically (Jopson 2012a). This has led to so-called 'hour glass' economies in developed nations, where the middle class consumer was squeezed between the very affluent and poor, leading to profound changes in buying behaviour (Frean 2011). In 2011 and 2012 any prospect of a return to sustained growth was stymied by the sovereign debt crisis, where developed economies (most notably PIIGS; Portugal, Ireland, Italy, Greece and Spain), having built expensive social welfare infrastructures unconnected to realistic levels of national income, moved towards default, threatening international financial 'contagion' through the collapse (or restructuring) of the euro currency.

Another economic factor that has threatened the viability of many multi-unit business models has been the increase in commodity prices, fuelling High Street price inflation and impacting consumption. The economic growth of developing countries such as China, Brazil and India has led to urbanisation and the sharp growth in demand for commodities such as wheat, cotton and natural minerals. Speculators have also added to the problem through commodity hoarding, encouraging artificial price distortions (Hall 2011b). This has forced up prices, creating price inflation for consumers in the developed world. The degree to which this is a temporary or permanent phenomenon is arguable; what is a matter of fact is that these developing nations are generating consumptive momentum that is likely to endure for the next 30–40 years. Commodity production or output increases will be needed to offset price rises; however, there is a finite level, in the absence of spectacular technological and scientific innovation, at which these essential items can be harvested and mined.

1.4.4 DISRUPTIVE EFFECTS

Taken together, the effects of these pressures upon multi-unit enterprises – squeezing item sales and margins – has been dramatic given the fact that they have high fixed operating costs (a consequence of heavy labour and property charges) that are difficult to mitigate. Those who have failed to successfully combine 'click with brick' or a 'market place with differentiated market space' have either gone bankrupt or had to scale back their estates. The Centre for Retail Research in the UK estimated that from 2008 to 2011, 148 medium to large multi-unit enterprises had collapsed, affecting 5,742 sites and 136,182 employees (Steiner 2012a). High profile casualties included publicly owned companies such as Woolworths (819 stores) and private equity-based firms such as Threshers (1,200 stores), Focus DIY (178), Habitat (30), TJ Hughes (40), Barratts (191), Past Times (46), La Senza (102) and Birthdays (154). With the future of the value fashion chain Peacocks (660 stores) hanging in the balance in early 2012, Euler Hermes, a global retail credit insurer, commenting on the prospects for UK retail market stated;

> ... we definitely do forecast that there will be a number of defaults in the retail sector. We are currently maintaining our cover, but we are not extending it despite the fact we receive requests to do so on a regular basis ... electrical retailing and clothing are the two sectors of UK retailing about which Euler Hermes is most concerned ... the vast majority of the population can easily postpone fashionable purchases ... many (people) are in survival mode ... (Felsted 2012b: 18).

By 2010 it was estimated by CoStar that 10 per cent of US retail space was vacant. In the UK in 2011 the BRC (British Retail Consortium) published its finding that 11 per cent of the UK High Street was vacant, with landlords also reporting a sharp increase tenants requesting rent 'holidays' and reductions (BRC 2011a). Retail locations had become an even greater determinant of success, with 'category killing' super-centre malls and out of town locations accounting for an ever increasing share of footfall (BRC2012a). This issue was examined, at the behest of the UK government, by the 'retail expert' Mary Portas, who recommended solutions including the removal of local car parking charges, reductions in business rates for independent stores and an increased emphasis upon 'community' through venues such as bingo halls (Portas 2011). Indeed, in addition to the aforementioned bankruptcies, many chains had taken action, or announced plans, to scale back their estates during the period 2008–2011, with the following commentary becoming common fare within the financial press;

> New Look, the value fashion chain, could close up to 100 stores during the next three years if it cannot secure better deals from landlords ... it has too many 'duplicate' stores with overlapping catchment areas ...It has also launched a successful mobile site and 'click and collect' service ... Other retailers looking to trim their estates include the Arcadia Group (possibly) 500 stores ... Thorntons 180 stores ... Dixons which is closing half of its high Street stores ... (Jopson 2012b: 18).

Similar announcements on 'estate rationalisation' had already been made in 2011 and 2012 by other multi-unit enterprises including Lloyds Bank, Thomas Cook, Game, Mothercare, Clinton Cards, HMV and JJB. Profit warnings amongst retailers became more frequent in the latter part of 2011 as 'one fifth of all quoted retailers issued profit warnings in the last three months of 2011 – more than any other in the FTSE sector' (Felsted 2012a: 18). By contrast, the leisure sector (in spite of companies such as Esporta, Punch, Enterprise and Luminar closing units during 2011) fared better over this comparable period, with modest like-for-like sales growth figures being posted by 'recession respite' companies such as Whitbread, Mitchells and Butlers, Greene King, Greggs and McDonalds, due to consumers being willing to 'splash out on small value treats or experiences they value' (Goodman 2011). It should be noted, however, that whilst sales have remained resilient, margin has been diluted by lower pricing, discounting and heavy couponing by several enterprises operating within this sector.

1.5 Challenges of the Multi-Unit Firm

Combined with these disruptive forces there are a number of distinctive issues that emanate from the operation of the standard multi-unit model. The ability of multi-unit enterprises to mitigate their effects, harnessing the principal benefits of standardised scale, has a major influence on the performance of these enterprises. The main challenges faced by the multi-unit model fall into five categories, as follows;

1.5.1 OPTIMISING UNIT-BASED HUMAN CAPITAL

Standardised multi-unit enterprise retail and hospitality chains are heavily reliant on 'aesthetic' and functional human capital for their operational execution. Two major issues arise from this model: first, its necessary restriction of human autonomy due to standardisation and, second, due to labour being such a large percentage of sales, its dependence upon poorly paid service operatives to deliver the product offer. In the case of the former, unlike other structures such as the multi-divisional model, the multi-unit form places emphasis on limiting error by decreasing autonomous decision-making. In part this is a reaction to the fact that the Centre feels that its inability to supervise unit managers at an operational level compels it to, in some cases, create detailed rules and procedures in order, first, to satisfy itself that the units 'are doing as they are told', and, second, ensure that any regulatory investigation or inspection will find operator error, rather than Central processes being at fault for any breaches. For these reasons the central principles of 'lean' or Fordism – standardised mass production, repetition and procedural adherence – have been brought to bear in many multi-unit environments limiting staff capacity for innovation and self-expression.

Allied to this, the fact that many entry level jobs in multi-unit enterprises are perceived as having low status, being largely unskilled, poorly paid with long and/or inconvenient working hours, leads companies to wrestle with the conundrum as to how they can engage and motivate their 'inter-generational' mix of, (in many cases) part-time, female and migrant, front-line service providers to 'delight the customer' without increasing the labour ratio (Grugulis and Boskurt 2011). The problem is particularly acute with young Generation Y workers who are able express 'self' and identity through vehicles such as YouTube, Facebook, blogs and Twitter but are restricted by the strictures of the standard multi-unit environment; a juxtaposition that can lead to conflict between generational groups, resentment, detachment, resistance and (sometimes) sabotage. Added to which the workforce of many multi-unit organisations is rarely homogenous given their regional, national and, in some cases, international spread. Different socio-cultural behaviours need to be accounted for in designing a service-based offer. This is a non-trivial issue in an environment where multiple and frequent transactions take place, with numerous customer touchpoints.

1.5.2 CONSISTENCY OF STANDARDS

Given the number of units in multi-unit organisations and their wide geographical spread problems of time, distance and space constantly threaten consistency and dependability of the offer (Olsen et al 1992). Ensuring uniformity is difficult given the remote nature of the units and, in spite of technology and physical infrastructure, its dependence on *functional and emotionally-led* human execution makes it susceptible to quality, service and standards breakdowns. Spatial and span of control issues are the enemies of the coordination of standardised product quality and service. Consumers experiencing variable and indeterminate quality across a range of, supposedly, standard units are unlikely to trust the offer, leading to high levels of non-repeat business and low net promoter scores.

1.5.3 STANDARDISATION VERSUS CUSTOMISATION

In spite of this drive for consistency, one of the myths of multi-unit is that all firms impose total operational standardisation. Factors such as non-standard unit footprints (due to site availability constraints), regional tastes and customs, customer demographics, levels of ambient competition and differing local labour markets all impinge upon the operations of single site units. It should be understood that, in effect, each unit within a multi-unit portfolio operates within its own local micro-market, in which multi-unit firms often make an effort to customise their operations in order to maximise revenues. Some firms operate according to a principle of fixing perhaps 80 per cent of their operations, allowing the other 20 per cent to vary according to local needs. This tension between conformity and flexibility is a constant problem within the multi-unit model, with the Centre favouring uniformity (and therefore certainty) and the Unit arguing for greater operational latitude with regard to wages, layout, promotional offer and range. The dangers of increased customisation are obvious – complexity, sub-optimal decision-making and (potentially) increased cost – threatening the very premise upon which multiples were founded; namely, consistency and efficiency.

1.5.4 FORMAT AND CHANNEL PROLIFERATION

Multi-unit enterprises have a propensity, either organically or through acquisition, to develop new brands, formats or channels. Constant refreshment, innovation and adaptation are necessary in order to meet changing demands and requirements. Acquiring and/or developing new brands/formats or opening up additional multi-channel routes to market as an adjunct to existing offerings, is, however, problematic for the extant estate which might be threatened with capital and knowledge starvation to fund new ventures. In the case of new format development within existing brands, several format types (such as smaller 'micro click and collect' sites and 'pop ups' in retail and 'food mobiles' and 'wagons' in catering) can proliferate within any given chain, making the operation of the enterprise complicated. Also, given the vital importance of *location* to site performance, multi-unit chains will often designate units 'core' and 'non-core' leading to twin-track capital and people investment programmes. Again this is problematic to both consumers – who will notice inconsistency – and unit staff in the 'non-core' units who feel like victims of an informal class system; neglected and under threat, resenting their lack of access to resources in comparison to 'higher caste' members within the system.

Thus, constant brand development, format extension and/or site acquisitions, coupled with changing external micro-market dynamics, creates a high degree of complexity within the portfolio for both policy makers and the operational line. How do policy makers adapt their offers to a 'two-speed' estate? How does the operational line manage new 'omni-channel' innovation (integrating postal, internet and 'click and collect') alongside bricks and mortar operations? Often, firms will react to the changes in their estate profiling by re-shaping operational segmentation, geographies and responsibilities (usually at the beginning of financial years) in order to focus effort. Whilst rational from an organisational point of view, constant boundary revisions are extremely disruptive to relationships within the operational line.

1.5.5 CENTRE VERSUS LOCAL TENSIONS

One significant aspect of multi-unit enterprises is the existence of boundary tension and conflict between Centrally-based functions (such as Marketing, HR, Audit and Supply Chain) and field-based operations. On paper the Centre dictates strategy, pricing, promotions, policies and positioning whilst the field-based operation busies itself with flawless implementation. In practice, however, major issues arise when dislocations occur in communication and consultation with the operators on new guidance, initiatives or projects. A lack of information transmission both upwards and downwards through the enterprise due to the dispersion of units is a serious rate limiter in multi-unit enterprises.

In firms where a lack of coordination exists at the Centre and/or the firm is reacting quickly to regulatory or competitive pressures, constant requests for information and new dictats can seriously disrupt the operational rhythm of the business. Customer facing operators can be distracted by endless bureaucracy and administrative compliance rather than providing great quality service. The introduction of new technology since the mid-1990s which has enabled the Centre to communicate with Units in real time, might have given the Centre the illusion that it has more control when, in actual fact, its constant stream of requests and changes to procedure create anxiety, stress and despondency at Unit level resulting in reduced levels of commitment and discretionary effort.

1.6 The Multi-Unit Leader (MUL)

One of the most pivotal organisational actors in ameliorating some of the aforementioned challenges is the MUL (more commonly known as Retail Operations Manager, Area Manager or Regional Business Manager) who can be defined as somebody who is directly responsible for the performance spectrum of two or more standard managed or franchised units. Within the organisational hierarchy they typically report into a Vice President, Regional or Area Director but their main defining characteristic is that they have direct P&L accountability for a defined number of units. The questions addressed by this section are what do we know about their history and what does previous academic research tell us about them?

1.6.1 HISTORY OF THE ROLE

As multi-unit organisations grew in the late nineteenth century, more layers of senior management were created, the hierarchy of larger chains mimicking the command structure of mechanistic and bureaucratic forms of manufacturing organisations. At first, in the absence of central technology, these managers assumed a policing role at unit level, being titled 'agents', 'store supervisors' and 'store inspectors'. As businesses developed paper-based stock taking, pricing and merchandising and ledger systems these 'inspectors' ensured that units were run professionally according to company policy. However, in spite of this pre-supposition that these actors assumed a mainly auditing function, some commentators have suggested that area managers made a considerable impact on the genesis of multiple retailing (Mathias 1967). In the case of Liptons, which experienced significant growth from the late 1890s, Mathias notes that 'an infusion of management skill and strength also had to come at shop inspector level' (1967: 24). In the case of Boots, during the period of US ownership (1909–1933), one significant innovation was the introduction of the Territory Manager (Greenwood 1977), implying a more diverse set of responsibilities extending beyond the merely 'supervisory'.

One major innovation that has brought the importance of MUL into sharper focus has been the growth of franchise retail. For instance, in the US it is assumed that a significant factor in the 'McDonaldisation' of fast food offerings has been the area manager, although observers have noted how little is known about their early duties, responsibilities and impact (Ritzer 1993). However, given the systemisation of food production and strict franchising rules most contemporaneous analysis and research has indicated that they have played a pivotal role in ensuring consistency of execution (Umbreit and Smith 1991).

1.6.2 PREVIOUS RESEARCH

To date there has been little research on this *specific* role by academics, Goss-Turner commenting that there is 'a lack of published research material, both on the contemporary multi-unit role…and on the HRM implications' (Goss-Turner 1999: 40). In essence there are three literature streams that are relevant to the subject in question, none satisfactorily explaining what constitutes an effective MUL.

The first literature stream, the 'middle management genre', has an orthodox 'blocker' narrative which posits middle managers, described as 'non-strategic' implementers, as potential barriers to performance, change and progress (Drucker 1955). Its principal argument follows the Burns and Stalker (1961) observation that mechanistic machine bureaucracies tend to produce inert and ossified structures in the middle of their organisations. In this literature academics have busied themselves with suggesting solutions as to how firms can motivate and liberate a cohort that stands accused of being the reason why strategy fails to translate into action. An honourable exception is Henry Mintzberg in his seminal work *Managing* (2009), who argues that it is not that middle managers are constraints per se, rather they are victims of a number of intractable conundrums that limit their capacity for action. The main issue with this 'middle management genre' literature is that it is mainly a commentary on multi-divisional types of organisation and fails to account of the multi-unit form and, in particular, the vital role of the MUL. It has not sufficiently differentiated between types of middle managers, failing to acknowledge that their function and impact might be different in certain contexts. Also, excepting Mintzberg, it plays back to organisations and senior managers their own prejudicial view of what the role is and why it breaks down.

The second literature that should deal with the role of the MUL, the 'retail management genre', is virtually silent on the subject. The most popular academic text on retail management, Berman and Evans' *Retail Management* (2010) – now onto its eleventh edition – makes passing reference to the role. How can we account for this? First, these general texts concern themselves with organisational and unit level analysis, with the presumption that within the standard multi-unit model, strategies and policies from the Centre are translated into action at Unit level. MULs are assumed to be conduits for this transmission. In fact, some argue, given the rise in technological intermediation, is there any need for the role at all given the ability of the Centre to monitor standards and performance 'by the wire' (Haeckel and Nolan 1993)? Second, due to the paucity of research in this area, these texts rely on generic academic commentary and tools relating to enacting organisational intent. Thus, models that can be applied across management, sometimes derived from completely different starting-points (such as manufacturing and FMCG), are used as frameworks to unpack the intricacies of quite distinctive multi-unit processes.

The third literature, the US and UK 'multiple restaurant genre', is the most serious attempt to research and explain the role of the MUL. Tracking the explosive growth of casual and quick service dining in the US, commentators have sought to explain the key performance dimensions, success factors, training and development needs and transitional difficulties of multi-unit managers (Umbreit and Tomlin 1986, Umbreit 1989, Mone and Umbreit 1989, Umbreit and Smith 1991, Ryan 1992, Muller and Campbell 1995, Reynolds 2000, Di Pietro et al 2007, Rivera et al 2008).

Umbreit's (1989) five job dimensions of multi-unit managers was the starting point for the research. First, he elicited the most important job tasks and dimensions from a panel of five fast food executives, denominated as Financial Management, Restaurant Operations, Human Resource Management, Marketing and Promotions Management and Facilities and Safety. Umbreit then weighted these dimensions through surveying 300 'fast food executives' with a follow-up analysis of high performers' dimensional ranking. The conclusions of his ground-breaking study were that fast food multi-unit managers ranked the importance of the different dimensions of their job in the following manner; i) Restaurant Operations, ii) HRM, iii) Financial Management, iv) Marketing and Promotions and v) Facilities and Safety. He noted that that the multi-unit managers in his study expressed concern over poor levels of training and stated that their greatest transitional issue from moving from Unit Manager to multi-unit manager was HRM (Mone and Umbreit 1989). With respect to high performers, by analysing a cohort of successful multi-unit managers, chosen as exemplars by their line managers, Umbreit and Smith (1991) concluded that they;

> ... believed that they were successful because they spend a great deal of time developing their management team, constructing a positive work environment and instilling a sense of pride ... (1991: 454).

Further studies validated the importance of HRM as a critical job dimension and success factor for multi-unit managers. Ryan (1992), using Umbreit's five job dimensions, found in his study of college and university food service multi-unit managers that HRM was ranked first as the most significant performance dimension (followed in order by Financial Management, Food Service Operations, Facilities and Safety Management and Marketing and Promotions). Financial Management and HRM were ranked first and second as providing the greatest challenges for Unit Managers transitioning to multi-unit managers. Likewise, Muller and Campbell (1995), surveying a sample of 627 managers in a single fast food chain, found that HRM was prominent amongst the job dimensions ranked most important to become a competent multi-unit manager, with weightings following a similar order to previous studies by Ryan and Umbreit; i) HRM, ii) Restaurant Operations, iii) Finance and Control, iv) Marketing Management, v) Facilities Development. Similarly, DiPietro et al (2007), in their focused study of 54 multi-unit managers in a single casual dining chain, concluded that out of eight 'key success factors' (which disaggregates Umbreit's five part model into more factors which include components such as crisis management, community affairs and visiting units);

> When exploring the means or importance of these (eight) factors, it is clear that the factors of effective leadership, visiting restaurants, and human relations are the most important (key success factors) based on the mean scores of the various components that comprise the factors ... (2007: 532).

In a follow-up study Rivera et al (2008), considering key training needs for multi-unit managers, concluded that, due to the systemization of operations, they were evolving from 'task masters' to 'people' developers, stating;

> *The Multi-Unit Managers in the current organization believe that human resource skills need to be developed in order to help them in their current jobs, as well as to help them develop to the next level of supervision. These training needs could be as a result of a lack of skills to perform specific HR duties such as staff training,* effective leadership (author emphasis), *unit manager development, modeling values, team building and acting as a district resource … (2008: 626).*

In the UK, Jones and Inkinci (2001), using Umbreit's (1989) five part model, conducted a quantitative analysis of multi-unit managers in UK restaurant organisations. Their findings were remarkably consistent with prior US research, indicating that there is little difference between the UK and US contexts for multi-unit managers (although parallel studies by Goss-Turner and Jones 2000 and Goss-Turner 2002 noted the differing evolution and industry structure of casual dining in the UK). Restaurant operations and HRM were rated as the highest performance competencies and the major problems encountered by Unit Managers transitioning to multi-unit managers were, in rank order; i) HRM, ii) financial management, iii) restaurant operations, iv) marketing and promotions, v) facilities and safety.

However if HRM is a dominant factor in the key job dimensions and success factors of multi-unit managers, what are the explanations for termination, turnover and/or burn out? Executive failure is typically framed as being derived from issues with interpersonal relationships, inability to hit targets, incompetent team leadership and lack of adaptive capacity – particularly during change events (Van Velsor and Leslie 1995, McCartney and Campbell 2006). With regard to multi-unit managers, Umbreit (1989) found that rates of turnover (typically 10-15 per cent per annum) were related to lack of HRM skills (45 per cent) and job stress (25 per cent). Alongside promotion, Ryan (1992) found that multi-unit turnover correlated to the fact that the 'position was too demanding' and 'lack of human relations skills'. In part these reasons stemmed from the career origins of most multi-unit managers, as ex-Unit Managers.

Many newly promoted multi-unit managers retained a 'one dimensional management style' (Umbreit 1989) compounded by the fact that they no longer directly controlled daily operations and were expected to manage flows of information and cope with supervising managers at a distance (Jones 1999). Having been promoted for their technical ability, deficiencies in behavioural and cognitive skills became exposed. New multi-unit managers had to learn to 'manage the managers' rather than 'managing every unit' (Umbreit and Smith 1991). Thus, interpersonal relations, motivational, leadership and analytical skills were essential to the success of newly promoted multi-unit managers, but rarely trained into new recruits at multi-unit management level (Jones and Inkinci 2001, Suboleski 2006). A major survival technique, *delegation*, was rarely taught and seldom deployed by newly promoted multi-unit managers in spite of the acknowledgement by one executive in Umbreit's study of its vital importance;

> ... *the key for a new multi-unit manager is to learn to delegate responsibility quickly, for it is impossible to spend as much time in each multi-unit on day-to-day details as before* ... *(1989: 54).*

Additional skills and behavioural training such as learning to establish an immediate rapport with staff through direct personal interaction and transitioning from being 'hands on' to becoming an individual coach were also neglected by organisations. More specifically the lack of preparedness of newly promoted multi-unit managers to conduct 'visits with a purpose' hampered multi-unit manager effectiveness;

> ... *each new unit multi-unit manager must learn the secret of managing remotely, which involves learning how to deal with unstructured time, establishing priorities and making each visit to individual units a high quality, productive visit* ... *(Umbreit 1989: 58).*

Further research by Batrus Hollweg International (2005a,b), reflecting '35 years of multi-unit manager assessment profiles' identified the specific leadership skills required by the role, which organisations routinely failed to address. Their study concluded that multi-unit managers have different interpersonal and leadership requirements from unit managers. Multi-unit managers need to learn how to practice virtual management, effectively structuring their time, extending their behavioural skills beyond technical 'comfort zones' and creating broader support networks. In essence Unit Managers promoted into multi-unit positions need to;

> ... *accept, embrace, and enact the paradoxical skills of management and leadership* ... *(McCartney and Campbell 2006: 191).*

In another stream of research on multi-unit manager leadership styles, Goss-Turner (1999) argues that they vary according to firm growth patterns. Following analysis of data from interviews with senior executives from hospitality organisations and multi-unit management job descriptions he concluded that during start-up and early growth stages multi-unit management leadership styles are 'values and culture' driven, whilst maturity and scale (bringing with it bureaucracy) forces a more 'command and control' approach. In addition he proposed four key themes for multi-unit managers (job scope, organisational congruence, geographic density and unit conformity) with three mediating factors (firm size, property portfolio and brand portfolio). In his view the 'maturity-dynamism' continuum explained four different definitions of multi-unit managers as a result; the entrepreneur, the business manager, the multi-brand manager and the 'archetype'.

Overall this literature is highly pertinent to this study, surfacing the primacy of HRM and leadership skills for multi-unit managers. Issues and gaps relating to this genre centre around three main points: first, its lack of cross-sectoral calibration (being mainly located within fast food and casual dining hospitality); second, its absence of a unifying integrated framework which explains effective multi-unit leadership; and third, its failure to take into account the views of unit managers.

With regard to its lack of a cross-sectoral comparison, some evidence of sectoral congruence between critical job dimensions is provided by Brzezicki (2008) in his comparative study of hospitality and care home multi-unit managers. Using Umbreit's (1989) framework as the comparator his study concluded that;

> ... except for the statistical differences in Facilities and Safety Management it would appear that, the management competencies in the home care industry and food service/quick service industries do compare favourably ...It would appear from this study that all the management competencies are transferable from one industry to another ... (2008: 77).

Yet, Brzezicki fails to provide a unifying integrated framework, conflating – like the other researchers before him (ie Muller and Di Pietro 2006) – HRM and leadership inputs with operational and financial outputs. An opportunity exists to disaggregate MUL characteristics from behaviours and operational impact; linking causal drivers with preferred outcomes. Also, most significantly, all studies fail to take account of the views of a key cohort – Unit Managers. What are the MUL competencies and behaviours they believe are the most motivational, given their importance as recipients and, potentially, followers?

1.7 A Model of Effective Multi-Unit Leadership

This book is an attempt to address the aforementioned gap, namely, to date there has been no extrapolation of an integrated conceptual and theoretical framework for MUL. This section will outline, first, the research base for constructing a model of effective MUL and second, what that model is. It is this framework that informs the structure of this book.

1.7.1 RESEARCH AND METHODOLOGY

As stated, the principal questions that the research for this book sought to address were;

1.   What do effective MULs do? What do they focus upon?

2.   How do they operate effectively, overcoming extant contextual issues and barriers? What behaviours do they drive amongst their followers? How and with what practices?

3.   What characteristics do effective MULs possess?

At this juncture, it is necessary to consider the method of data collection and analysis for this study, followed by a consideration of its strengths and limitations.

1.7.1.1 Data collection

The data collection method for the primary research for this book followed an inductive, multi-method approach from 2007–2012 where different cohorts of managers and staff across retail, leisure and hospitality multi-unit enterprises were asked the open questions outlined above. The enterprises selected for analysis were *mainly* UK-based, due to the author's location, networks and access capability. Such a multi-method approach – an attempt to bolster the validity and reliability of the study – is supported within the academic research literature by Denzin:

If each method leads to different features of empirical reality, then no single method can ever capture all the relevant features of that reality; consequently, (researchers) must learn to employ multiple methods in the analysis of the same empirical events ... (1970: 30).

Indeed the process of using as many sources as possible in order to facilitate the triangulation of findings can, in addition to increasing reliability, 'help with the problems of establishing the construct and internal validity of the case study evidence' (Yin 2003: 97). As regards this study, the primary data sources are highlighted in Figure 1.1;

Method	Level*	Sectors*	Co*	N*
Focus Groups	UM,MUL	R,H,L	8	223
Semi-Structured Int.	UM, MUL, SE	R,H,L	21	163
Engagement Surveys	UM	H	2	2,627
Accompanied Visits	MUM, SE	R,H,L	12	23
Psychometric Testing	MUM	R,H,L	5	68

* *Level; UM (Unit Managers), MUL (Multi-Unit Leader), SE (Senior Executive).* **Sectors**; *R (retail), H (hospitality), L (leisure).* **Co**; *companies.* **N**; *numbers of participants.*

Figure 1.1   Method of data collection

The detail behind each method of primary data collection was as follows;

- Focus groups; held amongst Unit Managers and MULs on the Multi-Unit Leadership and Strategy (MULS) Programme at BCBS 2010–2012.

- Semi-structured interviews; conducted by the author and consultants amongst Unit Managers, MULs and Senior Executives across a range of UK-based and international multi-unit enterprises over the period 2008–2012.

- Engagement surveys; Unit Manager surveys held in two major UK hospitality organisations in 2009 and 2010. Questions relating to personal supervisor support (ie MUL) extracted and examined.

- Accompanied visits; Unit visits conducted by the author with MULs and Senior Executives over the period 2007-2012.

- Psychometric Testing; Mental Toughness test (MTQ48) applied to MULs on the BCBS Programme during the period 2010–2012.

In addition to this primary data capture, the author was also a participant observer, holding the position of Group HR, Service and Productivity Director for the UK's largest casual dining organisation (44,000 employees, 2,000 units, 22 brands and 136 MULs) up to July 2010. In this position he had privileged access to internal sources of confidential data relating to MULs. In addition, on an external basis, the author interacted with senior executives from other multi-unit enterprises in environments such as industry bodies, award ceremonies, workshops and best practice seminars. For recruitment purposes the author was also involved in interviewing and appointing senior staff from a plethora of multi-unit enterprises (such as hotels, health clubs, fast food, banking, multi-site services, electrical and supermarket retail).

Over the duration of the research the author also secured access to documentary sources such as;

- MUL job descriptions and competency models;

- MUL training and development material;

- MUL communications and briefs;

- Company, Regional, Brand, District and Unit KPIs and balanced scorecards;

- Operational manuals etc.

Other sources such as trade magazine, financial press cuttings, annual reports, blogs and web-based data also provided additional data – particularly with regard to company strategising in response to disruptive forces.

1.7.1.2 Data analysis

Having completed data collection the researcher must engage in a process of data analysis, being comfortable with both ambiguity and fluidity (Miles and Huberman 1994). In the case of this research, its pattern of setting a broad research question (ie what constitutes effective multi-unit leadership?) rather than hypotheses, the selection of complementary research tools and identification of suitable multi-unit enterprise data sites followed Eisenhardt's (1989) recommended route of data analysis and conceptual construction.

The first step of the data analysis process was, as previously outlined, a 'cross-site analysis ... which give[s] investigators a rich familiarity' with the data (Eisenhardt 1989: 540). Second, the interview, focus group and survey evidence captured from informants, when combined with observational and documentary data, was analysed to expose important critical aspects of the subject of analysis (ie the effective MUL) from which iterative narratives began to flow. The third step involved structuring emerging patterns and themes from these narratives into an integrated account. This posed a particular challenge, although the emerging thematics presented a compelling storyline fulfilling Dumez and Jeunemaître's (2006) criteria of an *'end result'* (MUL focus upon standards, systems and service), *'start point'* (MUL personal characteristics of energy, EI and expertise) and a *'pathway or plot in between'* (MUL behaviourally-based practices of commitment, control and change). The fourth stage, that of 'sense testing' the integrated conceptual framework, was completed with a range of multi-unit actors during July–October 2011.

The benefits of such a multi-method, multi-level, cross-sectoral (UK and limited international) approach were threefold. First, it allowed the functions and characteristics of MULs to be investigated across a range of multi-unit service organisations. Second, the views of Unit Managers, hitherto neglected by previous research, were analysed; an important dimension, given that they are the principal recipients of the practices of MULs. Third, and most significantly – in comparison with previous research methods – it afforded a degree of qualitative triangulation between the views of different sets of managerial cohorts in differing sectoral contexts, previous research methodology having almost exclusively relied upon cross-sectional quantitative data within fast/casual food dining. Conversely, its weaknesses or drawbacks include its scope for repeatability (given its multi-method dimensions, time and context) and, to date, its lack of rigorous scientific testing of its emergent conceptual framework (in spite of its positive 'sense testing' with notable multi-unit actors). The author also acknowledges that his position as a 'situated observer' (as an ex-executive and MUL) affords accusations of contamination and bias with regard to research construction, data collection and interpretation.

1.7.2 CONCEPTUAL MODEL OF EFFECTIVE MUL

The conceptual model (see Figure 1.2) which emerged from the in-depth research is based around four drivers; context, personal characteristics, behavioural practices and activities, which comprise the following elements;

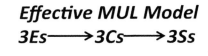

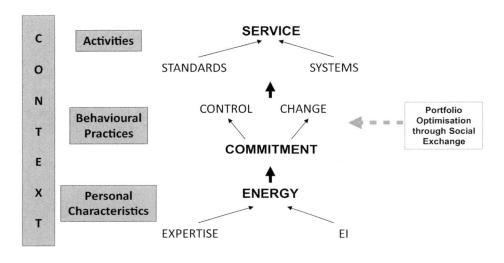

Figure 1.2   Effective MUL model

The linkages in the model in Figure 1.2 are as follows.

1.7.2.1 Drivers and clusters

As stated, the model is framed around four drivers (see shaded boxes); context, personal characteristics, behavioural practices and activities. The overall *context* of the multi-unit enterprise – its positioning, business model, leadership, culture, strategy and organisational design – creates the environment within which MULs operate. The three dominant clusters which are detailed include *personal characteristics* – the underlying technical, cognitive and behavioural competencies of effective MULs. These equip effective MULs with the skills and capability to make *practice-based behavioural interventions* that determine the execution of vital *activities* for the organisation. These clusters are linked; for instance, *without appropriate personal characteristics MULs will be ill-equipped to enact appropriate practice-based behavioural interventions, ultimately failing to effect optimal outcomes.*

1.7.2.2 Critical dependencies

Each of the three clusters (ie 3Es, 3Cs and 3Ss) has three factors that have their own critical dependencies. Within personal characteristics, *Energy*, given the terrain of MUL is the dependent variable, but is only viable and effective if supported by behavioural, technical and cognitive factors of *EI* (emotional intelligence) and *Expertise*. With regard to behaviour-based practices, *Commitment* is the crucial mediating variable, impacting the MUL's ability to effect *Control* and *Change* behaviours. Finally, within activities, effective *Systems* and *Standards* implementation are the precursors to sales-led *Service* execution, the dominant desired outcome. The items in the model in bold – *Energy*, *Commitment* and *Service* – are crucial linkages, but are reliant on the existence of the other items for effectiveness.

1.7.2.3 Theoretical underpinning

This model is underpinned a guiding theory; 'portfolio optimisation through social exchange' (POSE) which operates both *vertically* and *horizontally*. It is borne of the overwhelming insight from the research that MULs are, first and foremost, 'portfolio optimisers'. According to the economically-based balanced portfolio theory (Markowitz 1959) rational investors will seek to limit risk and optimize returns through spreading assets over a range of investment vehicles. Likewise, at a company level within multi-unit firms, strategic policy makers will seek to limit risk and optimize outcomes through allocating tangible assets such as capital in an optimal manner, taking into account factors such as site, product and likely demand. At a local level, MULs charged with implementing systems, standards and sales-led service take a 'softer' approach to portfolio optimization, leveraging scarce intangibles such as people and knowledge in order to secure optimal outcomes.

As MULs are measured and incentivised on an area basis and have a high level of interdependence with their followers (due to the same measures and metrics of success being applied), they gain an understanding of the micro-dynamics of each site (people, layout and market) and then leverage scarce people, knowledge and, in some instances, physical and capital resources across their portfolio to optimal effect. But in order to achieve these resource flows they have to transact *vertically* through social exchange; a theoretical perspective that advances the notion that organisations and managers can only achieve sustainable performance through trust-based socio-emotional transactions with followers, where perceived benefits outweigh costs (Cropanzano and Mitchell 2005, Saks 2006);

> *Social exchange theory (SET) argues that obligations are generated through a series of interactions between parties who are in a state of reciprocal interdependence. A basic tenet of SET is that relationships evolve over time into trusting, loyal, and mutual commitments as long as the parties abide by certain "rules" of exchange (Cropanzano and Mitchell, 2005). Rules of exchange usually involve reciprocity or repayment rules such that the actions of one party lead to a response or actions by the other party ... (Saks 2006: 603).*

Thus, social exchange theory conceives of work-place relations being governed by the law of reciprocity where a general social *indebtedness* is shaped, forming the basis of a community that can be kept in balance over time and across teams (Meeker 1971, Emerson 1976). There are six archetypes of exchange, including; love, status, information, money, goods and services (Foa and Foa 1974, 1980). Given the distance of the MUL from the units (juxtaposed against their high level of interdependence with their subordinates), coupled with Central interventions (often badly conceived and explained), effective MULs transact vertically with their subordinates through currencies such as protection from punishment, support and development, promise fulfillment etc. in order to secure optimal outcomes. Such transactions are governed by the laws of reciprocity in which clear mutual gains are made by each party through transmission mechanisms such as mutual goal attainment, free market exchange, compensated costs and the uncovering of hidden value (Gouldner 1960, Blau 1964, Cohen and Bradford 1989).

Importantly, in keeping with the observations of a few scholars operating in this area (Ladd and Henry 2000), MULS also transact *horizontally* with their peers and actively encourage horizontal reciprocation between their units. With regard to their colleagues, horizontal transactions are likely to take place around knowledge transfer and people (particularly in overlapping multi-brand geographies). At unit level, in order to optimise resources within the portfolio, effective MULs, either formally (through structures such as local clustering) or informally (inter-store relationships), facilitate exchanges relating to soft and hard assets such as human capital, knowledge, stock and equipment.

1.7.3 BOOK STRUCTURE AND ARGUMENTS

The structure of this book follows the conceptual framework outlined in Figure 1.2. Thus, the Introduction and Chapter 2 'Strategic Responses to Disruption' outline the broad context within which MULs have been expected to operate; particularly with regard to cost leadership, differentiation and value-led approaches. It also alludes to best-practice organisational design principles and internationalising multi-unit enterprises. It concludes that the inherent adaptive capacity of multi-unit organisations to cope with emerging threats has had a major influence on the way in which MULs are expected to discharge their duties and that the preferred strategy recently pursued by many multi-unit enterprises has been to pursue a cost leadership approach.

Chapter 3, 'Activities and Issues', outlines the activities against which organisations measure, reward and punish their MULs – operational systems, brand standards and service and sales execution. In particular it discusses the negative effects of concentrating upon operational systems, to the exclusion of maintaining brand standards and service and sales execution. It argues that the degree to which organisations place undue emphasis on cost-led systems such as labour scheduling and compliance at the expense of sales-led service execution can have a debilitating influence on MUL authority and room for manouevre and, consequently, Unit Manager morale and performance.

The next three chapters discuss how effective MULs overcome some of these hurdles and barriers, by examining the both the literature and empirical evidence (illustrated with case study examples) relating to Commitment, Control and Change practice-based behavioural interventions.

Chapter 4, 'Generating Commitment', outlines the 'psychology-based' service operations, leadership and HRM literatures before outlining effective MUL commitment practices; *local visioning and tactics, cross-portfolio involvement, 'talent matching', tailored support and development, recognition and positive reinforcement* and *openness, trust and promise fulfillment*. It argues that these commitment-based practices can be located in much of the aforementioned literature, albeit they conform more to notions of 'local situational leadership' and best practice HRM, rather than other genres. In addition, the deployment of commitment-based practices can be seen as an attempt by effective MULs to set the foundations for *portfolio optimisation* through facilitating forms of *goal attainment*, *free market* and *compensated cost-types of social exchange* that enable them to exert control and implement change.

Chapter 5, 'Ensuring Control', takes more of a 'sociological managerial' perspective, outlining first, theories of managerial control and the 'critically-based' management literature and then second, empirical evidence relating to control-based practices deployed by effective MULs. These practices include; *Pareto prioritisation, social network optimization, distributed delegation, sanctioned autonomy* and *added value deviance*. It is argued that in spite of the previously discussed literature, effective MULs are able to exert control through applying managerial practices rooted in notions of *goal attainment* and *free market-based* social exchange. Nevertheless, their ability to manage must be set within the context that they have demonstrated the commitment-based leadership behaviours and practices outlined in the previous chapter.

Chapter 6, 'Implementing Change', combines both psychological and sociological perspectives in order to understand how effective MULs enact transformational and incremental change processes. Following an elucidation of the practical difficulties of change and the 'top down' versus 'bottom up' streams of change literature, effective MUL change-based practices are outlined; *shaping mindsets, benefit up-selling, patch ups and workarounds, continuous process improvement* and *portfolio best practice diffusion*. It is argued that whilst the effective MUL acts as important conduit and facilitator for change initiatives within multi-unit enterprises, they have a major capacity to uncover *hidden value* through effecting micro-process improvements that enhance operational performance given the idiosyncratic nature (in relation to size, layout and position) of their units.

Following consideration of these behaviourally-led practice interventions, the book then turns to the final cluster of items in Chapter 7, 'Characteristics of Effective MULs'. Three areas are considered; Expertise, EI (emotional intelligence) and Energy. The components of Expertise are outlined as being *knowledge* (both explicit and tacit), *judgment* and *confidence and adaptability*. EI comprises *self-awareness and mental toughness, awareness of others and authenticity* and *relationship management and conflict resolution*. Energy is made up from *stamina, executional edge* and *passion*. It is argued that these characteristics are the vital factors behind the MUL's ability to drive the three Cs outlined in the previous chapters. Overall these characteristics are an amalgam of the technical, behavioural and cognitive capabilities necessary for effective multi-unit leadership.

The final chapter, Chapter 8 'Conclusion', brings together all the themes and insights of the previous chapters. In particular it considers the nature the *commitment-control paradox* within multi-unit leadership, a recasting of behaviourally-led practices as *currencies of vertical and horizontal exchange* and suggestions for further research.

2

Strategic Responses to Disruption

The previous chapter briefly outlined the disruptive forces and challenges that confront the standard multi-unit form in the second decade of the twenty-first century.. As a precursor to understanding what constitutes effective MUL today, it is important to delve deeper into the context in which MULs operate. In terms of this overarching context, this chapter will elucidate and analyse strategic, organisational and best practice design responses within contemporary multi-unit firms to the new environmental paradigms. Two overarching questions inform this chapter. How have multi-unit firms evolved their strategy and structures to deal with emergent challenges? What are the opportunities and constraints for multi-unit firms that internationalise their operations? This broader contextual analysis will enable relevant consideration of MUL activities, practices and characteristics in succeeding chapters.

2.1 Mediating Factors

The strategic responses that multi-unit firms have deployed in response to the disruptive trinity – challenging economic circumstances, technological disintermediation and changing consumer expectations – have varied according to two dominant factors. First, firm agility has been crucial. It will be argued that the degree to which the firm has been flexible enough to respond to the changing external environment has been contingent on three factors; its ownership structure, life cycle positioning and level of leadership expertise and adaptability. Second, the starting point of their strategic positioning (cost, differentiation or value) has been fundamental to their room for evolutionary manoeuvre, affecting the type and level of their response. The succeeding section will argue that many firms have used the emergent challenges as a 'burning platform', enabling them to either make or speed up dramatic changes to their cost base or customer facing offer.

As stated, as an entry point to the consideration of the range of strategic responses to disruptive forces, it can be argued that corporate agility that has been one of the main contingent variables affecting whether or not multi-unit enterprises have been successful or not in coping with headwinds. It is the contention of this study that, in recent times, the three most important factors in determining levels of firm agility have been ownership structure, stage of firm life-cycle and degree of leadership adaptability and expertise. These will be examined in turn.

2.1.1 OWNERSHIP TYPE

The type of ownership structure – public, private or private equity – has had a major impact on the way in which multi-unit firms have been able to respond to emerging pressures. In the case of publicly owned firms with open share registers, many US and UK company boards had been encouraged by corporate advisers and analysts, in the halcyon years of cheap capital in the late 1990s and new millennium, to take on debt in order to make large acquisitions or issue share buy-backs (often for shares priced at the height of the market). Firms that hoarded cash were deemed to be using capital inefficiently by financial 'experts'. The net result of following this self interested advice (it being exceptionally beneficial to advisers in terms of fee generation and, in turn, highly lucrative to incentivised senior executive 'agents' of capital) was that many multi-unit companies entered the downturn in 2008 with a high level of short and long-term debt on their balance sheets that, at best, constrained their flexibility, or at worst, threatened their very survival in the face of declining revenues and profits. This situation was exacerbated for some firms when they required refinancing at the height of the financial crisis, as onerous new repayment rates and severe headroom restrictions were imposed by the equally cash strapped banks. For example, in the UK leisure sector, Punch Taverns, the country's largest registered pub company (constructed by means of a deadly combination badly timed debt-fuelled M&A and asset-backed securitisation instruments), came close to defaulting on their large interest repayments. Such organisations essentially became 'zombie' debt repayment mechanisms with cash-starved operational companies attached (Wallop 2011, Fortson and Marlow 2012).

Multi-unit enterprises owned by private equity firms or 'buccaneer entrepreneurs' backed by corporate lending arms of some major banks, suffered a similar fate as a result of inept 'financial engineering' (Steiner 2012a, Fortson and Marlow 2012). Having been used as 'assets' to attract cheap credit in order to fund audacious acquisitions at the height of the market – attaching suicidal rates of debt to the acquired entities in order to minimise tax liabilities – many multi-unit firms under these types of ownership limped through the downturn or went bust. In the retail sector in the UK, the ownership of many high street chains (wholly or partially) lay in the hands of individuals backed by Icelandic banks (such as Iceland, Karen Millen, Oasis, Whistles, Jane Norman, House of Fraser, All Saints, Principles etc). Some 'entrepeneurs' (such as Robert Tchenguiz), backed by the same institutions, partially owned companies (in his case Sainsbury's and Mitchells and Butlers) believing that their 'activist' pressure on 'inert' management would 'unlock value' from land-based freehold multi-unit portfolios, accelerating the equity value of the organisation, leaving them with handsome profits on exit (Steiner 2012a). Such plans were largely exposed as 'casino tactics' when the credit tide turned in 2008.

Those multi-unit firms which had experienced more of a stewardship approach, either in the public or private domain in the run up to 2008 recession, fared better. It is an interesting fact that public enterprises, for instance, those that retained a high level of family ownership and stewardship in the hospitality (eg Fullers and Youngs) and retail domains (eg Primark) were set up to benefit from the downturn. Unencumbered with debt, having taken a long-term strategic view (unpopular with some financial 'experts' at the time) they were able to purchase prime assets cheaply from cash-strapped multi-unit competitors seeking to raise cash to pay down debt, and/or pick up vacant sites from the receivers of failed companies.

2.1.2 SERVICE FIRM LIFE CYCLE

Where multi-unit enterprises lay on the life cycle curve also proved significant as to whether or not they were in a favourable position to respond to the new paradigms created by disruptive forces. According to Sasser et al (1978) service firms follow a typical S curve of life, transitioning through the stages of introduction, multi-site rationalisation, growth, maturity and decline. During introduction, firms introduce an innovative new concept with modest sales which they roll out in multi-site formats, rationalising the estate once they have proof tested it's positioning and 'locational fit'. Having established a successful model, firms then drive profitable multi-site growth through rapid roll-out, facing limited competition at this stage as their concept has not been copied or understood by competitors to any great extent. However, maturity follows as the competition catches up and sales level off, leading many firms to drop into the decline stage where sales and profitability drop to levels that threaten their viability.

Those firms that entered 2008 downturn in an advanced state of maturity or decline were extremely vulnerable to business failure. Businesses in decline, such as book/music/card/video games retailers, off licence liquor stores, value furniture and some electrical and white goods chains – where their offers had been incorporated into other retailers' offerings or cannibalised by more cost-effective web-based platforms – saw steeper rates of decline and/or went into administration. However, as other commentators have noted, there is a high degree of determinism surrounding the firm life cycle model (Jones 1999, Lechner and Kreutzer 2010). Not all firms respond according to their life stage positioning. In maturity, firms have a range of choices that management can take and some multi-unit enterprises were skilful in adapting their positioning, formats and service offers. This speedy and resourceful adaptation will be explored in greater depth below, following consideration of the final enabling/inhibiting factor, adaptive expert leadership.

2.1.3 ADAPTIVE EXPERT LEADERSHIP

A major determinant of firm agility and responsiveness to challenging circumstances was the degree to which the leadership of the organisation could, according to its level of flexibility and expertise, successfully adapt their product to new patterns of demand. According to the firm life cycle concept, the types of leadership style required during start-up, rationalisation, accelerated roll-out and maturity differ (Reynolds et al 2007). The fluid and organic styles allied with systems of 'soft' HRM are required in the early stages of development in contrast to the mechanistic and administrative leadership style melded with a 'hard' HRM approach required during maturity (Tichy 1983, Schuler and Jackson 1987). Often, following concept development and initial roll-out, visionary pioneer-leaders require replacement by rational professional managers who have the skills to leverage multi-unit scale efficiency. However, problems occur when this administrative cadre is faced with major discontinuities that threaten the enterprise's business model. Their default style of standardised compliance and control leadership is insufficiently flexible to deal with fast changing external environments as they are locked into outmoded thought patterns that are suited to old, rather than new, paradigms.

They lack the imagination and ingenuity to galvanise their organisations around a 'big idea' that is a clear point of market difference, clearly understood by internal and external stakeholders.

In such circumstances shareholders, responding to rapid financial deterioration, have forced the Chairs and boards of many multi-unit retail and leisure chains to refresh their company's leadership. The turnover of multi-unit retail and leisure Chief Executives and Finance Directors in the UK rose dramatically from 2007 onwards, particularly in mature or declining businesses leading to the observation from one financial commentary;

> *A raft of bosses, from retail to finance and leisure to travel have found themselves heading for the exit as the going gets tough ... when times are tough firms have to focus on driving their core business hard – cutting costs and finding* innovative *(author emphasis) ways to win market share ... Instead of throwing up the flak of a transformational M&A deal to mask more deep-seated problems, cost cutting has become the mantra of the boardroom ... (Steiner 2011: 73).*

Examples in UK retail included the departure of CEOs at JJB, Mothercare, Dixons, Lloyds-TSB and New Look and the CEOs of Mitchells and Butlers, Punch, Esporta, Luminar and Gala Coral, in UK leisure and hospitality. In addition to the aforementioned cost pressures, the view that many boards took, admittedly after external pressure, was that their company's senior management was ill equipped to deal with the new challenges and/or were culpable for strategic mistakes leading up to the recession that were amplified when the economic tide turned. Those CEOs that had driven growth purely through acquisition, discounting and/or a failure to invest in their offer, amenity and infrastructure prior to the downturn were particularly vulnerable.

However, in other multi-unit businesses leadership continuity has been essential in enabling them to weather the dramatically changing retail and leisure landscape. One notable feature of this continuity has been the faith that boards and shareholders have shown in leadership teams which have actively demonstrated that they are taking decisive action in seeking to improve and meld their offers in response to changing demand. For example, the shareholders and board of WHSmith in the UK have backed CEO Kate Swann whose 'big idea' has been to reposition the product offer away from a reliance on books and compact disk revenue towards magazines and stationery on the high street, selling off non-core businesses such as the newspaper distribution arm, cutting costs, to concentrate on developing and expanding higher margin 'travel-based formats' (Sibun 2011). Thus, one of the first multi-unit retail companies in the world, that many would have argued was in a severe state of decline in the mid-2000s, has been stabilised by returning to its roots; clustering outlets around travel nodes. It is pertinent, perhaps, that Swann is a retail veteran, having worked for or run other high street retail chains such as Argos, before her appointment in 2004.

Thus, some leaders and businesses have sought to evolve their multi-unit offers to fit the new challenges that they face. The next section will consider how firms have responded according to their primary competitive positioning.

2.2 Strategic Responses

According to Porter (1980) there are three main viable long-term strategies that firms can choose to undertake in order to secure sustainable competitive advantage; *low cost*, *differentiation* and *focus*. It can be argued, given contemporary trends, focus can be recast as *value* (Fox and Sethuraman 2006). This section will consider how multi-unit companies working within these cost, differentiation and value paradigms have adapted their business models in response to prevailing challenges. Such analysis is important as a precursor to a consideration of effective multi-unit leadership, given that the communication and implementation of many of these changes has required the attention and assistance of MULs.

2.2.1 COST LEADERSHIP

The central premise of a cost-based strategy is that firms operating within this model construct the most efficient operational structure, affording them a more competitive price positioning than their competitors. The benefit to multi-unit firm operating in this mode is that it gives them competitive advantage during periods of economic disruption when consumers are particularly sensitive to price. Exemplars of this approach are 'every day low price' (EDLP) discount food retailers such as Aldi and Lidl, 'dime stores' such as Poundland and variety retailers such as Wilkinsons, who, through reducing complexity and generating lower supplier prices through a limited product range (typically 1,400 SKUs and items compared to 40,000 in Tesco and Walmart), cheaper sites in poorer demographic areas, multi-skilled 'skeleton staffing' and a 'no frills' approach (price promise guarantees, and consumers bringing their own bags), are able to sustain consistently lower prices than other retailers (up to 30–40 per cent in some categories of goods).

In recent times multi-unit enterprises operating within this paradigm have, in order to maintain or reduce pricing further – in the face of commodity inflation and a reduction in consumer discretionary spend – had to become more efficient through addressing practically every element of their value chain. However, it is important to state that *other multi-unit operators previously believed to be working in other strategic paradigms have also adopted many of the cost-minimising approaches* of firms that have typically operated in this domain. Approaches adopted within this paradigm have included;

2.2.1.1 Supply chain efficiencies

As the largest proportion of a multi-unit enterprise's costs, firms have redoubled their efforts in seeking savings through:

- Consolidation – further consolidating their number of suppliers through centralisation and eliminating product proliferation, thereby gaining better terms from the fewer remaining suppliers who were guaranteed higher volumes. In some cases firms have attempted to impose mandatory 'across the board' price reductions by offering sole supplier status or better payment terms (90 days instead of 120, for instance).

- Opportunistic buying – firms became far more adept at the spot-price buying of products that would offer better short-term value to their customers. Some firms, particularly in value casual dining, dropped some higher price protein products (such as steak), constructing their menus around cheaper options (such as poultry). Forwards and bulk buying also became levers to unlock hidden value in the supply chain, dependent on whether or not firms could guarantee sales.

- Bespoke products – in some cases, firms negotiated exclusivity on a range of bespoke products, often in smaller pack sizes, which gave lower price entry point advantage. This was particularly the case in 'dime stores' where FMCG suppliers were forced to remodel their supply chain to produce bespoke SKUs (stock keeping units) and items that reached a set price point.

- Supplier management – some firms handed over downstream demand forecasting and just-in-time replenishment systems to their suppliers, reducing their costs and management time spent in this area. However, some companies have come to rely more upon 'proximity sourcing', engaging locally-based suppliers to offset distribution costs or – in extreme circumstances – returning to vertically integrated supply chains to ensure quick turnaround times (particularly in fashion retail) or assured quality control.

- Seasonal slots – offering listings to suppliers in return for lowest price and/or over-riders, particularly during valuable high peak, seasonal demand periods. This was a common practice applied by supermarkets in the alcoholic drinks category; producers tendered 'best price' for the key trading slots during the summer and Christmas trading periods.

- Procurement team – a few companies consciously refreshed or swapped around their procurement buyers in order to ensure that any 'soft' relationships were broken and any unidentified opportunities were captured. This expedient tactic had been used for many years by supermarket multiples, most notably Tesco.

- Logistics efficiencies – companies such as Bookers have assessed 'hub' network, capacity and picking efficiencies, whilst others have outsourced their fleet requirements to solus logistics firms.

2.2.1.2 Labour efficiencies

The second largest cost in multi-unit firms resides in their labour line. In retail service firms labour costs (wages, National Insurance, pensions, incentives, holidays, sickness etc.) can amount to 26–30 per cent of sales; in leisure and hospitality typically 22–26 per cent. Small savings or efficiencies from such a significant overhead cost can have a disproportionate effect, feeding right through to the profit line. During the recession multi-unit enterprises deployed a myriad of labour saving and productivity enhancing initiatives:

- Layoffs and delayering – many multi-unit companies reviewed their staffing requirements, particularly in their 'back office' functions. There was a plethora of redundancies in functions such as HR, Marketing and Finance across the service sector. The 'survivors' were expected to do more, or certain 'non-core' transactional head office tasks were digitalised and/or outsourced (such as facilities, training, printing, payroll, pensions administration, IT support etc.)

- Rostering – in order to control labour costs many firms either applied strict labour cash targets at unit level or improved their rostering science in order to bolster capacity utilisation and throughputs; driving sales per employee per square foot. The former, a blunt instrument which estimates (based on sales trend data) what labour the unit manager requires, was juxtaposed against the latter, involving more sophisticated algorithmic methods. Thus, systems from companies such as Red Prairie, an IT labour deployment specialist, were introduced by some multi-unit firms to ensure that sufficient staff covered 'fat' (low demand) or 'thin' (high demand) periods.

- Skills deployment – in addition to the previous point, firms also sharpened their practices with regard to the 'right people' being deployed at the 'right time'. Particular scrutiny and attention was paid to ensuring the people with the right attitudes, behaviours and skills were deployed during critical high-intensity trading sessions in order to maximise sales. Attention was paid to what the 'A' and 'B' teams were in some companies; with an emphasis on the 'A' team being deployed during key trading sessions.

- Labour contract flexibility – one interesting feature of the recent downturn (in comparison to previous recessions) was the use by many multi-unit organisations of inventive means of retaining knowledge and talent through contract variations. Thus, the use of shorter working hour contracts, more flexible working, sabbaticals and increased unpaid holiday entitlement all contributed to some organisations being able to reduce their wage bill whilst, simultaneously, retaining key workers. Unlike previous recessions firms were keen to retain key staff through the use of inventive contract variations rather than reducing costs (and losing significant knowledge) through downsizing.

- Benefit cuts – some organisations used the 'burning platform' of the economic recession to dispense with expensive benefits such as defined benefit pension schemes. These schemes that guaranteed a pension linked to length of service multiple of final salary on retirement, had, since the early 2000s, following regulatory intervention (such as the 1997 cessation of the pension share dividend tax break), began costing large multi-unit firms a large amount in both contributions and 'liability bridge' payments. Early movers to close these schemes included Debenhams and WHSmith, although multi-unit organisations such as Boots and Mitchells and Butlers soon followed. Other benefits that firms cut related mainly to paternalist legacies, such as generous sickness schemes, death in service provision and annual health care contributions.

- Incentive arrangements – some firms removed bonus and incentives for 'non-core' head office staff, whilst others reduced the potential payout range. In the main however, given the aforementioned benefit cuts and the drive for firms to introduce a 'performance culture', many companies actually extended the range and application of their incentive schemes.

2.2.1.3 Site, plant and building efficiencies

The cost to companies of maintaining their land based estates, given the rise in regulatory 'red tape' and commodity prices, compelled organisations to take a number of actions:

- Energy saving schemes – rising gas and electricity prices forced most multi-unit firms to implement energy savings schemes as fixed costs escalated as a proportion of turnover. For example, enterprises with legacy estates containing poor building stock, convenience stores with a large chilled product range in fridges, large multi-unit sites with large air conditioning plants and restaurants using high gas consumption for cooking purposes took a number of measures to kerb usage. 'Soft' measures included introducing new energy practice codes to be implemented at unit level with, in some cases, incentives for staff to reduce year-on-year energy consumption. 'Hard' measures included the installation of new energy monitoring devices, replacement of old inefficient energy sapping equipment with more efficient plant and, following heat leakage assessments of buildings, preventative maintenance (such as lagging, sealing, window double glazing etc.) to reduce emissions. In part companies could sell these changes to their staff as part of an 'eco-carbon agenda', although in truth, the motivation for such interventions was rising costs.

- Rent and rates renegotiations – the second highest cost for operators with leased estates is their monthly/quarterly rental bill combined with local business rates (BRC 2012b). In terms of business rates, many companies took the opportunity to reduce their liability in the face of declining revenues by obtaining revaluations from local authorities.. Concerning rent, firms with sites coming to the end of term were well placed to renegotiate the original terms of their lease, many achieving more favourable deals such as dramatic rent reductions (pragmatic landlords deciding that a tenant paying business rates on the property was better than no tenant at all), the recasting of upwards only inflation linked increase clauses, reductions in length of term and service charges, more break clauses and disappearance of onerous 'put and keep' provisions. Some firms with sites in mid-cycle leases, finding themselves locked into uneconomic terms, attempted to bargain with their landlords. Some multi-unit enterprises such as JJB in the UK threatened their landlords with voluntary administration in order to exit sites or reduce rent charges.

- Relocation – rather than staying in the same sites many companies relocated to lower rent options or rationalised their estates by pulling out of 'low-traffic' areas completely. Some 'secondary' and 'tertiary' high streets and malls were badly affected by this trend, disused outlets leading to lower footfall and a downward spiral of business for the remaining tenants. This has, however, created a degree of innovation with some multi-unit organisations trialling 'pop-up' shops in these vacant spaces. For instance Signet trialled three pop-up H. Samuel shops in high street locations leading up to Christmas 2010.

- Capital spending efficiencies – in order to preserve cash some firms reduced the amount of capital investment in their estates. In terms of large scale projects, firms concentrated on customer-facing improvements, saving on back of house upgrades. Hence cash was spread across the estate on 'sparkle' improvements rather than large one-off projects. In addition maintenance budgets were reduced, many firms tightening up authorisation procedures for 'non-urgent' maintenance requests, with units expected to gain approval from their MULs or the Centre before proceeding. For instance in one large leisure organisation maintenance spend was reduced by 50 per cent in 2008, the net effect being a huge build up of work; some of which had (expensive) unintended consequences (eg as the budget for gutter clearance – leaf removal – was cut completely, water run-off caused residing wall damage in some properties that amounted to far more than the original 'savings').

2.2.1.4 Operational efficiencies

Some operators made significant attempts to optimise end-to-end service cycle efficiency by improving the layout, space management and point of purchase speed. Back of house they also reviewed process efficiency, improving IT functionality and speed of decision-making. Good housekeeping practices such as availability, shrinkage and wastage were also targeted by many firms:

- Layout and space – in reviewing their ranges (in some cases reducing product proliferation) retailers also addressed layout and shelf space with the objectives of increasing service cycle efficiency and propensity to purchase. Pinchpoints preventing the ergonomics of efficient customer movement were removed and/or space was used far more effectively. Greater use has been made of store hotspots (eg gondola ends, front of store promotion areas etc.) to drive impulse promotional spend. Given that in March 2011 it was estimated that 40 per cent of purchases in UK supermarkets were made 'on promotion', efficient use of space has been a major priority (Hall 2011a).

- Point of purchase – increasingly operators have resorted to self-service technology which has the dual benefit (in theory) of reducing labour costs and increasing shopping speed for the customer. As queuing is one of the main detractors in retailing, self-service technology provides a perfect solution for both retailers and customers. In the UK operators such as Tesco and Asda have pioneered self-service technology, although not always with intended results. A study has purportedly shown that such devices fail to reduce labour because of the help that customers require in using this nascent technology. In the US, Tesco found that self-serve technology in its 'Fresh and Easy' convenience concept proved particularly unpopular with customers. There is little doubt however, that as this technology becomes more user friendly, more chains will resort to self-service methods. In the fast casual dining sector in the UK, operators such as Nandos and Gourmet Burger have compressed the restaurant service cycle by getting customers to pay up front for their meals and drinks. This has the effect of reducing dwell times and, consequently, increasing table turns as it has cut out the time that customers spend (compared to a full service environment) ordering between courses and waiting to pay the bill. Nascent 'pre-pay' and 'cashless transaction' technology has also been introduced in some chains in an attempt to increase purchasing speed for the customer and reduce labour.

- Back of house processes – in some cases multi-unit firms have made attempts to increase efficiency through the better central systems coordination and quicker decision-making. Some companies formed cross functional teams with a view to improving process flows, such as getting procurement and marketing insight to work together on what customers want with where these products could be most effectively resourced. In some cases key strategic functions were joined together in order to speed up decision-making and collaboration; for instance, service departments being subsumed by HR to optimise staff engagement and IT functions being integrated into Finance to leverage efficient data management.

- Availability, shrinkage and wastage – in terms of good housekeeping, best practice firms have, first, concentrated on improving availability through targeting the replenishment of key sellers (such as milk, bread and tobacco in convenience) through more accurate monitoring and measurement. Second, in terms of shrinkage (theft and pilfering by customers and warehouse, logistics and retail staff) security in many high street stores has been tightened through better deployment of CCTV and more thorough auditing of delivery and stock-keeping processes. Third, wastage has been targeted, particularly fresh goods in supermarkets and 'spoilt' product or overproduction in the food and beverage sector. Taken together, all these measures, with significant unit-level operational input, have made a significant impact on some retailer margins. For instance, more accurate measurement of 'per ounce' portions of meat plated in Toby Restaurants, the UK's leading carvery brand, yielded major food margin enhancements over the period 2009–2010.

2.2.1.5 Promotions and sales efficiency

Many firms have tightened up the way in which they have analysed both the targeting and effectiveness of price promotions. Some have also addressed issues such as opening hours and better capacity utilisation through extending or changing their offer:

- Promotional effectiveness – one feature of the 2008 downturn was the extent to which firms had to pay attention to what made promotions pay. In particular, firms have had to have a better understanding of the terminal effects of constant promotions (ie BOGOFs – buy one get one free) that degrade margins when consumers, in challenging economic circumstances, only purchase promotional products. Up to this point some companies had taken a fairly unscientific approach to promotions, not fully understanding the concept of price elasticity (the recovery in volume and cash profit required to compensate for reducing price). In this regard finance personnel have had to become far more commercial, working with sales and marketing to provide insight and intelligence rather than just data.

- Multi-media channels – companies have had to become far more adept at utilising cheaper sales, marketing and promotional channels, hence the use of social media such as Facebook by some companies as a cheap, highly penetrative marketing channel which reaches core demographics for products such as clothing and beauty. The use of voucher sites (such as Groupon, mysupermarket, toptable, Savoo, MoneySavingExpert etc.) and direct selling/ promotional marketing through customized apps has also extended business-to-consumer promotional reach. Within leisure gaming, the development and co-existence of web-based sales channels has been encouraged alongside land-based multi-unit – offering firms valuable off-peak sales opportunities.

- Capacity utilisation – with a large fixed overhead some firms have examined ways to make more effective returns through means of attracting more customers during non-peak trading periods and/or longer opening hours. For instance, Greggs in the UK extended its opening hours to start breakfast trading, giving it a far more efficient use of its assets. Grosvenor Casinos introduced 24/7 opening on the basis that the costs of closing down and then opening again in a very short time period were greater than remaining open for business.

- Format spin-offs – some multi-unit enterprises have taken elements of their core offer (eg home and furniture in John Lewis and clothing in Tescos and Asda) and set up standalone land-based sales entities. Thus, higher growth or margin areas of the business can be expanded in smaller, cheaper spaces in areas with low sales penetration.

2.2.2 DIFFERENTIATION

The other long-term sustainable strategy identified by Porter was differentiation. In respect to multi-unit enterprises this can be defined as the extent to which firms are able to create an identifiable advantage over their competitors with regard to controllable elements of their offer. Such organisations created distinctiveness around elements such as customer service, the shopping/eating experience and product quality. This can be a costly strategy designed to appeal to a segment of the market which is willing to pay extra for a higher degree of added value. Alternatively, companies might seek to understand *cost-value* relationship of various elements of the customer offer, in some cases discovering what the customer values most, which might be of minor or inconsequential cost to them! This section will now consider the various elements in turn.

2.2.2.1 Amenity and experience

Organisations that pursue this generic strategy understand that alongside meeting the functional needs of customers, making an emotional connection can secure long-term relationships and loyalty. Chains that make the in-store experience stimulating, exiting and fun are sure to engage the consumer's imagination and, consequently, stimulate their propensity to purchase. This approach goes beyond functional rationality. The means through which some firms have pursued this goal include improved amenity and environment, inventive zoning and special events:

- Amenity and environment – sensory stimulation is a key objective of firms that wish to differentiate. What consumers hear, see, touch, feel and smell will lead to indelible conscious or unconscious levels of recognition and association (Sorenson 2010). Thus, great attention must be paid to the art and science of designing the store amenity and environment. In the past retailers have paid special attention to all elements of the fit out; lighting, fixture quality, floor covering, ceiling height, elevated areas, colours etc. Some high end retailers, like Burberry, have used new technology as a key inbuilt element of their offer; web-based holographic big screens to bring scenes, accompanied by evocative music, of international catwalks showcasing their brands and in-store touch screen 'garment browsing' applications. Through these means Burberry aims to make a powerful and enduring emotional connection with its customers.

• Zoning – in the past it has been a common tactic of department stores to zone their offer in order to provide shoppers with variety, choice and interest. This approach has been replicated by other retailers to varying degrees of success; stores have tended to segment their space according to gender or product type rather than a series of exciting spaces addressing occasionality (ie low energy regular or high energy special purchase). Now high-end retailers are zoning stores according to special occasionality. For instance, the upmarket jeweller Ernest Jones is creating zones for high end special purchases such as a 'Rolex' zone, where customers feel that they are entering a space befitting the 'specialness' associated with purchasing such a premium product.

• Events – special events that act as a promotional device and provide amusement, diversion and excitement in-store have been a regular feature of stores wishing to differentiate. Signings, tastings, demonstrations and celebrity visits have all been means by which stores have been able to generate publicity and footfall in their local micro-markets. Today, even if customers are unable to visit, chains are able to convey the impression, by showcasing and streaming these events live through multi-media channels, that their offer is dynamic rather than static.

2.2.2.2 Product distinctiveness

Chains that can claim uniqueness for elements of their product offering are better placed than those that have merely replicated or copied their competitive set. This point of difference serves as a powerful footfall driver if the product is high quality and possesses inimitable attributes. Distinctiveness can be conveyed in three ways; merchandising and packaging, private label brands and exclusive supplier brands:

- Merchandising and packaging – in the past, multi-unit retailers have paid considerable attention to designing planograms with the objective of displaying merchandise in order to attract shopper attention and transmit subliminal messages. Thus, supermarkets have arranged colourful perishables, such as fruit, front of store to emphasise the freshness and abundance of the general product offer. In premium environments the placement of signature products that create a 'halo', 'hero' or 'signature' effect for the rest of the store offering has been a common technique. Also many chains have worked with suppliers on the distinctiveness of their packaging, which also acts as key purchase trigger point. Today upscale chains are using techniques such as digital imagery on their web sites to convey the quality of their merchandise; as such it acts as another form of shop window to attract and/or reinforce the views of customers.

- Private label – own label products that emphasise special benefits are another form of differentiation. In supermarkets, products based on distinctive recipes which emphasise attributes such as health and ingredient quality will attract consumer attention, particularly if they are priced beneath well-known brands. In fashion, proprietorial brands that are exclusive only to that chain and are not sold through other channels are a powerful attractor. In the UK both Sainsbury's and Waitrose have had considerable success in establishing 'treat-led' own label premium ranges that undercut establish brands and value-led everyday 'essentials' ranges. Leveraging the endorsement of 'celebrities' or domain experts, further bolsters the credentials and authenticity of own label offers (ie Gok Wan styled fashion in Sainsbury's and Heston Blumethal crafted premium food in Waitrose) The UK chemist Boots has had considerable success with its own label beauty products; particularly its No7 anti-ageing range (Walsh and Goodman 2011).

- Exclusivity – chains that are able to claim exclusive access to a range of manufacturer products can lay claim to distinctiveness that serves them well in terms of competitive positioning. The payback for manufacturers is that they are assured a contract run of orders and higher penetration in-store due to product support from the retailer. In the UK, premium beer producers such SAB have restricted the supply of products such as Nastro Assuri and Peroni to specified upscale pub and restaurant chains. This preserves their price premium status whilst affording the vendors special status.

2.2.2.3 Customer promise and service

Most chains state that their primary stakeholder focus revolves around 'engaging their employees' and 'satisfying their customers'. Implicit within this is the notion that both factors are linked, although it is surprising how few firms *scientifically* evaluate the connections between the two as a basis for action. Providing superior levels of customer support is a major form of differentiation that is a major controllable lever for most organisations. Those that differentiate in this respect do so in the following regard: explicit and valuable promises that generate trust with customers; employee empowerment to immediately rectify customer concerns/complaints at source, and HRM systems that improve employee skills, knowledge and behaviours:

- Promise and trust – some companies formalise their relationships with customers by making visible, explicit promises that set them apart from their competitors. These promises can include price guarantees (such as Sainsbury's successful 2011–2012 Brand Match campaign which granted customers coupons at point-of-purchase, refunding any price differentials with Asda and Tesco on key brands), no quibble returns, assurances on ethical sourcing and a commitment to environmental and social causes. For instance the John Lewis Department Store chain in the UK makes the promise 'never knowingly undersold', employing price checkers to visit local competitors in order to ensure that, at worst, their prices are matched. If customers have bought the same product cheaper elsewhere John Lewis promises to refund the difference. In terms of building trust John Lewis also trains its partners to advise customers on the most suitable goods for their needs by motivating them through good salaries, equitable PRP with senior executives and market-leading terms and conditions rather than commission-based compensation. Other firms have built trust through making it explicit their policy never to sell anything that might be deemed objectionable to customers (such as children's clothing with inappropriate messaging) and safety standards that exceed minimum regulatory requirements. For instance, some restaurant chains have built 'open' kitchens where customers can see for themselves the high standards of hygiene and cleanliness taken during the food preparation process. Finally, some chains have built trust with customers by never putting poor quality food and garments on display through stringent in-house quality control testing systems.

- Rectification and recovery – there is one common practice that binds multi-unit firms that offer superior customer service together; the extent to which they empower front-line employees to rectify complaints immediately. Empirical research demonstrates that at source resolution recovers perception, actually leading to higher levels of customer satisfaction. Generally the customer expects to be referred to a higher authority ('sorry there's nothing I can do; I'll go and get my manager') or some anonymous central function. This can lead to high levels of customer anxiety and frustration. Perception exceeds expectation when front-line staff deal instantly with complaints through rectification methods such as immediate apologies, money-back and/or an offer of a substitute product or vouchers. For instance, the Four Seasons Hotel chain grants total autonomy to its staff when dealing with customer complaints. Having put its staff through appropriate induction and training in the values of the chain, it trusts its staff to respond appropriately and swiftly to any customer complaints. Unsurprisingly, this business has been consistently ranked in the top 5 businesses in the world for customer service.

- Best practice HRM – another feature of differentiated companies is the extent to which they invest in best practice HRM systems (see Chapter 4 for definition). Companies that devote investment to high quality selection, intensive training, good pay and benefits (with equitable differentials), two-way channels of communication and have an ethos of autonomy, status parity and meritocratic career development, are more likely to generate sustainable levels of good customer service. In addition companies that hire employees with a knowledge and passion for the sector market (such as 'foodies' for high-end supermarkets, 'wine buffs' in drinks units and 'techies' in electronics stores) and the provision of specialist product training for staff, free samples, tastings and visits to suppliers are likely to gain far higher levels of commitment, motivation and discretionary effort.

2.2.3 VALUE

The inevitable question that arises, following consideration of cost-led and differentiated strategies, is whether or not firms can pursue both strategies as a form of long-term sustainable competitive advantage? Academic and empirical evidence would suggest this is possible under the banner of value-led strategies (Heskett et al 2003). Here companies pursue elements of the strategies outlined above, including aspects such as relatively low prices combined with product quality, differentiated goods and a superior customer experience (for a full overview see Berman 2010: 173-197). Thus, when UK supermarkets such as Morrisons advertise their offer with the strapline 'pay less, eat fresh' and Sainsbury's 'quality where it matters', they are signalling to the customer that they are offering quality in the areas that count to consumers without compromising a relatively low price approach. In this respect they are addressing a core customer need, in that 60 per cent of consumers rank 'good value for money' as the most important factor in choosing a grocery store (ACNielson 2007). Within the Casual Dining sector in the UK, value for money is cited by 64 per cent of consumers as being important to their overall experience, with food quality standing at 76 per cent (Peach Report 2011).

The value profit chain outlined in an important contribution by Heskett et al (2003) is a useful way of understanding the main drivers behind a value-led strategy. In their model they highlight the main elements of 'value' as being 'results' + 'process quality' divided by 'price' + 'customer access costs'. What is significant about this framework is the notion that price, being one part of the mix, can be offset by superior customer experiences in relation to product quality (results), service speed and politeness (process quality) and location (customer access costs). This section will use this framework to outline value strategies pursued by multi-unit enterprises, albeit the detail relating to each part of the equation will be limited given their elucidation in prior sections.

2.2.3.1 Results-based solutions

In Heskett et al's (2003) model the notion of results highlights the fact that firms need to go *beyond* product to emphasise solutions. For instance, firms can maximise the results element of the value proposition by bundling various attributes and benefits that meet consumer *needs* and *values*. Hence in grocery, products that are locally sourced might be positioned as addressing *needs* such as health and freshness, whilst attending to *values* such as sustainability. In apparel stores, *needs* can be met through no quibble returns policies or services such as free alterations to garments purchased at full price, whilst *values* are addressed through ethical production and sourcing methods. Further examples of solutions that extend beyond merely product include the following approaches;

- Quality – extensive product testing by the retailer

- Warranties – inclusion of warranties alongside product quality promise

- Benefits – product freshness, taste, safety and health benefits (ie. food that is low in salt, additives, fat and cholesterol).

2.2.3.2 Process quality

This portion of the value equation includes superior customer service (such as high quality customer interaction), high levels of service fault rectification, smooth and efficient service cycles, ease of access and good availability, short queues and speedy service and a quality shopping environment (HBR 2008). Process quality exceeding customer expectation can be a powerful *attractor*, enabling firms to position their offer beyond merely price. Examples of superior customer service factors include the following:

- access – accessibility and availability of product (eg 'click and collect' services)

- flow – layout flow and ease of store navigation

- speed – ease of payment and short queues

- politeness – positive staff-customer interaction

- experience – exciting and engaging in-store experience

- rectification – outstanding service rectification (money back or substitution).

2.2.3.3 Price

The importance of price is high, notwithstanding other elements of the value proposition that might offset its critical influence. Of the aforementioned 60 per cent of consumers who ranked value as being the most important factor in choosing a grocery store, 80 per cent defined value as 'promotions and discounts' and (somewhat confusingly) 70 per cent 'everyday low price' (ACNeilson 2007) . Retailers must therefore balance this essential conundrum of providing costly elements of the value profit chain (ie service and product quality) whilst simultaneously addressing the price element of the equation. In 2012 research by the consumer analysts Mintel on supermarket retailing in the UK established that 'own label' sales accounted for 54 per cent of new products, compared to 46 per cent for 'big brands' (Steiner 2012c). Own label has become a very powerful price tool in this sector, enabling companies to retain more margin – rather than giving it to the *upstream* brand owner – whilst delivering price value *downstream* to the consumer. Other means have included:

- unbundling – deconstructing the offer to reduce 'bad' purchase costs (allowing customers to choose elements of the greatest value to them)

- upselling – price promotions offset by upselling non-discounted products.

- 'range pricing' – offering 'good, better, best' product lines with different 'price point entries' enabling customers to choose whether or not to trade up or down.

2.2.3.4 Customer access costs

In the final element of value profit chain, addressing negative customer experiences will reduce customer access costs, increasing propensity to visit and purchase. If customers perceive high barriers to entry with regards to 'personal' cost and time they are unlikely to return. Thus, firms must scientifically address *detractors* in order to reduce perceived penalties such as;

- travel charges – removing car parking charges or providing free public transport

- security and safety – increasing security infrastructure (ie CCTV-based 'face recognition' files that can be downloaded to the police) to prevent car vandalism and hooligan behaviour in-store.

- one visit offer – enhancing 'one stop' shopping experience through extensive offers and ranges

- opening flexibility – extending opening hours

- fees – reducing or scrapping onerous 'membership' fees.

It is important to emphasise that the *numerators* of value – results and process quality – are perceived as major attributes by customers (Berman 2009: 193). Both elements can be used by firms as powerful differentiators. They can offset the *denominators* of the value profit model, price and access costs, but only to the extent that their perceived value outweighs any increased costs. Therefore, service companies that pursue a value strategy have to tread a very fine line in trying to balance the numerators against denominators, with those charging too much for little perceived benefit risking serious drop offs in footfall and dwell time.

2.3 Organisational Design

Pursuing a definitive strategic path is essential but will ultimately fail unless the firm accompanies strategy with structural congruence in order to ensure optimal execution (Pugh 1984). Quite simply, how people are organised is critical to the effectiveness any strategy (Chandler 1962). This section will, after briefly considering types of organisational structure, examine the structure and form of the multi-unit firm. What does the archetypal multi-unit firm look like? What are the roles and responsibilities within these organisations? How do successful enterprises configure themselves to operate in an optimal manner?

According to Mintzberg (1979) basic organisational form is determined, alongside strategy, by external issues such as market complexity (product, geography and customer) and internal factors such as firm-life, professional elites and ideology. Organisations are designed around six building blocks:

the strategic apex, techno-structure, support staff, ideology, middle line and operating core. The dominance of any of these building blocks is contingent on factors such as the level of supervision required, degree of standardisation of work, skills, outputs or norms. Mintzberg's six ideal forms – simple, machine bureaucracy, professional bureaucracy, divisionalised, adhocracy and missionary – are configured as a consequence of these situational factors and key design parameters. Other commentators, developing Mintzberg's framework, also identify six basic structural forms – simple, functional, multi-divisional, holding company, matrix and network. In many ways it can be argued that the multi-unit enterprise is similar to the simple Weberian bureaucratic form which has organisational principles based around standardised roles, a defined managerial hierarchy and a central chain of command.

In fact, the multi-unit firms analysed for this book exhibited remarkably similar structural characteristics. In all instances firms had Mintzberg's six building blocks. The strategic apex in these enterprises, usually comprising the functional heads and the operational MDs, sets the goals and direction of the organisation. Data and insights for its actions was supplied by the techno-structure; specialist marketing, property, HR, finance and risk and compliance personnel, who also performed the function of translating executive decisions into actions. Support staff generally assisted the middle line and operating core in implementing new processes, policies, procedures and initiatives.

Differences between organisations related mainly to ideology. The introduction referred to the issues relating to multi-unit firms, namely consistency, customisation versus standardisation, Centre versus field and perceived lack of autonomy in the operational core. It is interesting to note that this research exposed two archetypal multi-unit models which could be classified displaying either a 'hard' or 'soft' bias. 'Hard' versions of the multi-unit model had a tendency to impose total standardisation, restricting autonomy through exercise strict control from the Centre. In this model the strategic apex and techno-structure had complete primacy, with little involvement with, or input from, the operational line. In this form expertise was deemed to reside centrally, hence initiatives, innovation and change flowed from top to bottom with virtually no consultation from the line. In 'softer' versions of the multi-unit model, there were established feedback and communication mechanisms from the line, enabling the Centre to adjust and improve its interventions. Thus, whilst on the surface structures seemed remarkably similar, there were nuanced differences in *how* organisations processed information and implemented strategy.

Why did organisations exhibit 'hard' or 'soft' characteristics? First, the size of the multi-unit firm was a factor, with larger firms with greater spans of control having to impose 'hard' order and discipline through large networks of multiple units for the sake of consistency and dependability. Second, the type of strategy pursued was significant, with low cost operators operating a far harder control and compliance model than those pursuing a differentiated path. Cost, functionality and simplicity accounted for the fact that low cost operators like Aldi and Netto had far more standardised regimes than other differentiated and/or value operators such as Sainsbury's and Tesco. Third, choice as to whether or not a 'hard' or 'soft' model was applicable related to the required levels of local customisation. In companies where a high degree was required, companies tended to operate a 'soft' multi-unit model in order to ensure a high level of flexibility and adaptability to local markets. Lastly, the economic crisis precipitated in 2007, tipped many multi-unit firms into 'hard' operational mode with a need for companies to ensure maximum efficiency through reducing cost, particularly through labour overhead control. Local autonomy and discretion has been curtailed with the Centre requiring final sign-off on many items of spend such as maintenance and repair.

2.3.1 BEST PRACTICE DESIGN PRINCIPLES

Whilst there were a number of generic structural characteristics relating to the multi-unit enterprises analysed during the course of research, there were also some clear best practice design principles. A few enterprises studied during the course of this research had built in processes and mechanisms that facilitated strong alignment, gates that filtered initiatives and information sent out to the line, feedback and review loops, re-set mechanisms and rapid decision-making forums.

2.3.1.1 Alignment mechanisms

Unlike many other organisational forms, operational roles within multi-unit enterprises are general rather than specialised. This means that accountability and responsibility for many metrics and processes is shared by the different operational levels. It is important, therefore, that organisations pay sufficient attention designing optimal overlap of 'roles and goals'. That is not to say that there is unnecessary duplication, rather, the organisation provides a 'multi-layered net' (Garvin and Levesque 2008) that is capable of dealing with systemic threats through shared accountability. Hence, service performance issues are shared at all operational levels rather than being 'outsourced' to front line operatives. Best practice companies observed by this study (such as Sainsbury's) had balanced scorecard mechanisms that translated into KPIs that were remarkably consistent from the top down, lending consistency of purpose and line of sight.

2.3.1.2 Gates and 'filtration' processes

Prior to initiatives being launched some best practice organisations ensure releases are regulated and 'sense checked' prior to release. This is problematic. In many multi-unit enterprises few operators (voluntarily) opt for transfers into the Centre because as one retail senior operator remarked during the course of this research 'we are too well incentivised, and, if truth be told, incapable of doing the job and frightened of being on the receiving end!' This causes issues when operational plans and initiatives are conceived by central staff with limited knowledge (due to their prior experience and distance from the line) as to how to translate them into finely tuned action plans. It is at this point – between conception and implementation – that best practice organisations deploy resources that focus upon shaping and moulding the content and process of initiatives into workable solutions. Initiatives that flow from the Centre in an unfettered manner, without any input from personnel with direct operational experience, are likely to fail.

In addition to this 'moulding' activity, well designed multi-unit enterprises have structural checks and balances in place sifting the quality and quantity of information that flows from the Centre to the units. In some organisations specific support function roles are assigned at the Centre, such as Operational Services Managers (OSMs) who will oversee ERP (Enterprise Resourse Planning) systems (with a calendar of events and releases), regulating the flow of initiatives and new policies to the units. OSMs often have responsibility for the Operations Administration teams supporting the units, reporting directly into Divisional Directors. In ideal circumstances OSMs worked closely with decision-makers in the line to decide whether or not specific information releases or initiatives are commensurate with operational priorities, preventing the onward transmission of non-value added instructions. In some organisations information releases and downloads were restricted to certain times of the day (usually pre-opening) or week (typically Friday) in order to prevent distracting unit managers with a constant barrage of data.

Companies that had robust gates through which information was checked and regulated prior to release to the operational line had far fewer complaints from unit managers that they were unable to discharge their duties due to 'admin' and information overload than those that allowed unregulated, free-flowing communication to the Units from all functions at the Centre. Unfortunately, as Chapter 3 will demonstrate, such organisations were the exception rather than the rule.

2.3.1.3 Feedback and insight loops

Another best-practice design principle was built-in feedback loops from the line to the Centre which afforded real time information and (more importantly) insights on the impact and success of certain launches and initiatives. For instance at international fashion retail company Zara (5,500 stores owned by Spanish firm Inditex) qualitative feedback is sought on the latest launches from unit managers by the Centre the day after placement (Keeley 2012). 'Trend information' on what colours and designs the customers liked is sought immediately and, when linked to quantitative data, informs decision-making on succeeding ranges:

> A system is in place for retail staff to transmit information (on ranges) straight to the design team at Arteixo (Hume 2011: 23).

> Store Managers hold daily staff meetings to discuss hyper-local trends, such as which colour of pastel trousers are selling well in Dubai, or what hemlines are it in Bogota. Information which is then fed back to headquarters ... (Johnson and Felsted 2011: 13).

Also, some companies such as Timpsons (the UK-based cobbler and key cutter chain) hold regular feedback meetings between operators and senior managers, considering a range of issues such as which product lines work, which practice changes are required and what operational improvements can be made to increase efficiency and effectiveness. What was noticeable, however, was how such feedback loops were absent in most of the multi-unit enterprises examined for this research.

2.3.1.4 Re-set mechanisms

One of the main problems that multi-unit organisations have is sets of legacy practices and systems that have lost their relevance. Organisations are notoriously bad at reviewing and reducing redundant reportage, 'red tape' and ossified operational instructions. However there was one organisation reviewed during the course of this research which made regular efforts to 're-set' its operations following regular reviews of all its practices and procedures. This organisation, a major UK supermarket, took a unit every couple of years and analysed all its systems, policies, practices and processes. It did so in order to address the questions; what is mandatory for legal and operational excellence and what is superfluous or 'nice to have'? They then experimented by resetting operations in the pilot unit, measuring outcomes with regards to process and operational efficiency. The interventions that worked and improved operations then became standard across the estate. This company was almost unique in this approach amongst managed service operations; less so amongst franchise firms (such as McDonald's).

2.3.1.5 Rapid decision forums

Another feature of best practice design was the presence of decision-making forums with the authority to make instant or rapid decisions. Outside the normal monthly central meeting cycle of Product, HR, Promotions, Pricing and Capital Executives some firms had lines of communications set up where units could seek instant decisions to practical operational problems. One organisation had a daily operational telephone conference call where a unit manager representing his/her district fed back operational issues and dilemmas for instant decision-making (eg how to shift non-selling general merchandise). This organisation believed that it resolved almost 90 per cent of the issues and problems that were highlighted by operations within 7 working days. The whole process worked due to the fact that a senior operational executive chaired the calls, lending it credibility and force. Also, participants in the process had reached a level of insight and maturity which ensured that only issues of consequence were raised for a high quality debate. Such a mechanism was notable for its almost unique nature within the companies studied for this book.

2.3.1.6 Talent planning processes

Given the critical nature of the human element of multi-units, organisational design principles should incorporate sufficient mechanisms for constant talent review and calibration. Many companies examined for this research apportioned significant amounts of time during operational meetings to assess capability and deployment and/or schedule regular manpower planning sessions to take stock of requirements, gaps and solutions. The HR team often worked closely with the operational team at all levels to forecast manpower demand and then run selection, training and career development programmes to meet operational requirements. Informally, a constant process of assessment and judgement occurred in most multi-unit enterprises where operations personnel identified and located talent, acting as coaches and mentors to certain key individuals for significant periods of time. Often unit managers would switch districts to work for their former mentors and supervisors and district managers; tracking trusted former superiors into new regions (or companies if they moved out of the organisation). The issue around this best practice design principle was not so much that it was absent as a process, rather it lacked the authority to move talent across regions, areas and brands (if multi-branded). Operators were exceptionally territorial and parochial – nurturing their own talent within their own spheres of influence.

2.3.2 OPERATIONAL ROLES

Because of the dispersed nature of multi-unit enterprises the operational core plays a vital role in ensuring strategic implementation. Typically there are four levels of manager that sit in this area, fulfilling strategic and non-strategic implementation roles according to their levels of seniority; divisional director, regional director, district manager and unit manager. In the view of Garvin and Levesque (2008), who refer to these managers as 'the field', this cohort is key;

> ... *the success of the multiunit corporation depends on the competence, capabilities and commitment of field managers, who embody the brand through their actions, oversee daily operations, and implement new initiatives ... (2008: 6).*

What is significant about these roles is the degree to which, first, unlike other business structures, they have a high degree of *mutually interdependent accountabilities* and responsibilities to create a 'multi-layered net' that prevents operational breakdowns (Garvin and Levesque 2008). Second, their jobs are less specialised than those of middle managers in classic bureaucratic organisations, having a set of general management functions that involves the supervision of standards, systems and service.

As previously stated, it is the contention of this book that the key role in the operational hierarchy, and indeed throughout multi-unit organisations, is the district manager (MUL). Indeed in Garvin and Levesque's model of overlapping responsibilities (2008: 5) *eight out of the 10 fundamental priorities* of the operational line fall within the MUL domain, a far higher number than for the three other operational management cohorts (unit, regional and divisional).

While the role of this essential group of employees is discussed in great depth in later chapters, a brief synopsis of the main roles and responsibilities of the operational line is pertinent in order to provide context at this stage.

2.3.2.1 Unit managers

Unit managers are expected to fulfil the least strategic role of the operational line. Typically they operate under tight controls from the Centre, often to a defined operational blueprint that details the operational processes, policies and procedures of the brand or chain. They have little input into issues such as pricing, promotions, store and shelf layout and stocking policies. In addition to the operational blueprint, well organised multi-unit firms regulate the operational rhythm of the units by daily or weekly electronic 'management action systems' which supply guidance on new initiatives, stock and promotions to unit managers. They are tightly appraised – with very little consultation – on a multitude of targets which involve output (financial and operational, safety, wastage, availability etc.) and input-led (customer service and employee satisfaction) indicators. The degree to which organisations place emphasis on either output or input measures is likely to rest with the financial position of the firm and/or its dominant ideology. Firms operating within the 'hard' paradigm are more likely to be concerned with outputs, whilst those operating within the 'soft' paradigm are more likely to have more of an input focus.

Autonomy for unit managers lies in three areas. First, unit managers must exercise discretion with regard to the recruitment, training, deployment and motivation of their staff. Second, they play a key role in regulating the implementation and execution of new initiatives and key calendar activities. Third, in some multi-unit firms, unit managers are granted limited autonomy in matters such as product display, price markdowns to shift end of date/ season stock and the ability to order certain goods locally.

The contribution that unit managers make to the P&L can be significant. Retail firms surveyed for this book estimated that a good unit manager could add 10 per cent to store turnover, whilst leisure companies, with a far higher degree of emotional customer connection, anything up to 30 per cent. Their added value contribution lies in three main areas; maintaining and improving *standards* such as store cleanliness, effectively using labour deployment *systems* and overseeing superior customer *service*. The main detractors from these value added activities are lack of delegation, failure to lead teams effectively and general inability to plan, prioritise and organise tasks and processes. The latter point is significant. The role of a unit manager as a trouble shooter and problem solver – resolving issues such as late deliveries, customer complaints, damaged fixtures and fittings and optimally organising workflows – is a key contributor to the unit's success.

2.3.2.2 Area/District/Regional managers (MULs)

The nature of the role of the area manager or MUL is the subject of greater analysis later in this book. At this juncture, however, it is necessary to understand how the role meshes within the operational hierarchy. Essentially, area managers, who typically oversee 12-20 units in a defined geographic area (although hard discounters like Aldi and fast food operators such as McDonalds generally allocate 8 with large 'big box retailers' extending to 32), have three main functions; ensuring that there is consistent execution of *standards* at store level, that performance *systems* are improved and talented people are deployed to enact perfect execution and sales-led *service*. As they are measured on an aggregate of the measures applied to their stores (financial, operational, service and satisfaction) they have congruent objectives with their unit managers; any improvement in their unit manager performance being directly beneficial to themselves. Like unit managers, however, area managers have little input into their budgets, pricing and property investment decisions and promotions.

Additional responsibilities do lend the role a degree of discretion and autonomy. For instance, area managers will be heavily involved in new store openings and will have some input into pre-opening site design meetings. They are also, in some organisations, able to provide input to the Centre on new product and service initiatives through being co-opted onto cross-functional design groups. However, their added value to the organisation manifests itself in four principal ways. First, they generate *commitment* at unit level through the key role of appointing the right unit managers, coaching them and managing their career development. Seeking to optimise their portfolio of stores, area managers will also concentrate on building significant in-store bench strength, in order to move and deploy skills across the district to maximise standards and service (see Chapter 3) . Second, they perform an important *control* and audit function, ensuring that units are compliant with company policies and procedures (see Chapter 4). Third, they act as important intermediaries in *change* processes by leading the implementation of any new initiatives or projects at district level (see Chapter 5). Fourth, their knowledge of formal and informal networks at the Centre enables them to act as 'fixers', solving problems at store level through their knowledge of key people at the Centre.

As will be highlighted later on, successful area managers are able to balance the commitment-control paradox through adapting their leadership style and engaging in sophisticated levels of negotiation and *social exchange*. Poor area managers will do more auditing than coaching, operate a static, inflexible leadership style, fail to delegate important tasks across their districts and are insufficiently attuned to the importance of talent management.

2.3.2.3 Regional/Zone director

The regional or zone director, who commonly has direct responsibility for about eight area managers, plays a more strategic role in the organisation. These managers focus internally upon any resolving systemic problems in their regions and externally upon the dynamics of their regional markets, noting what their competitors are doing and identifying any growth opportunities. They are the vital strategic link with the stores, spending half their time in their operations, reinforcing goals and identifying trends, and the other half at the Centre where they provide input to projects, work groups and site selection. Typically, the regional director has dotted line reports including marketing, HR, finance, audit and sometimes property, who provide another direct link to the Centre.

The added value they provide is three-fold. First, acting as hubs between the Centre and operations, they transmit valuable operational insights upwards and drive corporate priorities downwards. They perform a particularly valuable role in ensuring that the Centre's plans are turned into viable action plans and their regional team is aligned with its purpose and intent. Second, they act as interpreters of competitor activity and important consumer nuances within distinctive local markets. To this extent their input is essential in corporate policy making with regard to promotions, range, pricing and labour. Third, they are directly responsible for the P&L for their regions with many of their performance objectives overlapping those of their district and unit managers.

Effective regional directors avoid being accused of being 'barons', interested only in their own fiefdoms, through even handed engagement upwards and downwards in the multi-unit enterprise. They are able to balance corporate priorities with local needs, concentrating on driving consistency within their own particular regions. Poor behaviours amongst this cohort include obsessing with compliance to the detriment of service, mindless resistance to well designed Central initiatives or subservient acceptance of poor ones. Interestingly, this research revealed that this cohort was actually being granted extra power and autonomy by many multi-unit companies (one company renaming them Brand Operations Directors) in order to bolster regional customisation (such as the stocking of local products and community impact projects).

2.3.2.4 Divisional/Managing directors

Like regional directors, this cohort of operational executives fulfils a largely strategic role although, unlike their direct reports (usually numbering about six), they have more corporate power to enact change. The main objectives of this role are to guide and inform the organisation on the strategic path required for operational success and to act as a *integrating* force between the Centre and the operational line. Although they are less connected to day-to-day issues than regional directors and area managers they will spend approximately 25 per cent of their time in the field gauging understanding of the organisation's strategy and the impact of various initiatives and programmes. Their main added value to the organisation relates to their formulation of divisional plans and objectives that are sensitive to corporate priorities but also specific divisional business needs. Acting on divisional data and insights the divisional director (or managing director) might, for instance, meld the annual plan to monitor and measure improvements in perceived weaknesses such as service, due diligence or labour ratio measures. Given their positional power in the organisation they are also able to mobilise central resource to provide support for these priorities.

Effective divisional directors will have good planning and communication skills and an ability to set a clear direction and inspire their divisions to meet their goals. They will generate trust whilst being discreet in relation to some of the market sensitive intelligence that they will have on the future of the brand and estate. Like the best regional directors, they will be able to establish and utilise strong formal and informal networks at the Centre. Those who regard the Centre as an irritant are likely to be destructive both to the company and, ultimately, their divisions. Divisional directors who are able to make a clear distinction between their role and that of their regional directors are also likely to be far more successful. They are not close enough to customers and competitors on a regional basis to fully understand their trends and dynamics but by listening and incorporating intelligence from their regional directors into corporate plans (such as talent, property and capital decisions) they can fulfill a vital role.

2.4 Internationalising Multi-Unit Enterprises

In comparison to FMCG producers and other industries such as car manufacturing, domestic multiple chains have been slow to internationalise operations. Although notable exceptions existed in retail (US variety retailer FW Woolworth in the UK in the early twentieth century and C&A around Europe in the late 1960s) the hotels sector (Holiday Inn and Hilton from the 1950s onwards) and fast food (McDonald's from the 1970s onwards) multi-unit enterprises have taken a cautious approach to international expansion until the latter part of the twentieth century. Why? First, multi-unit enterprises were more concerned with gaining domestic and regional ascendancy through organic growth and local M&A activity than foreign expansion. Second, the levels of capital required for land-based expansion are high, with investors being nervous about costly foreign adventures that might end in failure (high profile UK examples in the past including Sainsbury's in the US and Marks and Spencer in France). Third, related to the previous point, well established domestic and regional multi-unit enterprises in some sectors provided formidable competition to aspirant entrants in many developed markets.

Over the past 20 years, however, there has been a marked growth in the globalisation of multi-unit enterprises. This section will consider the reasons for this trend for internationalisation and then consider the expansion routes and market entry strategies adopted by firms. It will then consider the reasons why international expansion has failed or succeeded. Finally, the role of the operational line – in particular MULs – will be considered in relation to internationalising multi-unit firms. How significant are they in ensuring that companies are successful when pursuing this strategy?

2.4.1 WHY INTERNATIONALISE?

The growing trend for multi-unit enterprises to internationalise their operations has been assisted by macro factors such as the globalisation of business generally, increased travel and the spread of social and commercial media. There are, however, four specific reasons why multi-unit firms have chosen to internationalise:

2.4.1.1 Diversification and growth

Like firms in other industries, multi-unit enterprises have sought to internationalise their operations in order to balance their portfolios. Seeking to mitigate the effects of domestic economic cycles, organisations have expanded abroad in order to hedge against a dependency on a single domestic market. Gaining international reach has also had the additional benefit of making firms more resistant to takeovers as the winners in the race for international scale have insulated themselves from bids through accelerating their market capitalisation beyond most suitors.

2.4.1.2 Developing markets

In the same way that chains disrupted independents in western economies at the beginning of the twentieth century, developing countries are experiencing the same pattern of events (increased urbanisation, growth of the middle classes and better transport) leading to demand for better goods and services. Although indigenous chains have grown up to service these needs, the scale and economic power of nascent international multi-unit enterprises has meant that they have been well placed, through a variety of means, to enter these new markets.

2.4.1.3 Efficiency

Increasing scale through foreign expansion has also enabled certain organisations to make efficiency gains through reducing their buying costs for certain goods through greater volume sales and better utilisation of their technology platforms. Supermarket chains have been able to renegotiate contract prices with large FMCG producers based on increased sales. Hotel companies like IHG (International Hotel Group) have been able to utilise their sophisticated booking platforms to leverage growth from international travellers in locations they have opened in developing territories.

2.4.1.4 Defence

Another reason for internationalising lies in companies seeking to defend their country of origin businesses against the competitive threat from foreign entrants. This so called 'follow the competitor' strategy allows firms that have expanded abroad into competitor territory to retaliate to aggressive moves such as price discounting and promotions in their home markets.

2.4.2 HOW DO MULTI-UNIT ENTERPRISES INTERNATIONALISE?

Internationalisation theory (Rugman 1981, Rugman and Hodgetts 2003) dictates that internationalising firms typically adopt a low risk strategy to enter markets due to lack of perfect information in uncertain foreign environments. With regard to multi-unit enterprises there are five types of market penetration approaches, with graduating degrees of risk:

2.4.2.1 Web-based penetration

Advances in web-based technology have enabled multi-unit firms to adopt a new low risk market penetration strategy of setting up online order catalogues. For instance, Marks and Spencer re-entered the French market in 2011 with one showcase store backed up by a website that offers over 30,000 goods for guaranteed two-day delivery anywhere in France. This approach is designed to raise consumer awareness, minimising capital outlay on store infrastructure whilst the next stages of expansion are examined.

2.4.2.2 Franchising

A slightly higher risk strategy involves the licencing by a Franchisor to a Franchisee (single or multiple) of the intellectual property (typically the operational blueprint and design) of their standardised format in exchange for a fixed fee. Additional fees might also be charged for use of proprietorial technology, marketing and promotions support and supply chain access. Risk here lies for the Franchisor in the form of Franchisees undermining the essence of the chain through imperfect execution. Also, insufficient support to Franchisees (along the lines of those promised in the licencing document) could lead to costly claims and reputational damage for the Franchisor.

2.4.2.3 Green site

Firms can enlist local consultants (such as consumer insight, marketing and property) to help their management build a business in foreign territories on a site-by-site basis. This is the strategy that has been adopted by Tesco in the US with their Fresh & Easy convenience chain and Nandos in the UK with their fast casual dining format. Both companies have eschewed any form of partnership agreement or acquisition in favour of patient organic growth. Theoretically, the merit of such a strategy is that the right sites can be purchased for the brand and the firm avoids any integration issues that arise from M&A. Issues arise, however, if firms select the wrong sites due to lack of market knowledge and/ or fail to adjust the consumer proposition appropriately if the initial stores fail to deliver to initial expectations. For instance, Tesco has admitted that it failed to properly understand its US consumers during its expensive launch of Fresh & Easy convenience stores, having to make adjustments to its pre-packed fruit offer, increase its frozen lines, include more brands than own label and reduce self-service terminals (Felsted and Jopson 2011).

2.4.2.4 Joint ventures

Partnering with local companies is another means of mitigating risk. Companies might choose this as a soft route to entry, framing a local joint venture agreement where it utilises the knowledge and expertise of a local firm to roll out its standardised product, whilst ensuring that risk is equally spread between both parties as the local partner is strongly incentivised (due its financial tie-in) to make sure that the venture succeeds. In time the internationalising firm might grow in confidence to the extent that it assumes majority control of the jointly owned asset. Common drawbacks to such arrangements relate to issues such as cultural incompatibility or lack of trust between the two parties.

2.4.2.5 M&A

Buying a local firm lies at the extreme end of the risk profile for internationalising firms. The advantages are that through M&A it gains complete control of an asset that it can either modify or change to mirror its own standardised format, acquiring knowledge, presence and a springboard to rapid roll-out in one bold step (eg Tesco in Poland and Thailand: Felsted 2012). However, as most academic research has shown, most M&A ends up having a value destructive, rather than enhancing, effect. The reasons for this, which will explored in greater detail below, relate to financial, strategic, integration and socio-cultural issues.

2.4.3 KEY SUCCESS FACTORS OF M&A

The success of internationalising multi-unit enterprises through M&A is contingent on two broad factors; financial analysis/strategic intent and integration effectiveness/socio-cultural fit. This section will consider these factors in turn.

2.4.3.1 Financial analysis and strategic intent

It is self-evident that M&A must satisfy financial objectives as a starting point for eventual success. Classically, establishing the embedded net worth of a target company is achieved through applying market-based measures (acceptable multiples of the last three to five years EBITDA (earnings before interest, tax depreciation and amortisation) or cash flows which are commonly matched against recent comparable transactions), EPS (earnings per share – the impact of the price paid as a determinant of its dilutive or accretive influence on the acquirer's share price) and/or DCF (discounted cashsflow – the value of the target to the acquirer with regard to its stream of future cash flows over an extended period – usually a five-year time horizon – with its terminal value discounted at the combined entity's cost of capital).

However, it is the task of the selling organisation to optimise the price of its assets in order to satisfy its shareholders by generating an auction amongst several bidders to force the price up. Thus, whilst the acquirer may have embarked on a logical financial assessment of the price of an identified target, it is most likely that in order to secure the asset they will have to pay a premium which will have to be justified through some form of synergy rationale (Fuller 1975, Hitt et al 2001). Typically these synergies are explained as cost synergies (overhead reductions) or, more pertinently in relation to multi-unit, revenue synergies (turnover and profit enhancers), market power synergies (increased dominance leading to enhanced pricing leverage) and intangible synergies (people and knowledge).

The tendency amongst firms to almost always pay a premium above the standalone value in order to gain control of a target – outlining to their own shareholders the means by which they will 'capture synergies' or 'release value' – has been described as the 'winner's curse' (Sirower 1997). During the asset auction the target's merchant bankers and deal advisers are incentivised to engineer, if possible, intense competition between the bidders, driving up the price not only by playing the bidders off against each other but also by factoring the likely synergy capture of each interested party into the sale price. Conversely, on the buying side, the bidding parties vie with one another to 'talk the price down', although in an intense competitive process this is likely to prove an unsuccessful strategy. It is typically through such a process that an 'escalation of momentum' occurs such that, eventually, the acquirer wishes to make the deal whatever the financial state of the target firm or the theoretical bolt-on benefits of the acquisition (Lubatkin 1983, 1987, Jemison and

Sitkin 1986). There are numerous examples of multi-unit firms that have been adjudged to have overpaid for assets, a move that constrains their ability to provide investment and funding improvement and/or expansion.

The financial imperative underpinning a bid will be reinforced (or reverse engineered) by a strategic rationale that numerous commentators, agencies and scholars have attempted to categorise over the past 30 years. In the 1960s, during the conglomerate M&A boom where unrelated assets were incorporated into large MNCs for capital reasons, five dominant strategic approaches to M&A were noted: conglomerate, horizontal, concentric marketing, concentric product and vertical integration (Kitching 1967). In the 1970s the fashionable descriptors of ideal M&A strategies were shaped by the definitions of the Federal Trade Commission (1975): horizontal, vertical, product extension, market extension and unrelated. For the purposes of this book, however, a more up-to-date conceptualisation of acquirer strategic intent is provided by Bower (2001). His research started from the insight that most existing research tends to lump all types of acquisitions together, even though they represent fundamentally different phenomena that need to be studied and managed differently. In his extensive Harvard-based research into the strategic rationale underpinning M&A activity in the 1990s, Bower identifies and describes five distinctive M&A strategies pursued by acquirers; overcapacity, geographical roll-up, product or market extension, R&D substitution or industry convergence M&A. With regard to multi-unit M&A the strategic intent is typically governed by geographical roll-up, product or market extension or R&D substitution intentions.

The problem with this rational assessment of strategic intent, however, is that organisations may choose to pursue multiple elements of these strategies in order to achieve their objectives. For instance, a company may pursue a geographical roll-up strategy but, because there is some minor duplication of activity within the target, may simultaneously seek an overcapacity or cost-elimination objective. In addition, such a prescriptive account of M&A strategy excludes other, irrational, reasons for M&A, including ego-trips and self-aggrandisement on the part of a CEO, knee-jerk decision-making in response to crises, 'landgrab' brought on by competitive pressures and M&A activity that is driven solely by 'financial engineering' purposes: here, taking a public company private allows the buyer (usually private equity) to 'load' the organisation with debt, thereby reducing its corporation tax liability, leading to an observation by the leading financial commentator in the UK that in the present economic climate perhaps 'better management at home is more important than sticking flags around the world...maybe shareholders don't want an Empire!' (Felsted 2012a: 9)

2.4.3.2 Integration and socio-cultural compatability

When an acquirer has identified a target they should immediately, on the basis of their financial and strategic rationale, begin to formulate a plan as to how they intend to integrate the organisation into their structure (Weston et al 2001). In the case of M&A activity, organisations should seek to achieve optimal consistency between themselves and the acquired entity, the fulfilment of which will lead to positive financial outcomes. This is in preference to a lack of integration or alignment which, according to the M&A literature, will in all likelihood lead to value destruction and failure. There is common agreement in the literature that, apart from getting the financial side/aspect and the strategic rationale right, the management of the post-acquisition integration process determines the extent to which the latent potential of the deal is achieved (Chatterjee et al 1992, Mirvis and Marks 1992, Carlton 1997, Lublin and O'Brien 1997, Angwin 2000). Success will be contingent on the degree to which organisations structure themselves (Perlmutter 1969, Bartlett and Ghoshal 1989), pursue the effective alignment (Bower 2001, Schweiger 2002) and implement the right integration process (Jemison and Sitkin 1986, Haspeslagh and Jemison 1991).

There is a vast amount of literature pertaining to 'best practice' forms of integration planning and implementation (see Lees 2003 for an overview). Most scholars agree that the sooner organisations plan for integration (perhaps pre-deal, during the due-diligence stages) the more likely it is that buyers will achieve favourable results (Jemison and Sitkin 1986). Hence, creating a transitional structure (to deal with integration planning during the exchange and completion window) complete with a merger integration office, headed by a powerful integration champion who is well briefed on the real financial and strategic imperatives, means that the transaction is more likely to be successful. The reality, however, is that research has consistently demonstrated that buyer executives and their advisers, being understandably focussed on 'getting the deal away' during the transaction process, give scant regard to the intricacies of post-closure integration processes. For instance, Rankine's (1998) study of 350 European organisations involved in M&A showed that, of the issues inadequately considered during the transaction stage of integration, matters such as the structure of the new entity, communications plans and assessments of the target management and of the cultural fit between the two organisations featured particularly highly. Because of a lack of preparation and planning, forced assimilation is the dominant type of mode of integration (Schweiger 2002). In this approach, adopted consciously or subconsciously by the buyer, a 'superiority syndrome' informs the behaviour of the acquirer managers, who act unilaterally in forcing the combination on their terms, an approach that inevitably elicits resistance amongst target company employees.

The process of bringing together two related (or unrelated) organisations with differing histories, size profiles, cultures and (potentially) national characteristics, presents enormous challenges in terms of integration. Depending on the extent of required integration and the way in which the acquirer sets about the task, the integration process can provide fertile conditions for conflict to be generated between the parties at organisational, group and/or individual level.

Typically, however, conflict during M&A is portrayed as arising for two main reasons. First, at an individual level, M&As are portrayed as traumatic, unsettling events that cause enormous stress and anxiety for managers and employees, worried about the potential impact upon jobs and working practices (Hayes 1979, Marks 1982, Schweiger et al 1987, Larsson 1989, Schweiger and Walsh 1990). Secondly, at an organisational level, cultural differences between the two organisations in terms of their procedures, standards, norms and values, derived from their past histories and traditions, and, in a cross-national context, from their national settings, give rise to the potential for immense friction during integration (Schweiger and Goulet 2000, Aguilera and Dencker 2004). Indeed, some scholars argue that the chances of M&A success are enhanced only when the business cultures of the two combining organisations are closely related (Cartwright and Cooper 1996).

The concept of culture as providing an explanation for variance in firms' performance gained credence in the 1980s through the work of notable scholars such as Harrison (1972) and Schein (1985), also being popularised through the work of commentators such as Peters and Waterman (1982). Given its antecedents in anthropological theories of organisation, scholars operating in this area have, as their starting point, structural notions that the basic values, beliefs and assumptions held by members of a corporation translate into a dominant culture of shared outlooks and meanings within organisations.

Earlier studies on culture clashes in M&As were mainly situated within Berry's (1983) theory of acculturation, the essence of which refers to the fact that as an acquisition develops through courtship and marriage, both acquirer and target will go through phases of polarisation, creation of monolithic structures and ethnocentrism. Put simply, because of the M&A change process, which itself defines salient organisational characteristics more sharply, the two organisational cultures become more tangible and coherent, with individuals from both parties placing greater emphasis on and belief in the norms and values of their own particular organisation (Navandi and Malekzadeh 1988).

As a result of this insight, culture clashes have been conceptualised in terms of disturbance of human rights (Walter 1985), cultural retrenchment/countercultures (Buono and Bowditch 1989) and cultural rejection (Sales and Mirvis 1984). The assumption behind most of this literature is that the degree of employee resistance that flows from the individual and collective opposition of employees to the combination, and subsequent integration of the combining firms, is associated negatively with M&A performance (Chatterjee et al 1992). This opposition is typically portrayed as both active (voice, voluntary exits and sabotage), and passive (absenteeism, disobedience and shirking), leading to significant dilution of synergies during the integration process.

2.4.4 INTERNATIONAL MULTI-UNIT LEADERS

During the process of internationalising, multi-unit firms must address two related questions. First, to what extent should it appoint home country or local operational personnel? Second, in appointing local operators how can it ensure that they are aligned and engaged with the firm's mission and product?

Given the socio-cultural issues and tensions outlined above most multi-unit firms adopt a local resourcing approach at unit, district and regional level complemented by a country of origin approach at strategic director level. Reasons for local resourcing relate to factors such as language, local customs, legal and legislative context and leadership style preferences. From a labour perspective it is vital that first and second line leadership speak the same language as the workforce, understanding local employment laws and the type of leadership style that delivers the most effective performance; especially during rapid roll out. As Howard Leigh of Cavendish, a leading UK M&A boutique, commented;

> *If you buy a business with good local management and that management is absolutely compatible with your business then that will work. The choice example being Walmart buying Asda ... (Felsted 2012a: 9).*

In addition, knowledge of local markets is advantageous at this level in order to provide feedback to policymakers on how to shape and customise the product to consumer needs. As Philip Clarke, the former head of Tesco International stated;

> *International retailing is all about the nuances. There are many, many similarities in the world – we walk on two legs, we all eat food, we all wear clothes – but in global retailing it is the differences that matter ...* (Hall 2011a: 35).

At a more strategic level it is not unusual for companies to appoint country of origin directors who form a bridge between the home company and local subsidiary. Through such mechanisms the international multi-unit firm can achieve a balance between ensuring central control and consistency whilst addressing the nuances of the local market.

Other means of ensuring the alignment of local personnel deployed by internationalising multi-unit enterprises include comprehensive communication programmes, education and placements of local staff in the home country operation. Enhanced digital technology has allowed home country operations to communicate in real time with multi-unit staff. For instance, Burberry has quarterly briefing sessions in which their Chief Executive and HRD present to all staff via webcam, taking any questions that are posted on the in house Q&A site. In terms of education, firms have invested in orientation and skills programmes. In China, McDonald's has established a Hamburger University where local personnel are taught the 'McDonald's way'. Also, companies have brought foreign operators into their country of origin operations to understand the way in which they do things and the standards expected.

2.5 Summary

This chapter began by considering the context of the contemporary multi-unit enterprise and its responses to the disruptive forces it has recently faced in developed economy contexts. It has argued that organisations have responded to the challenges they have faced by adopting classic Porterian cost leadership or differentiation responses, or an amalgam of the two, a value-based approach. Within these paradigms, companies have been restricted by the degree to which they can exercise agility and also by their imagination around carving out a definitive market space around a 'big idea'. Also, whilst there is a degree of isometric convergence in the way in which most multi-unit enterprises are structured, some are exemplars of certain best practice design principles that enable free-flowing communication and instant operational action. Within the structure, the MUL has an important position in the operational line, being responsible, according to Garvin and Levesque (2008) for more operational priorities than any other level in the line; underscoring its pivotal positional importance to the organisation. Also, within internationalising multi-unit enterprises, given socio-cultural barriers and issues, the MUL is an important organisational actor in connecting organisations to local markets with idiosyncratic nuances.

The overwhelming impression of any analysis of the context of the multi-unit firm over recent times, however, is the rate, extent and pace of change. Particularly with regard to cost-led strategies, where most multi-unit firms have had to react swiftly and decisively with a range of new policies in order to ameliorate the effect of economic, customer and technological disruption on sales by reducing fixed costs. In order to do this, organisations have structured the activities and KPIs of MULs in a certain manner, concentrating efforts, as the succeeding chapter will demonstrate, upon the execution of operational systems – focussing on cost-control and compliance activities at the expense of a sales-driven service activities. To some degree this a pragmatic and necessary response to the extant environment, but it has had consequences upon the morale and engagement of the MUL 'messengers' and implementers.

Activities

3

Activities and Issues

Having considered the context of the multi-unit enterprise it is now appropriate to consider what activities organisations expect MULs to do. Previous research (Umbreit 1989, Jones and Inkinci 2001, DiPietro et al 2007) conceptualised activities in the form of job dimensions or critical job success factors. By contrast, this chapter will examine the functions of the MUL by, first looking at their prime activities which are elucidated in the order that organisations generally prioritise them; namely, enforcing operational systems, controlling standards and service execution. Second, the manner in which they address these activities will be discussed with particular reference to the way they are measured and expected to organise their work. Third, the chapter will consider the particular issues and problems that MULs feel they have in discharging their functions, using empirical evidence to highlight dominant themes and issues. The argument that will be followed in this chapter is that most multi-unit enterprises examined during the course of this research, due to the aforementioned disruptive forces and consequential cost-led strategies, have placed inordinate emphasis on operational systems compliance at the expense of service execution. The net effect upon MULs is that they feel that are merely transmission mechanisms for enforcement and punishment; a state which elicits stress, anxiety and paralysis. Following chapters will outline the practices that effective MULs deploy to overcome these challenges and the personal characteristics they need in order to do so.

3.1 Core Activities

From an organisational perspective MULs have limited input into factors such as pricing, product and place; their principal focus lying in enforcing and executing the operational blueprint of brand or concept and, in pursuance of this goal, also implementing specific organisational imperatives that are designed to strengthen this platform. A definition of what the purpose of the

MUL role is was defined by one organisation reviewed during the course of this research as being:

> ... *to flawlessly execute the offer to the customer with the highest standards of safety, quality and service, resulting in the growth of sales and delivery of profit targets ...*

In order to assist the operational line, the blueprint of most retail and leisure brands systematically details all the operating functions which must be performed at unit level including their particular characteristics, responsibilities and timings. Often enterprises will have multiple blueprints for different operational processes, standards and sales-led service duties that might be conducted independently or simultaneously. Imperatives detailed within job descriptions, procedural manuals, KPIs, balanced scorecards or incentive schemes are usually an attempt to leverage those elements (ie systems, standards and service) of the operational blueprint that the organisation deems critical to its success.

3.1.1 OPERATING SYSTEMS

The starting point for operational effectiveness is the proper application of a multi-unit enterprise's system and associated processes. Many of these might be invisible to the customer but have an enormous impact upon the standards and service levels that they experience. The operational system can be defined as a series of interlocking, critically dependant processes which are concerned with turning materials, information and/or customers into value added outputs through the intervention of 'transforming inputs' such as staff, technology, machinery and buildings (Slack et al 2009). To a large extent process success is contingent on the correct strategy and design principles being followed by the multi-unit enterprise prior to implementation, with review mechanisms ensuring correction and improvement. Strategy, design and review apart, however, the main objective of MULs is to ensure that the vital processes flow efficiently, meeting prime objectives of cost, speed, quality, dependability, safety and flexibility. While it is impossible to detail within the confines of this book the diversity of multi-unit enterprise operational systems and processes, it is important to highlight the key activities and processes that the research for this study found that organisations generally deemed to be critical to MUL role.

The first area that MULs are responsible for – indeed the starting point for understanding the role – are all processes that relate to cost control and procedural/legal compliance. The degree to which organisations place an overdue emphasis on these areas will be dealt with later on in this chapter, but there is little doubt that whatever the rhetoric that many organisations wrap around the role, a qualifier for MUL success is, as the HRD of a major multi-unit enterprise explained, is to 'get the substance of the role right'. The dominant processes that MULs are expected to oversee in most multi-unit enterprises are as follows:

i) Labour processes

- Labour ratio tracking; ensure units keep to forecast ratios and/or budget/cash targets.

- Rostering and deployment; ensure that units are fully staffed to undertake duties required during peak and non-peak trading sessions. Check seasonal rostering plans; ensure sufficient labour quality and capacity to service volume. Check 'right person, right place, right time'.

- Legal compliance; ensure that units are operating legally (ie following working time directive, foreign workers have permits and passports, statutory training compliance, proper age, equality and diversity regulatory adherence etc).

ii) Standard operating procedures

- BOH (back of house) tasks; ensure standard back of house task lists and section 'details' are adhered to (ie data uploads, delivery checks, storage, security etc). Monitor food production procedural adherence within catering and dining contexts.

- FOH (front of house) tasks; monitor front of house tasks such as pre-opening procedural adherence, 'daily duty manager' sweeps, section accounting, till procedures etc.

iii) Availability, stock and waste processes

- Availability; ensure appropriate stockholding is in place to service demand. Monitor replenishment to ensure constant availability.

- Reconciliation; ensure cash takings reconcile with sales and stock.

- Theft and shrinkage; check security and surveillance processes to minimise pilfering, 'knock-offs' and shrinkage.

- Waste; monitor and minimise non-consumable *and* perishable waste.

iv) Sales and pricing monitoring

- Daily/weekly sales; check daily and weekly sales against budget and last year.

- Timeslot analysis; monitor sales flows by timeslot; check throughputs and efficiency.

- Pricing accuracy; check coding exception reports; ensure pricing accuracy.

- Ad hoc discounting; check 'end of line'/'out of date' pricing and sales times (are pricing concessions granted too early?).

v) Due diligence and essential maintenance processes

- Safety; check fire safety compliance (smoke alarm testing, extinguishers etc). Monitor on-site customer incident books.

- Hygiene; check adherence to statutory and company procedures. Ensure food hygiene standards are compliant (ie one hundred per cent food hygiene training for food handlers). Check pest and rodent control systems.

- Legal compliance; make sure the store is 'operating legally' ie. one hundred per cent under-age alcohol sales training in supermarket retail.

- Hazards; ensure all essential maintenance requests are actioned on time and to specification.

vi) Ad hoc processes/change initiatives

- Refurbishment/new build pre-opening; oversee new opening processes; staffing, stocking, training, handover etc.

- New product launches; train and communicate new product launches.

- Change initiatives; act as conduit for all new change initiatives (ie promotions, operational systems etc).

- Defective internal processes; act as a troubleshooter and 'progress chaser' to resolve internal pinch points ie delivery, POS (point of sale) and product quality issues.

3.1.2 BRAND STANDARDS AND ENVIRONMENT

In addition to monitoring and implementing back of house systems and processes for cost and compliance purposes, MULs have a large role to play in enforcing front of house standards, ensuring the customer-facing store environment is kept to a high standard:

i) Merchandising and display

- Planogram checks; ensure merchandise is displayed according to specification (ie facings and perishable range display).

- Promotions; check promotions (signage, posters, shelf pricing, gondola ends etc).

ii) Internal environmental management

- Cleanliness; check cleaning rota and cleanliness (especially toilets and trading areas). In addition check BOH stock rooms, staff changing and rest rooms etc – the cleanliness of these areas will be linked to FOH standards.

- Sound, lighting and 'smell'; ensure all *'sensory'* sound, lighting and (where appropriate) 'smell' systems are functioning appropriately. Check speaker systems and background music loops, ensure the store is properly lit for security, safety and product illumination purposes and check 'perfume' and ersatz 'odour' systems.

- Air conditioning and heating; check functionality and effectiveness.

- Fixtures and fittings; ensure fixtures and fitting are maintained and presented to the required standard.

iii) External environment

- Social responsibility; check links with local community (ie charities, fund raising, job schemes, perishable food distribution etc).

- Local PR; ensure units have a high degree of local visibility through the local press or (where permitted) local social media channels (ie facebook, twitter, targeted e-mail updates etc).

- External agencies – fulfil a troubleshooting and problem resolution role with local authorities, landlords, environmental health, safety executives and external auditing agencies engaged by the organisation.

3.1.3 SERVICE EXECUTION

Clearly systems/process efficiency and standards adherence are important inputs into service effectiveness. In addition, as the previous chapter outlined, the business model of the multi-unit enterprise influences the elements of service that are an operational necessity in order to guarantee customer satisfaction. Organisations operating in a low cost paradigm are more likely to concentrate upon functional speed and efficiency whilst firms seeking differentiation will emphasise emotional attributes of service; staff politeness, knowledge and engagement. Customers will have pre-set service expectations based on variables such as price as to the levels of service that they will receive; service companies must ensure at the very least that they ensure that their perceptions (ie judgement as to *actual* levels of service) meet these expectations (Johnston and Clarke 2008). Managing the perception expectation gap is a science that many multi-unit enterprises are devoting a lot of time and resource to at present, the execution of which is a key function of the MUL.

In order to impact levels of sales-led service execution MULs are generally tasked with the following functions;

i) Unit-based HR

- Roles and responsibilities; check that roles and responsibilities are clearly denominated, assigned and understood. In particular, ensure shift leaders have clearly specified pre- and in-session duties and tasks.

- Recruitment and selection; appoint managers and assistants with appropriate attitudes, behaviours and capabilities. Check store recruitment systems and hiring mechanisms to ensure attitudinal and skills testing.

- Coaching and training; ensure that appropriate coaching and training mechanisms are in place and are being rigorously followed.

- Compensation; check compensation levels against local market; ensure that sufficient talent is being attracted and retained.

- Performance appraisal; ensure that regular staff appraisals are taking place to the required standards of development and performance metrics.

- Store leadership; check and audit staff satisfaction/engagement, absence, grievance data etc.

ii) Service concept adherence

- Service flow; ensure that customer 'touches' are applied in the appropriate manner at each stage of the service cycle.

iii) Customer survey follow-up

- Mystery customer; monitor and action outputs from mystery customer visits.

- Online surveys; monitor and action outputs from online survey data.

- Web-based feedback; regularly check and (where permitted) answer feedback on web-based forums and channels.

iv) Service promise and complaints resolution

- Service promise; check that the service promise (ie no quibble return) is fulfilled – particularly in relation to 'click and collect' services.

- Complaints; ensure that complaints are answered and rectified both in-store and at Head Office in accordance with company procedures.

3.2 Reports and Measurement

The data for measuring many of the above activities is generally bundled into daily, weekly and monthly reports. MULs can access data through web intelligence reports and, increasingly, through vehicles such as daily reporting apps (which generally convey sales and labour data). The main issue for MULs, as will be discussed later (particularly those new to the role or organisation), was the volume, frequency, accuracy and format in which the data is conveyed. In one organisation MULs were the recipients of 23 different reports on a weekly basis, some in Excel format, others in PDF and Word files, making the extraction and tabulation of data into usable form complicated and time consuming. Naturally, MULs would concentrate on reports that related to their KPIs and incentives.

3.2.1 KPIS AND INCENTIVES

Typically, MULs would have KPIs which clustered around three main areas; business/operations, customers and employees. Generic metrics included:

- Business/Operational KPIs; sales (revenue and/or items), margin, labour, other management costs (non-consumables, energy, waste, shrinkage etc), safety, availability etc.

- Customer KPIs; mystery customer scores (net promoter, overall satisfaction, individual elements such as knowledge, speed and quality) and complaints (per cheque or transaction).

- Employee KPIs; satisfaction, turnover, stability, absenteeism, disciplinary levels, and succession.

Different sectors within the multi-unit universe were apt to apply disproportionate incentive weightings to metrics that were regarded as specific drivers of commercial success; retail supermarkets (items sold per customer and availability), leisure (new member recruitment), builders' merchants (active accounts), retail banks (new accounts and cross-sales), fast food (speed of service), casual dining (food quality), hotels (revenue per average room) and apparel (stock movement and customer conversion).

Incentives were generally structured for annual performance with some element of tactical quarterly bonuses (usually relating to labour targets). Overall the multi-unit enterprises examined for this research tended to concentrate more on business and operational metrics (ie outcomes) rather than employee and customer metrics.

3.2.2 FORMAL APPRAISALS

Formal performance measurement against these KPIs was generally assessed and monitored through performance and competency-based appraisal systems;

- Performance Appraisals; these usually include 'balanced scorecard' KPIs outlined above. As stated, the weightings that organisations applied to each measure varied relative to sector, but also culture, business model and/or competitive position.

- Competency Assessment; often organisations had input competency measurements for MULS, against which they are scored according to range statement 'fit'. One organisation had six competencies; 'leading to win, understanding organisations, interpreting people, curiosity, impact and influencing and courage and conviction'. Issues with using such methodology relate to its validity, interpretation and 'real life' application.

3.2.3 LEAGUE TABLES

League tables were a regularly used method of performance measurement in multi-unit enterprises. They helped organisations to calibrate general performance against the mean whilst generating competition amongst MULs within specific regions or areas. Common league tables included; sales (against budget or last year), margin, stock control, training compliance, hygiene scores, margin, wastage, new customers, labour turnover and/or staff stability, customer service, voids and refunds etc. The degree to which these tables were genuinely used as a 'carrot' or another form of subtle 'stick' with which to beat MULs is a moot point. Many respondents in the research for this book had a view which accorded with the latter; that in many cases league tables were there to name and shame rather than recognise and praise.

3.3 Planning and Organising

In order to ensure that MULs discharged their responsibilities effectively most multi-unit enterprises offered guidance (sometimes mandatory) on how they *should* allocate their time to maximum effect. In extreme circumstances companies dictated the minutiae of MUL movement; for instance one organisation used a vehicle-based telematics tracking system that recorded MUL journeys to ensure that they kept to their defined 'structured ways of working' parameters! The schedule in Figure 3.1 is an example of how one organisation mandates its MULs (who have on average 15 sites each) to use their time.

In terms of the major activities' MULs are expected use their time in a specific manner.

3.3.1 ADMINISTRATION, ACTION AND PLANNING DAYS

MULs typically spend a day working from home, examining their reporting pages (sales, cash, costs and stock) and web intelligence (hygiene and margins) in order to analyse the performance of their units and decide on any remedial action required. It is also an opportunity to examine e-mails relating to new initiatives and promotions and consider actions that might be pending relating to forthcoming promotions, initiatives, capital investment etc. In organisations with ERP (enterprise resource planning) systems, MULs can review and consider the calendar of activities scheduled for the next month. It is also an

Activity	Days
Admin, Planning and Action	47 (1 day per week)
Unit Strategy Meetings	30 (2 days per quarter)
Unit Operating Reviews	30 (2 days per quarter)
District Meetings	9
Unit Mgr. Appraisals	10 (2 x 5 days one location)
Flexible days	74 (1.5 days per week)
Area Meetings	12
Conferences/Roadshows	4
Quarterly Appraisal	4
Profit Review	6 (0.5 days per month)
Total	*226*

(Time Available; 260 working days minus 34 days holiday = 226 days)

Figure 3.1   MUL Activity Planner

opportunity for MULs to phone and e-mail their units to chase up specific issues and, in some cases, take the opportunity of having telephone conference calls which involve the whole district in order to monitor and review the progress of particular priorities. Although some companies have tried to introduce e-mail embargos for MULs and their Units during the week, with specific downloads only allowed at pre-set times of the week, it is common, with current technology, for MULs to devote another 15 hours per week at various other times to administration and progress chasing by phone and/or e-mail.

3.3.2 BUSINESS STRATEGY MEETINGS

This meeting is intended to be a forwards looking meeting in which past performance is reviewed through analysis of the balanced scorecard (people, customers, sales and profit) as a basis for future action. The MUL meets the unit manager on-site to observe the business and the offer delivery in order to agree specified actions which should be recorded on an agreed action plan. This meeting is designed to be different from performance appraisals or compliance reviews as it concentrates on the actions that will improve the execution of the offer through people deployment and, in some cases where allowable, targeted promotions.

3.3.3 OPERATING REVIEW MEETINGS

This meeting – sometimes called the standards or due diligence review – is designed to concentrate solely on operational compliance aspects of the business. In essence these visits are about keeping the site 'safe and legal' through ensuring, by checking the bookwork, interviewing the manager and staff and personal observation that the business is fully compliant with legal and company regulations. Thus, in casual dining environments, the MUL will conduct a staff and guest safety review examining areas such as the kitchen and checking hygiene and safety standard compliance. The unit's due diligence paperwork will be reviewed to ensure that operatives are monitoring fridge and food preparation temperatures, undertaking mandatory training programmes for new starters and carrying out vital health and safety precautions such as regular pest control visits. In multiple retail environments, the MUL will check items such as the customer incident book, security systems, trading standards documentation (such under-18 alcoholic drink sales refusals) and hazard maintenance progress. In all sectors the MUL will be expected to check the front-of-house standards of the operation, very often with a pre-designed checklist that produces an overall 'compliance score' for the business.

3.4 Issues

There are a number of issues that relate to way the role is structured and the key functions that are expected to be fulfilled. In the main, most MULs surveyed for this book believed that due to the role's emphasis on controls, there was little time to address value-added commitment-based activities. The principal issues highlighted were undue emphasis on compliance (which undermined their authority and capacity for action), the pressure they felt they were under to punish rather than reward and their immense workload. These will be considered in turn.

3.4.1 COMPLIANCE FOCUS

The major issue with standard multi-unit enterprises is the degree to which complying with the myriad of controls and procedures becomes an end in itself rather than an enabler for running truly great businesses. In many cases organisations placed far more emphasis on 'doing it right' rather than 'doing the right things'. Issues such as sales-led service and improving the offer were put on the back burner as MULs and their unit managers were compelled to concentrate on compliance minutiae to the detriment of improving the product. It was an almost universal complaint of MULs that they spent too much time 'checking', leading one retail MUL to observe:

> ... if I spent as much time on people, service and sales as I do on checking and policing the business I'm sure that I would achieve far better results ... the trouble is that there are so many things to monitor and 'police' I have very little time to spend with my managers developing the business ...

One major survey in a major multi-unit enterprise that this research was able to access found that MULs believed that they spent over 50 per cent of their time, whilst onsite, on 'compliance and checking' activities; with as little as 8 per cent of their time devoted to coaching and training and 12 per cent on reviewing performance.

Other aspects of compliance which MULs are expected to enact, amplified by the recent economic downturn, have included monitoring and limiting labour ratios, maintenance spend, wastage and stock losses. In the case of labour ratios some firms abandoned their extant systems imposing strict daily and/or weekly labour cash targets that units were not permitted to exceed. In one particular organisation, MULs were expected to monitor and review labour spend on a daily basis:

> ... and it got absolutely fucking ridiculous ... I had to report back to my boss on a daily basis on how much we were spending on labour meaning that I had to chase my guys almost hourly, or that's what it felt like ... this obsession with limiting staff wages took up almost all my time ... it was a joke ... a complete fucking joke ...

As has been previously stated, given that labour is the major cost in any multi-unit enterprise, it is little surprise that during tough economic conditions or a major business downturn that the organisation should seek to ensure that costs are kept to an absolute minimum. It is the degree to which MULs are made to be (seemingly) solely accountable, with little or no proper communication from 'the Centre' which led to another MUL to comment:

> We (the MULs) all understood the reasons why we had to clamp down on labour costs but it was not well explained by the 'grown ups' to the troops ... we were expected to carry the can ... it was a case of 'shoot the

*messenger'… it was unpleasant having to control costs with very little
buy-in or understanding other than us saying that we had to do it …*

Also, the consequences of 'squeezing' the labour line meant that fulfilling other
compliance tasks was made more difficult with less staff. In one organisation,
food hygiene compliance scores and stock gaps deteriorated rapidly because
there were simply not enough people resource to fulfil basic tasks, prompting
a casual dining MUL to observe:

> *… and the consequences of 'getting the labour ratios right' were dire
> … some of my houses started to register really poor hygiene scores
> that I could see were related to the freeze … and this coupled with the
> maintenance spend reduction…only essential works … that was a
> laugh … everything was essential! … meant that my due diligence was
> going to pot … but I'd get the blame … oh yeah! …*

3.4.2 ENFORCEMENT AND PUNISHMENT

A natural consequence of having compliance regimes is that they must be
enforced. This research discovered that many MULs spent a lot of time 'chasing
compliance' and, in many cases, felt under inordinate pressure from the Centre
to apply sanctions for non-conformance. For some acts of non-compliance,
many multi-unit enterprises provided strict disciplinary guidelines for MULs
to apply for issues such as stock losses or hygiene breaches. In one firm MULs
were expected to issue managers who had received a negative food safety rating
with an immediate final warning whatever the extenuating circumstances (ie
lack of staff or faulty equipment). One casual dining MUL commented:

> *We have strict guidelines on what we should do if our managers fail
> to comply on issues such as stocks, cash and hygiene … I am expected
> to go in and discipline the manager and I know that in some cases it is
> not his fault … in some cases he has not got the manpower or the kit to
> comply yet he gets punished anyway … the thing is I'm the one that the
> Company expects to take disciplinary action … it's not pleasant and in
> many cases it's not fair …*

In other instances companies issued new procedures, in response to disruptive
events such as extreme weather or new onerous government regulations that
made explicit the consequences unit managers would face if they breached
guidelines. For instance, one organisation, reacting to the snow and icy

conditions that hit the UK prior to the key Christmas trading period in 2010, distributed an e-mail to all its managers telling them to cut their labour costs immediately or face disciplinary action. As one MUL in the organisation recalled;

> ... and the weather wasn't expected but we had already geared up for Christmas trading and the rosters and shifts were organised ... we were manned up...then came the e-mail threatening our managers with disciplinary action if they didn't cut staff immediately ... it was a great way to head to Christmas where we would be expecting our people to work on Christmas day and over the break ... a great thank you for all the effort that they would have to put in after the snow had cleared ... actually, you couldn't make it up! ... twats ...

3.4.3 OVERLOAD AND INACCURACY

Given the spans of control that MULs have in most multi-unit enterprises and the time they spend travelling between units (up to 30 per cent in some organisations) it is essential that organisations are judicious in the allocation of tasks and data analysis expected of this operational cohort. It is clear that the amount of blueprint standards and procedures that MULs are expected to regulate is significant but, when coupled with overlays, changes and amendments, the workload for most MULs is vast. Most MULs interviewed agreed that it was almost impossible to analyse, cover and/or enforce every single policy, procedure or measure produced by the organisation.

In one company a study showed that each unit was subject to over 400 measures per week, meaning that the MUL was, theoretically, confronted by nearly 23,000 metrics per month to check their district against. Factor in the fact that data is frequently inaccurate or misleading then, as one MUL commented, it is very difficult for them to prioritise or convert data into meaningful information:

> We've got measures for everything and new exception reports coming out all the time ... you'd have to be Einstein to work out what it all means and what is important and what is not...we have measures that measure measures! ... if it moves we've got measures on it...I am expected to sift through a lot of garbage ... much of it wrong ... to get the nuggets I require ... I could spend my whole life looking at this information without getting anywhere ... its funny that the amount

of reports always seems to go up but never down ... despite what we're promised ...

A complicating factor might lie in the fact that many reports come from different sources within the organisation and, as previously stated, due to legacy IT infrastructure, on different systems and in different formats. The MUL is expected to interpret and prioritise this data into actionable outcomes, often with little assistance from the Centre. Also, organisational priorities might change, complicating the work of the MUL. A suite of reports that the MUL has relied upon as key performance metrics might become redundant if the organisation places emphasis on a new set of priorities.

In one company survey less than 40 per cent of MULs believed that Head Office understood the consequences that data and initiative overload had upon them and their sites, one MUL commenting:

Everything changes frequently ... the reports ... the different lines on the reports ... and then we're expected to put in new things that are measured again by new reports! ... I don't think that they (Head Office) have a clue about how they are overloading us with all this stuff ... and some of the new operating standards and procedures are plain daft ... you wouldn't have thought that anyone in operations had been involved in putting it together ...

The fact that new plans and initiatives might not have been designed appropriately might also be combined with the fact that processes within the organisation are defective. In one organisation, a new pricing strategy (which was found to be unworkable) was launched with virtually no briefing and training, leading an MUL to comment:

... not only was the new price policy shit, the process (by which) they launched it was shit too! ... so there we were apologising to our unit managers who were having to learn the new structure and deal with really unhappy customers ... it was changed, but by then the damage had been done ...

3.4.4 UNINTENDED OUTCOMES

There are a number of outcomes relating to these issues that bedevil the role, many of which have serious operational consequences.

3.4.4.1 'Busy fools'

MULs experiencing the above issues were apt to refer to themselves as 'firefighters' and 'troubleshooters'. One cohort of MULs surveyed for this book believed that in addition to the 50 per cent of their time spent on compliance monitoring an additional 20 per cent was spent creating 'patch ups' and 'work arounds' to unworkable policies and initiatives. As one MUL succinctly stated:

> I don't spend much time creating value I spend most of my time preventing the destruction of value through badly thought out things by them (Head Office) ... in effect I'm a busy fool running around clearing up messes without having any time to concentrate on what is really important ...

MULs also resented having to do 'Head Office's job for them', collating information for random data requests due to inadequate information systems, often with short timescales attached. In one business MULs were tasked with responding to a Head Office data request on foreign workers 'by tomorrow' because the organisation's HRM systems were inadequate. In another, MULs were given a couple of days to review car parking safety procedure adherence after an accident at one store. As one MUL commented:

> ... most ad hoc requests either come to me or go to the store and then back to me for querying ...like – 'do we really have to do this?'... it's wearing because it completely derails the day job meaning that I spend most of the time doing things that others should be doing rather than what I should be doing ...

3.4.4.2 Fear and loathing

A natural consequence of the imposition of a compliance culture is that MULs developed a fear of, as one MUL put it, 'the faceless bureaucrats at Head Office'. The notion that somebody was monitoring them over such a vast range of metrics, some of which were bound to be in negative territory at various junctures, fuelled feelings of resentment, anxiety and loathing. As one MUL put it:

> We really hate them ... loathe them ... they never fucking get anything right ... we are always picking up the pieces ... but you know what the bottom line is; we're scared! ... because they have got so much on

us ... if don't do what they say and then get it wrong...there might be consequences ...not today or tomorrow perhaps ... but somewhere down the line ... we'll be labelled as troublemakers, non-conformist, wreckers ...

3.4.4.3 Stress and paralysis

It is of little surprise that such feelings commonly lead to high levels of stress within this cohort. In one organisation with an excessively control-type regime, compounded by the economic crisis from 2008, 12 per cent of MULs were signed off sick with 'stress related illnesses' at one particular point. Those that were left were faced with increased workloads. As one MUL in this organisation remarked:

... some of the guys just couldn't take it anymore ... stuck in the middle ... being told to do things and then getting the kickback from the stores ... we were put in an impossible position ... you can understand it on the one hand but you really resent it on the other because their absence meant more work for us ... I had to take on x more stores to cover a colleague's sickness ... and it really paralysed the organisation because so much stuff wasn't done ...

Thus, discretionary effort drops, innovation and creativity is stifled and MULs survive and 'satisfice' rather than optimise the business.

3.4.4.4 Infantilisation

Another outcome of compliance, enforcement and overload was the degree to which MULs felt, in the words of one, being 'treated like children made us act like children'. Thus, in an extreme reaction to their perceived environment, reasonable requests from Head Office were now subject to routine cynicism, with some MULs 'complaining and moaning just for the sake of it'. Mature MULs, worn down by the constant demands and strictures issued from the Centre, started to behave badly, with a respondent MUL observing:

... we were reduced to the antics of the playground really ... you wouldn't have thought that we were grown men with families ... the abuse we gave to anybody turning up to our meetings from Head Office was appalling ... I know that one of the marketing girls was reduced to

tears by the way she was treated ... completely immature behaviour (on our part) ... it diminished us really ...

3.4.4.5 'Going native'

The degree to which MULs identify more with the needs of their units than the organisation is another issue created in extreme compliance cultures. There are two explanations for this. First, some MULs side with their units because of what they perceive as the injustices of the unreasonable demands and metrics they believe are being meted out. In this respect MULs see themselves as the guardians of their people and districts, or as one MUL put it:

> *I wouldn't call myself Robin Hood defending my people against the Sheriff of Nottingham but that's what it feels like sometimes! ... somebody has to stick up for them and in order to rest easy in my own conscience I'd rather side with them than with those people (Head Office personnel) ... it keeps me sane really ...*

Second, there are those MULs who will side with their unit managers for self-interested purposes. Given their own performance needs MULs recognise that in order to maintain some semblance of order and discipline they need to demonstrate both in word and deed, their support for their people. Hence, being seen to fight their unit managers' corner and challenging the Centre is a powerful way of ensuring, as one MUL said, that their unit managers are 'onboard':

> *... the only way I can get my guys to do things is by demonstrating I am on their side ... this means that at times I have to take up the battle on their behalf ... (like what?) challenging Estates about not mending things ... even if there is supposedly no money ...*

The problem with going native, however, is that it can potentially undermine the ability of the organisation to make merited changes and drive strategy. To what extent are MULs good judges of what is actually beneficial or detrimental for their units? There comes a point, as one operations director put it, when some MULs 'have completely lost their marbles and fight anything that is introduced on the basis that if it has come from the Centre it must be bad!'

3.4.4.6 Resistance and sabotage

Such feelings of fear and stress often manifested themselves in other ways such as through acts of wilful non-conformance. Evidence of resistance was common, with MULs recounting their ways of getting around 'the system' with relish. One such example was the MUL who elegantly circumvented new maintenance rules instituted by his organisation:

> ... and then they put a curb on all non-essential maintenance requests which really pissed my store managers off ... so it was quite simple really ... the maintenance I really wanted to get through I marked 'potential safety hazard' or 'could be harmful to children' ...that always gets them as nobody wants to be had up for not doing something that could have prevented the injury of a child ...

In terms of low level resistance some MULs admitted refusing to acknowledge e-mails or return phone calls, ignoring requests for information or central dictats on purpose. In one particular organisation resistance was evidenced through a high rate of resignations where one MUL stated in his exit interview:

> ... frankly we are only interested in compliance around here now ... this is not the Company I joined ... although I like my colleagues and the type of work I don't like what we are being asked to do now ... to some extent my position has become untenable as I can no longer ask my people to do things that I would not do myself ...

At the extreme end there is evidence that some MULs engaged in deliberate sabotage through slowing processes down or issuing incorrect instructions. In one organisation an MUL was reputed to have deliberately changed the postcode addresses on his stores for a promotional material drop in order to create havoc and chaos in the run up to a key seasonal trading period. When questioned as to why he had done it he replied ' ... it was my own strange way of getting my own back on those pillocks in marketing ... '

3.4.5 BUSINESS CONSEQUENCES

The unintended consequences of operating an unrelenting compliance culture are the very antithesis of what the organisation was seeking to achieve in the first place! This research found that the outcomes were actually opposite to those intended resulting in less control and worse performance.

3.4.5.1 Less control

The outcome of operating an unrelenting compliance culture – where enforcement and overload rules – will result in the organisation having less rather than more control. Accountabilities are avoided for fear of retribution, discretionary effort collapses and key people leave, draining the organisation of vital knowledge capital. In one leisure organisation MUL turnover reached 36 per cent in 2009, mainly through voluntary resignations. In 2011 the operations director at that time reflected:

> ... *as the business went backwards we tightened everything up and as we did so a lot of people left of their own accord ... when I look back we made a fundamental error because by hardening the culture and introducing controls we lost people ... meaning that things actually got worse! ... the new people we brought in didn't have a clue ... it was a complete car crash ...*

3.4.5.2 Worse performance

Connectedly, as an accompaniment to deteriorating control and alignment, performance suffers. Put simply, organisations that were doing well do less well and those doing badly perform worse. In one organisation which reverted to an aggressive compliance regime, with letters being despatched to MULs and unit managers threatening sanctions for non-conformance for a range of measures in late 2007, profit trends worsened from 4 per cent like-for-like declines to nearly 10 per cent; a significant underperformance within their market sector. Following a new leadership regime this organisation is now recording record like-for-like performance, outstripping its competitive set. Whilst many variables have contributed to this uplift there is no doubt amongst the survivors of the old regime that switching from a control to a commitment-based culture has been key to providing an uplift in performance. As one MUL reflected:

> ... *and all we were doing was control and more control ... squeezing the life out of the business ... our performance became shocking and was deteriorating badly ... we had a high turnover of managers and staff ... morale was appalling ... then x came in and got a grip ... we started doing things the right way ... stabilised the business and now we're driving it forwards ...*

3.5 Summary

The introduction and context chapter hinted at the reasons why so many multi-unit enterprises lean towards a compliance-type mentality including the need for the centre to apply strict controls in order to ensure standardisation and consistency within the dispersed geographical form of the multi-unit enterprise. The consequences of applying such an approach to the exclusion of everything else can be seriously damaging to the long-term financial performance of the firm, squeezing entrepreneurialism, innovation and discretionary effort. How do MULs assert some semblance of authority, legitimacy and consent in order to operate effectively in such in an environment? How to they enforce the needs of the Centre without demotivating and or disengaging with their staff? The following three chapters will explore how effective MULs address this conundrum, beginning with an examination of their commitment-based approaches that underpin any attempt to assert control or introduce change within multi-unit enterprises.

Behavioural Practices

4

Generating Commitment

In the organisational behaviour literature, commitment is portrayed as a construct that determines an individual's psychological attachment to their firm. The higher the levels of an individual's positive emotional attachment to the organisation the more likely they are to 'commit' to the firm's goals and objectives (Meyer and Allen 1991). But is organisational commitment necessarily the main determinant of positive attachment given the distance of the Centre from the units within multi-unit enterprises? The previous chapter referred to a number of barriers that confront MULs in attempting to discharge the main functions of their role, potentially eroding their own personal, and their teams', commitment to the organisation. Yet the research for this book uncovered effective MULs who outperformed their peers in both benign and adverse organisational contexts. The question that arises from this is, how do effective MULs generate commitment within their own sphere of influence to ensure that they meet their goals and objectives?

This chapter will argue that effective MULs are adept at optimising their portfolio through garnering psychological attachment from their unit managers and staff to the aims and objectives *of their units and district* through *exchange-based local leadership* practices. Given the constraints of time, distance and space within multi-unit enterprises where the goals of an organisation can seem abstract to the staff on the ground, the MUL plays an essential role in motivating people to higher levels of performance through clarifying goals and strong *local HRM* deployment which builds buy-in, serving as a form of *social exchange* that assures *reciprocity*. It is through these means that, as subsequent chapters will demonstrate, the MUL is then able to assert control and change within the multi-unit enterprise. Thus, the paradox as to how MULs are simultaneously able to balance commitment with control is explained; in order to exert control, MULs must first generate local commitment.

In order to understand how MULs generate commitment within their portfolios this chapter will first, as a means of set-up, elucidate relevant commitment literature with reference to service operations, leadership and HRM texts. What does this literature say and how does it help frame our understanding of how MULs generate commitment? Second, this chapter will outline empirical evidence relating to effective MUL and commitment, referring to the techniques and practices deployed for optimal outcomes. In particular, it will be argued that successful MULs are expert in the way in which they optimise human capital and HRM within their portfolios for added value outcomes. Through *creating a local vision, cross-portfolio involvement, 'talent matching', tailored learning and development, recognition and positive reinforcement* and *openness, trust and promise fulfilment*, effective MULs can make a significant impact upon the commitment of their people, regardless of the organisational context.

4.1 Understanding Commitment

The term commitment, used liberally by practitioners and organisational commentators alike, is usually expressed to denote worker willingness, readiness or a positive mindset. To this extent it takes an attitudinal perspective, its principal meaning being related to ensuring that 'people's hearts and minds are in the right place'. The natural inference of the commitment hypothesis is that if such a state of emotional attachment between workers and organisations is achieved there will be a concomitant behavioural dividend, translating into performance outputs (Guest 1997). Some academics would argue that a better explanation for increased worker discretionary effort might be framed more effectively from other constructs such as 'engagement' or 'job satisfaction'. However, it can be argued that commitment provides a valid lens through which to understand effective MUL given that many of the practices that are designed to elicit commitment are connected to engagement and job satisfaction initiatives. In short, rather than accepting the position of some academics that there are differences between commitment, engagement and job satisfaction, the view of this author is that the three are intertwined and inextricably linked to one another.

It should be understood that in addition to commitment being understood as 'affective emotional mind set attachment' to the organisation it can also be framed as in terms of 'continuance' and 'normative' mindset attachments (Meyer and Allen 1991). Unlike the former 'affective' state, where the individual identifies willingly with the organisational goals, both 'continuance' and 'normative' perspectives conceive commitment as being applicable when individuals feel that they might either suffer cost as a result of not committing or feel an obligation to commit. 'Affective commitment' – deemed the most desirable mindset due to its voluntarism – is conceived as being most usually the output of engagement interventions such as selecting the right people with the right values and attitude in the first place; putting in place a clear vision, mission and objectives; extensive two-way communications; teamwork and high investment in employee development. Hence inputs into commitment are conceived very much within the service operations, leadership and HRM paradigms, areas of enquiry that will be examined below, followed by consideration of what effective MULs actually do.

4.1.1 SERVICE OPERATIONS AND COMMITMENT

The service operations literature is concerned with identifying and isolating the key variables that result in organisations producing service that is perceived by the customer as being memorable; fulfilling – even exceeding – their original expectations (Albrecht 1992, Fitzsimmons and Fitzsimmons 2006, Johnston and Clarke 2008, Reichheld and Markey 2011). Customers define great service from organisations as 'being easy to do business with', which, from the their point of view, involves service providers doing four specific things; delivering the promise, resolving problems well, providing the personal touch and going the extra mile. Of these attributes, customers cite one area in particular as having a disproportionate effect upon their perception, namely the degree to which service providers are *empowered* to resolve problems and manage complaints effectively 'on the spot' (Lashley 1997 and 1999). But what are the key characteristics of organisations that conform to this customer definition of great service provision? Two perspectives within the service operations literature are pertinent – Albrecht's Service Management Concept (1992) and Johnston's (2001) Service Personality Framework – both being notable for their emphasis upon the importance of service provider *commitment* in effecting excellent service.

4.1.1.1 Service management concept

According to Albrecht (1992) and Albrecht and Zemke (1995) organisations that provide excellent service adopt a 'customer value package' (CVP) or *'service management concept'* (SMC) comprising three vital components. First, they take a *long term* perspective to generating enduring customer relationships and are focused upon realising substantial *lifetime customer value*. Second, such organisations adopt a *total service approach* in which the organisational values and objectives are directed towards superior service provision. Third, such an approach is underpinned by a *management focus*, whereby the organisational systems are designed to elicit maximum commitment and effort from front-line service providers. Such systems include the following characteristics:

- Resource availability – appropriate resources are provided to service providers in order to provide superior customer satisfaction.

- Local decision-making – service providers are granted the autonomy to deal efficiently and effectively with customer complaints and service faults.

- Service skills – supervisors are granted the necessary materials and time to concentrate on upskilling frontline staff in order to improve service levels and release discretionary effort in order to deliver key customer 'moments of truth' .

- Aligned reward – incentive systems are customer orientated with disproportionate emphasis on satisfying key customer service metrics (ie speed, quality, politeness, knowledge, rectification etc).

- Two-way feedback – mechanisms are provided for effective two-way feedback from service providers to managers (ie pre- and end-of-session briefings, team meetings, forums, focus groups and confidential surveys).

In such regimes, according to Albrecht and Zemke (1995), the roles of both the manager and service provider are redefined. The manager is transformed from an 'order giver' and 'controller' to a 'facilitator' and 'team leader', whilst the service provider is changed from being an 'order taker' into becoming an 'engaged participant' in the creation of a viable and sustainable guest satisfaction culture.

4.1.1.2 Service personality framework

The best practice service personality framework (SPF) conceived by Johnston (2001) – the result of empirical analysis of 70 organisations – views the service personality of a firm (ie the functional and emotional attributes of excellent service) being framed by four significant contingent variables; a service culture, leadership, committed staff and customer focused systems. Although Johnston concedes that the provision of good service is also connected to more employees and 'larger asset investment', Johnston argues that organisations which devote the necessary focus and resources to creating an identifiable service personality are likely to reap higher profits, margins and total return on assets. The main characteristics Johnston identifies as key to shaping a superior service personality are as follows:

1. A service culture;

   – Values – shared and well articulated values that revolve around service such as that of a major international supermarket retailer:
     ▪ No one tries harder for customers:
       ◊ Understand customers better than anyone
       ◊ Be energetic, be innovative and be first for customers
       ◊ Use our strengths to deliver unbeatable value to our customers
       ◊ Look after our people so they can look after our customers
   – Treat people how we like to be treated:
     ▪ All retailers, there's one team … The x Team
     ▪ Trust and respect each other
     ▪ Strive to do our very best
     ▪ Give support to each other and praise more than criticise
     ▪ Ask more than tell and share knowledge so it can be used
     ▪ Enjoy work, celebrate success and learn from experience

2. Good leadership;

     ▪ 'In touch' – senior managers, executives and directors who are seen to be very involved with the business and in touch with the business at a grass roots level (ie through walkabouts, back to the floor working etc).
     ▪ Openness – physical and emotional openness characterised by open plan offices and 'no bars' communication, receptive attitudes and transparent policies.
     ▪ No blame – mistakes are tolerated in the spirit of continuous learning and the shared desire to take risks and innovate.
     ▪ Trust – an implicit and explicit circle of trust where staff are empowered to do the right thing by the customer.

- 'Into the detail' – senior managers are involved with and concerned about getting the detail of service delivery right through the service concept design and proper allocation of resources.
- Lack of complacency – good is not accepted as 'good enough' – managers and staff are in a constant quest to improve their service offer.
- Passion – evident enthusiasm from top to bottom of the organisation expressed through behaviours, body language and tone.
- Concern for continuous improvement – a willingness and commitment to develop continually, and at times reinvigorate and reinvent, their service concept.

3.   Committed staff

– Having staff who are committed to the organisation, its service and customers through;
  - Adult relationships – sensible interactions between managers and employees exemplified by;
    ◊ Maturity in approach – implied and explicit contracts fostering 'a grown up approach' governing managerial and staff relations.
  - Positive attitude – encouragement of a 'can do, extra mile' attitude through;
    ◊ Team working – fostering a feeling of collective responsibility and accountability through close team working.
    ◊ Spirit of camaraderie – a sense of belonging, attachment and shared identity through ad hoc events, trips, visits and celebrations.

4.   Customer focused systems

– Systems that are well thought out and designed around the company's values – including six systems that are vital to developing and sustaining a reputation for service excellence;
  - Communication systems – great service-orientated organisations define themselves as 'communications organisations' first and foremost with regular face-to-

face executive forums with business units and cascade mechanisms such as colleague councils, newsletters, message boards etc.

- Feedback systems – embedded systems, such as regular surveys or intranet forums, that carefully collate feedback from staff and customers, generating insights for action for senior management around service delivery and performance.
- Training systems – training and development that encompasses both technical and softer 'behavioural skills' related to service.
- Appraisal, performance management, reward and recognition systems – joined-up appraisal, performance management and reward systems that are linked to balance score card metrics that encompass service measures plus formal and informal recognition mechanisms (ie newsletter citations, e-mails from the CEO etc).
- Complaint management systems – formal procedures for capturing and expediting customer complaints in an efficient and timely manner, with rectification feedback loops to improve processes, behaviours and procedures.

Echoing Albrecht (1992), Johnston concludes that service excellence requires a *total quality* approach, with all the above components being in place. He argues that it need not be expensive; rather, ineffectual and poorly designed systems that result in low staff commitment, high rates of turnover and dissatisfaction have far more costly repercussions.

4.1.2 LEADERSHIP AND COMMITMENT

What makes a great leader? Leadership is commonly defined as an individual's ability to organise and influence a group of people to *commit* willingly to achieve a common goal. As such the leader's role in generating commitment and psychological attachment to the organisation and its goals is perceived as key, with many studies purporting to demonstrate that effective leadership is a key determinant of firm success (Bass and Bass 2008). It should be noted, however, that the concept of leadership should not be restricted to the apex of organisations, with some commentators arguing that leaders can and should exist at all levels within the organisation (Goffee and Jones 2006). There are a vast number of frameworks and theories that advance models of effective leadership; this section will, first, consider what can be termed as *generic* leadership theories and second, with particular reference to the MUL role, *local* functional and team-based leadership models.

4.1.2.1 Generic leadership theories

Trait theory of leadership

The question 'what inherent qualities make a leader?' has exercised intellectual enquiry since the times of Plato and Plutarch a couple of millennia ago. The theory that good leadership is fundamentally based on identifiable individual personality characteristics – that great leaders are 'born not made' – is the basis for trait theory (Carlyle 1841). Preliminary enquiry attempting to separate traits from leaders and non-leaders identified characteristics such as intelligence, dominance, adaptability, persistence, integrity, socio-economic status and self-confidence (Bass and Bass 2008). More scientific studies from the 1980s claimed to have established significant relationships between effective leadership and traits such as extraversion, intellect and 'adjustment' (Lord et al 1986), experiential openness (Kickul and Neuman 2000), work ethic (Arvey et al 2006) and general 'self-efficacy' (Foti and Hauenstein 2007).

The trait approach to defining effective leadership can be criticised for three major reasons (Zaccaro et al 2001). First, trait theories mainly coalesce around the big five personality traits; *intelligence, extraversion, self-confidence, dominance and persistence*. Generally, the frameworks presented underplay important attributes such as ethics, morals, thinking/cognitive capacity, interpersonal 'social skills', guiding motives and technical knowledge. To this degree other contemporary studies leading from a psychological perspective are important, citing personality traits such as *drive, desire to lead, honesty and integrity, self confidence, intelligence, job relevant knowledge and extraversion* (Kirkpatrick and Locke 1991, Judge et al 2002). Second, trait theory fails to distinguish between leaders who adopt a fixed approach and those who are malleable and shaped by situational factors. Third, general trait theory fails to consider patterns or integrations of multiple attributes.

Behavioural and style theories of leadership

In response to the criticisms of trait theory, leadership style research in the mid twentieth century (influenced heavily by the concurrent human relations school) concentrated on establishing 'ideal type' behavioural models of leadership. Most pertinent was Lewin et al's (1939) study which found that leaders exercised managerial influence in group decision-making in three dominant stylistic approaches; *autocratic* (centrally controlled decision-making), *democratic* (consultation and participation) and *laissez faire* (devolved and autonomous decision making). In addition to these styles, other commentators (ie de Vries et al 2003), have added others such as *toxic* (where leaders leave groups worse off than before) or *narcissistic* (where decision making is a vanity project for the leader's own ego!) Building upon Lewin, Blake and Mouton's (1964, 1985) 'managerial grid' framework advanced five different leadership styles (*team, country club, middle-of-the-road, produce or perish and impoverished*) connected with leaders' orientation towards *people* or *production concerns*. Issues with this approach related to the fact that style was conceived, as with trait theory, as being in stasis, with little consideration being given to situational factors.

Contingency and situational leadership

As with behavioural and style approaches, situational and contingency theory was contrived as a response to the trait theory of leadership. As early as the late nineteenth century, commentators noted that it might be 'the times that produce the person' rather than the personal qualities overriding all. In essence, this theory based on contigual fit, arguing that different scenarios draw upon differing styles of leadership. According to this body of theory, there is no optimal personality trait of a leader because 'what an individual actually does when acting as a leader is in large part dependent upon characteristics of the situation in which he functions' (Hemphill 1949: 43).

Overall there are four main contingency or situational leadership models that have been cited exclusively that merit consideration:

- Situational favourableness (Fielder 1967); leadership effectiveness is conceived as an interaction between style, group control and situational favourableness. Fielder defines two types of leader: those who are *relationship orientated* and seek to accomplish the task by developing good relationships with the group; and those who are *task orientated*, their prime focus being task execution. There is no ideal leader; either approach can succeed depending upon 'situational fit'. Fielder argues that task oriented leaders are effective in *extremely favourable* or *unfavourable* situations, whereas relationship oriented leaders perform best in situations with *intermediate favourability*.

- Situational contingency (Vroom and Yetton 1973) – these scholars advance a taxonomy which can be used to describe how leadership styles and group decision-making approaches 'suitably fit' with situational circumstances. This model established credence through the notion that the *same* manager could deploy different 'group decision making approaches' according to the characteristics and attributes of each situation.

- Path-goal (House 1971) – The central proposition of path-goal is that effective leaders behave in a way that complements context and follower capability in order to counterbalance subordinate gaps and deficiencies; increasing their levels of engagement and discretionary effort. House's model locates four leader behaviours, – *supportive, participative, achievement-oriented* and *directive* – that will vary according to follower and environmental characteristics. This theory states that the four leadership behaviours are fluid, and that leaders can adopt any of the four approaches depending on the demands of the situation. The path-goal model can be classified as a contingency theory as it depends on the circumstances, but also as a transactional leadership theory (see below) as it emphasises reciprocity behaviour between the leader and the followers.

- Situational leadership (Hersey and Blanchard 1993) – this model suggests four (again!) leadership styles juxtaposed against and four levels of follower readiness. Their framework advances the notion that leadership styles should 'match' appropriate levels of follower readiness (with regard to job demands). For instance, leaders need to apply a *'task-based' style* to followers with a low level of readiness while applying a *relationship-based style* to sunordinates with a high level of readiness or development. The issue with this model (and the others above) is the notion that leaders have the self-awareness, time and space to adapt their styles or that their assessment of where their followers lie in terms of readiness is particularly accurate!

Transactional and transformational leadership

An influential contribution to the leadership debate is Burn's (1978) notion of the transactional and transformational leaders, the latter construct being subsequently built upon by emotional leadership theorists (ie Bennis 2001):

- Transactional leaders – such leaders are vested with authority to perform certain tasks and reward or punish the team's subsequent performance. Positional power grants the opportunity to the manager to lead the group and the group agrees to follow their lead to accomplish a predetermined goal in return for something else. Power is given to the leader to evaluate, correct and train subordinates when productivity is not up to the desired level and reward effectiveness when expected outcome is reached.

- Transformational leaders – these leaders motivate their teams to be effective and efficient within a commitment-based practice paradigm. Good communications reinforce and celebrate the achievement of goals, focusing the team on desired objectives and outcomes. The transformational leader is an activist visionary but uses a formalised command structure to ensure executional delivery. Hence, transformational leaders take a 'big picture' view, with a need for committed staff who 'take care of the details'. This type of leader is a 'prospector', continually scanning the horizon for insights and ideas that advance the organisation towards reaching its overarching vision. Subsequent theorists have built upon this theory with notions of emotion-based leadership, as outlined below.

Emotional leadership

The emotional leadership school uses as its base the notion that positive psychologically-based interventions (ie approaches such as servant leadership; Autry 2001) can lead to significant behavioural modification. This area of study has also been touched upon through approaches such as positive reinforcement, emotional intelligence and happiness theory.

- Positive reinforcement (Skinner 1976) – according to this 'pavlovian' theory, positive behaviour occurs and is sustained when it is reinforced by positive stimulus. For instance, the use of praise is conceived as a positive stimulus that, when applied judiciously and appropriately, will lead to positive repeat behaviour. The main benefit of this technique is that the use of positive reinforcement approaches, such as praise, encouragement and recognition can be inexpensive, stimulating higher levels of effort for relatively low cost!

- Emotional intelligence (Goleman 1996, 1998) – Emotional intelligence is defined as an actual or perceived ability to identify, assess and control the emotions of oneself, others and groups. The 'mixed' or trait model advanced by Goleman (1998) conceives EI as a set of competencies and skills that shape leadership performance, proposing a model based around four principal constructs; self-awareness, self-management, social awareness and relationship management. Within each of these areas he proposes a number of emotional competencies that can, in his view, be learned and developed in order to produce exceptional leadership performance.

- Happiness and flourishing (Seligman 2011) – the genesis of flourishing lies in happiness theory, a state that can be taught as well as acquired. According to Seligman, although happiness might be a passing mood reaching a state of human flourishing can be sustainable with highly beneficial consequences. Whilst pleasure and delight are important, a good life includes deep relationships with others, accomplishment, absorbing activities and a sense of serving something greater than the self.

4.1.2.2 Local leadership theories

With particular reference to MUL, there are two specific theoretical approaches that can be labelled 'local leadership' theories that merit consideration; functional and group/team leadership.

Functional leadership

The functional leadership view (McGrath, 1962) focuses upon leader behaviours required to impact upon *business unit* performance (Hackman and Walton 1986) . This approach conceives the leader's main role as being to address the needs of the group; thus, a functional leader is adjudged to have performed well when they have instigated and sustained *group effectiveness and cohesion* (Hackman and Wageman 2005). Scholars operating in this domain (see Fleishman et al 1991, Kozlowski et al 1996, Zaccaro et al 2001, Hackman and Wageman 2005, Morgeson 2005 and Klein et al 2006) generally elucidate four activities an effective functional leader performs, including:

- 'scanning'; internal/external environmental monitoring

- 'managing'; organising follower activities

- 'motivating'; coaching and teaching subordinates

- 'detail'; proactively understanding and rectifying group processes.

These activities require distinctive functional leadership behaviours. Taking a follower perspective, Fleishman (1953) observed that subordinates categorised their leaders' behaviours in *consideration* and *initiating* terms. *Consideration* behaviours included displaying subordinate concern or demonstrating support towards followers in both 'fair or foul times'. *Initiating* behaviours, which focused on task accomplishment, included clear role definitions, unambiguous performance standards and 'following through' on accountabilities.

Group and team leadership

- Group leadership – in preference to obsessing with individual leadership, some academics have focussed upon the utility of group leadership (where the collective rather than one individual provides direction) as a more efficient way of increasing creativity or reducing costs (Hemphill 1950). According to this approach, the main team member best able to handle any given phase of the project becomes the temporary leader. Additionally, as each team member has the opportunity to experience the elevated level of *empowerment*, it energises staff and feeds the cycle of success (Lashley 1995 a,b).

- Team leadership – in this paradigm team leaders are expected to demonstrate tenacity, persistence and excellent communication/ motivational skills to draw out similar qualities from their teams. According to the NBSA (2006) effective teams have the following overarching characteristics:

  – purpose: members proudly share a sense of why the team exists and are invested in accomplishing its mission and goals
  – priorities: members know what needs to be done next, by whom, and by when to achieve team goals
  – roles: members know their roles in getting tasks done and when to allow a more skillful member to do a certain task
  – decisions: authority and decision-making lines are clearly understood
  – conflict: conflict is dealt with openly and is considered important to decision-making and personal growth

- personal traits: members feel their unique personalities are appreciated and well utilised
- norms: group norms for working together are set and seen as standards for every one in the groups
- effectiveness: members find team meetings efficient and productive and look forwards to this time together
- success: members know clearly when the team has met with success and share in this equally and proudly
- training: opportunities for feedback and updating skills are provided and taken advantage of by team members.

4.1.3 HRM AND COMMITMENT

HRM, a psychologically-based analysis of organisational dynamics, has at its heart the belief that the purpose of various employment practices is to guide employee attitudes and behaviours (Wright and McMahon 1992, Ulrich 1997) in a positive direction. Based on various Human Relations experiments in the mid twentieth century, and important strands in the psychology literature, the eliciting, by employment practices, of commitment-based behaviours is believed by HRM scholars operating within this domain to be essential to generating optimum performance (Beer et al 1984). There are two strands of the HRM literature pertinent to this book, first the 'best fit' genre of HRM and, second, the 'best practice' school.

4.1.3.1 Best fit HRM

Building upon the Michigan School's view of HRM in the 1980s, that the congruence of strategy, structure and HRM were critical to firm performance (Fombrun et al 1984) the 'best fit' view of HRM can be divided into two distinct areas;

- strategic fit – HRM practices were vertically 'matched' either to strategy (Tichy 1983, Evans 1986, Schuler and Jackson 1987, Guest and Peccei 1994, Huselid 1995, 1998, Bird and Beechler 1995, Budhwar 2000) or shareholder expectations (Becker and Gerhart 1996, Becker et al 1997) in order to produce optimal outcomes.

- practice congruence – HRM practices were deemed to be most effective when they achieve congruence (Baird and Meshoulam, 1988, Wright and Snell 1991, Delery and Doty 1996, Lowe et al 1997,

Batt 2000), or are 'bundled' together into 'high performance works systems' (MacDuffie 1995, Huselid 1995).

Two specific models are worth considering in relation to the strategic fit approach. First, Guest's (1997) model (Figure 4.1) has as its starting point HRM strategy based on Porterian notions of competitive advantage.

Guest proposed this model as a theoretical construct based on a thorough consideration of all the important research and theorising on HRM to that date. Classifying what he deemed to be three themes in the HRM literature up until that time (HRM, performance and causal mechanisms linking the two), Guest put forward the framework in Figure 4.1 as a construct that might merit testing in further HRM research. Secondly, Becker et al (1997) begin their model with the notion of a 'business and strategic initiative' being the reference point for any subsequent HRM strategy, leading eventually to increased profits, growth and market value. This model has merit in two respects. Firstly, unlike Guest's model, it does not begin with Porter's strategic ideal types, but, rather more realistically, with a conception of strategy as an emergent rather than a planned phenomenon (Mintzberg et al 1998, Purcell 1999). Secondly, it utilises the notion of the effective design of the HRM system leading, sequentially, to an increase in the firm's value.

Other streams within this 'best fit' perspective include the strategic 'matching' school (Fombrun et al 1984, Schuler and Jackson 1987, Guest 1987, Lengnick-Hall and Lengnick-Hall 1988, Hendry and Pettigrew 1990, Becker

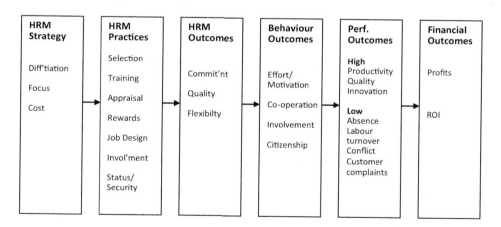

Figure 4.1   **Theoretical Model linking HRM and Performance**
Source: adapted from Guest 1997

et al 1997, Guest 1997, Sanz-Valle et al Guthrie et al 2002) and the school of 'contingent determinism', where the ownership of the company, life-cycle or industry sector is believed to be quite likely to act as an influence on HRM practices (Kochan and Barocci 1985, Cohen and Pfeffer 1984, Marginson et al 1988, Miles and Snow 1994).

There are two main issues with these 'best fit' approaches. First, they take a simplistic approach to strategy and its direct impact upon HRM. Few scholars operating within the strategic domain would accept any notion of the efficacy of the Ansoffian planned view of strategy (Whittington 1993). Rather, building upon the insights gained through Lindblom's (1959) 'muddling through' and Quinn's (1980) 'logical incrementalism', scholars would generally contend that corporate strategy is better described as emergent, a stream of decisions that responds to events as they unfold, rather than as a process of object determinism (Mintzberg et al 1998, Purcell 1999). Even if HR practices were fixed to planned strategy, doubts persist over its immediate consequences, given the lag that exists between HRM implementation and outcomes (Peck 1994). Second, the dubious causal links postulated by scholars operating in this area call into question any notion that there can be a tangible connection between vertically integrated HRM practices and positive performance outcomes (Golden and Ramanujam 1985, Paauwe and Richardson 1997; Truss 2001). Indeed, some scholars deny any causal relationship between the two (Paauwe and Boselie 2005) and no scholar has produced any hard evidence of financial or HR-related links (shown in retention, commitment, satisfaction or motivation) between congruent HR and organisational strategy (Wood 1999, Wall and Wood 2005).

With regard to internal congruence between HRM practices, the High Performance Work Systems or High Performance Commitment Systems genre which sought to examine whether particular bundles of practices such as communications, involvement, training and profit-related pay, when matched together, had a positive outcome on performance, was the subject of intense analysis by a number of HRM scholars (most notably Huselid 1995). Its conclusions were that certain bundles did indeed have a positive effect, with Delery and Doty (1996) noting that where congruence failed, 'deadly combinations' of HRM practices could have a deleterious impact upon performance. Other survey-based empirical studies such as the Workplace Employee Relations Studies (Cully et al 2003) have also purported to offer evidence that those companies with congruent bundles of 'commitment-based' HRM practices are more successful, in terms of productivity, satisfaction and performance, have also added to the debate. Such approaches suggest that rather than HRM practices fitting strategy or context, there are definitive 'bundles' of best practice HRM that have a universally transformative effect on organisational performance, a proposition that will be now considered below.

4.1.3.2 Best practice HRM

The best practice school of HRM is derived from a proposition from the '4Cs' Harvard school of HRM which emphasises the importance of commitment in the HRM mix (Beer et al 1984). Generally, HRM researchers define organisational commitment as an individual's psychological attachment to their organisation:

> ... *commitment human resource systems shape desired employee behaviours and attitudes by forging psychological links between organisational and employee goals. In other words, the focus is on developing committed employees who can be trusted to use their discretion to carry out job tasks in ways that are consistent with organisational goals ... (Arthur 1994: 546).*

As Arthur indicates, commitment is measured by three attitudinal factors: identification with the goals and values of the organisation, a desire to belong to the organisation and willingness to display effort on behalf of the organisation. For some commentators, an individual can be considered truly 'psychologically contracted' to the organisation only when all three factors are in evidence (Applebaum and Batt 1994, Guest and Conway 1997, Guest 1999, 2000, 2001).

An exemplar of the types of commitment-centred practices that yield competitive advantage was outlined by Pfeffer (1994 and 1998). From 'years of corporate research' Pfeffer argues in his 1994 book that companies should deploy 16 best practice HRM policies, although four years later he reduces this number to seven (see Figure 4.2).

The lists above differ in terms of the number of practices they list, but are notable for their emphasis on unitarist styles of managerial control, individualist approaches that preclude any significant role for independent worker representation or joint regulation. In this regard, they are representative of most of the approaches in the behavioural perspective in that they place a high level of emphasis on managerial determinism (Legge 1995a,b, Bach and Sisson 2000, Boxall and Purcell 2003).

'16 Practices for Competitive Advantage'	'7 Practices for Building Profits by Putting People First'
1. Employment security 2. Selectivity in hiring 3.High wages 4. Incentive pay 5. Employee ownership 6. Information sharing 7. Participation and empowerment 8. Teams and job design 9. Training and skill development 10. Cross-utilisation and cross-training 11. Symbolic egalitarianism 12. Wage compression 13. Promotion from within 14. Long-term perspective 15. Measurement of the practices 16. Overarching philosophy	1. Employment security 2. Selective hiring 3. Self-managed teams or teamworking 4. High pay contingent on company performance 5. Extensive training 6. Reduction of status differences 7. Sharing information

Figure 4.2   Best Practice HRM Prescriptions
Source: adapted from Pfeffer 1994 and 1998

There are three principal issues with the best practice school approach. First, where HRM scholars link best practice HRM to staff satisfaction and performance outcomes, a process of *reverse causality* might be a more likely explanation (Wright and Gardner 2003, Wright and Heggerty 2005). Best practice HRM is more likely to be in place as a result of firm performance, not the other way around. Second, notions of a link between commitment and best HRM are challenged by the reality that many organisations pursue cost-minimising 'hard' strategies – particularly during times of straightened economic circumstances (Boselie et al 2005, Legge 1998, 2001, Subramony 2006). It is more likely organisations superficially pursue a unitarist 'soft' HRM rhetoric thats mask a hard reality of tough working conditions, poor managerial practice and excessively compliance-driven regimes (Gratton et al 1999, Legge 2005). Third, HRM research, in general, stands accused of a narrowness in its research questioning, a lack of generalisability outside the confines of its research sites (mainly manufacturing and high technology) and national contexts (mainly US), and the problem of single respondents (usually HR professionals) to batteries of questions (Legge 2005).

4.2 How do Effective MULs Generate Commitment?

As has been previously outlined, the challenges facing MULs in multi-unit enterprises are significant. Situated between the Centre and the units MULs are expected to lead their units to deliver high levels of systems and process efficiency, superior standards and excellent service. This is in spite of the fact that, as the previous chapter outlined, they are sometimes supplied with inaccurate data, faced with irreconcilable aims and demands and, in many organisations, an expectation that they are principally charged with control and compliance activities. The question remains as to how MULs are able to generate commitment in such hostile and ambiguous circumstances? What the research for this book found was that in *both* benign and extreme contexts, effective MULs did similar things in order to generate commitment, although admittedly it was easier for MULs to achieve this in the former, rather than latter, paradigm. Thus, it can be argued that many of the instruments designed to elicit commitment can be denominated as being fairly universal, given their identification and observation in a range of situations.

4.2.1 PORTFOLIO OPTIMISATION

Our starting point for elucidating the commitment-based practices that MULs deploy for favourable outcomes is the fact that effective MULs concentrate on optimising their portfolio as a whole, rather than concentrating exclusively on managing individual units. To this extent they should be seen as portfolio optimisers, utilising and deploying human capital and knowledge in the most effective manner across their districts. There are three reasons for this phenomenon. First, MULs are measured and incentivised according to a district P&L and therefore their behaviour is somewhat conditioned to consider the performance of the whole rather than just the sum of its parts. Second, effective MULs recognise that in order to achieve optimal efficiency they have to utilise talent, knowledge and scarce resources across the portfolio, particularly the areas of starvation that have huge growth potential if the right skills and capabilities are 'matched' effectively. Third, because of geographical constraints and hoarding by fellow MULs, gaining access to resource outside the district is difficult, therefore effective MULs are forced to arrange their own portfolio effectively rather than relying on outside help.

4.2.2 COMMITMENT-BASED PRACTICES

As outlined in the introduction, the research for this book adopted a multi-method approach in seeking to find evidence of what effective MULs actually did to motivate and engage their people. In order to investigate the problematic, data was extracted from a number of sources including engagement surveys, semi-structured interviews and ethnographic observation with a range of multi-unit enterprises. The outcome of the analysis of this data is outlined in the sections below.

One particular quantitative experiment in one market leading multi-unit enterprise in 2009 merits particular citation. Here unit manager engagement data from 16 high performing (HIPO) MULs was matched with their 119 of their peers. These 16 MULs had been selected by the company as exemplars for the construction of a new cross-company leadership framework. They had been selected on the basis of their prior three-year profit and sales performance, compliance record (health and safety, cash and stock and standards), employee engagement (stability and turnover) and customer satisfaction (speed of service, quality and politeness). Would these high performing MULs (HIPO MULs) demonstrate better unit manager engagement scores than their peers? If so, in what areas? What *local leadership and HRM* characteristics did they demonstrate?

Following statistical analysis the HIPO MULs were found to have significantly better engagement scores than their peers (ie mean versus mean) with better mean scores in relation to support and development, involvement, direction, resource allocation, camaraderie and openness and honesty (see Figure 4.3).

Engagement Question	Variance*
My manager and I regularly discuss how I could improve through training, coaching or development	+7.2%
My manager involves me in setting our team's goals	+6.9%
The manager of our team gives us clear guidance	+6.6%
I feel as though I get fair recognition for a job well done	+6.7%
I have the resources I need to do my job to the best of my ability	+5.4%
There is a good spirit in our team	+5.3%
My manager is open, respectful and honest with me	+4.2%

Figure 4.3   HIPO MUL Engagement Scores versus Peers

Note: per cent deviation from mean versus mean

Two other findings emerged from this comparative analysis. First, HIPO MULs, while scoring disproportionately well in relation to their peers in 'personal supervisor support' attributes (as seen above), rated slightly worse (−0.04 per cent) in relation to the battery of questions relating to reward. This should be of little surprise as pay, conditions, budgets and incentives were set by the Centre in this organisation – HIPO MULs had little control over this hygiene factor. It is significant, however, that their perception regarding reward did not contaminate their overall assessment of engagement factors relating to their MUL. Second, HIPO MUL respondents scored the question 'I know what the company is working to achieve' −0.2 per cent worse, suggesting that they rated the local direction of their HIPO MUL more highly than their understanding of overall company strategy. Overall this survey indicated that high performing MULs achieved their results through effective *local leadership* practices, leveraging the human capital of their portfolio (through *local HRM practices*) more effectively than their peers. But what are the results of the broader research conducted for this book; what are the commitment attributes of effective MULs?

4.2.2.1 Local vision

The survey cited previously in Figure 4.3, found that HIPO MULs in a large multi-unit enterprise had a positive variance in engagement scores with their peers with regard to the question 'the manager of our team gives us clear direction' but a neutral reading on 'I know what the Company is trying to achieve'. What are the implications of these findings? Further qualitative analysis in this enterprise and a range of other multi-unit companies found that the ability of the MUL to synthesise the super-ordinate objectives of the parent organisation/brand with the focus of their district – creating what many respondents elucidated as a 'local vision' – was a key variable in effective MUL success. Why is a local vision required? What is its importance and how do effective MULs achieve a distillation and crystallisation of the overarching objectives of the organisation to create a compelling local agenda?

The requirement for a local vision was felt to be critical by effective MULs for three reasons. First, because of the physical and emotional distance of their units from the Centre, effective MULs felt that they needed to translate what might seem highly abstract goals into a plan with local relevance, thereby 'bringing the strategy alive'. Second, in some organisations the policy makers had presented a highly complex set of objectives that, at first sight, seemed mutually exclusive. Effective MULs felt a need to simplify this complexity by breaking down the overarching vision, strategy and objectives into a local digestible form where the linkages between each element could be made. On occasions they were adept at abstracting strategy from tactics; preserving the policy makers' original intentions, albeit with a more sophisticated tactical plan for local action. Third, while some best practice organisations had effective business objective cascade mechanisms in place, codified through performance management systems, their purported links with the strategic intent of the organisation was not always obvious. Effective MULs made subtle adaptations and iterations to this cascade in order to improve alignment and line-of-site at local level. Sometimes this was achieved in conjunction with their peers and operations director in their region, often it was done by themselves and their teams.

Effective MULs were passionate about creating a local vision for a number of reasons. Like strategic policy makers they were intent on creating a sense of local mission where collectivism transcended individualism. Getting unit managers to buy into a local portfolio vision helped portfolio optimization; acting as an enabling mechanism to get people to cooperate, putting aside their own self interest for the common good. This sense of collectivism was heightened in those districts where MULs actively involved their unit managers in framing a local vision; a process that is explored below. In addition, the elucidation of a local vision gave their teams a deeper sense of purpose and control. Often the district vision was used as a template at unit level by managers seeking to engage and motivate their staff. In terms of control, the existence of a local vision gave participants a feeling that they had some sort of influence over their destiny.

What did these local visions look like? The most unsuccessful were merely a rational reiteration of the district budgets and targets; a series of outcome-driven compliance measures and statistics, bolted onto the company vision. Such approaches left unit managers uninspired and bored. Effective MULs, on the other hand, created local visions that engendered:

- recall – abbreviations or patterns of numbers were used for instant recall purposes

- realism – stretching but realistic super ordinate district goals, creating a sense of 'optimistic momentum'

- relevance –focused upon closing the gaps between 'where we are now' and 'where we want to be'.

How do effective MULs give a clear vision and direction? Best practice observation suggests that they do the following:

1.   understand company objectives (weighting and importance)

2.   calibrate district *gaps* against higher order objectives

3.   understand input and output linkages and connections

4.   team goal setting to close gap and objectives

Case Study 1 – Unit Visioning at Rank

Ian Burke is the Executive Chairman and CEO of Rank Plc, the UK's largest multi-channel gaming company. Under his leadership the company has undergone a major transformation, simultaneously developing new land-based and on-line products. Previously Ian held CEO positions at multi-unit enterprises such as Holmes Place (fitness clubs), Thistle Plc and Holiday Inn EMEA (hotels) and Gala (leisure). The excerpt below is a blog posted by Ian in August 2011, stressing the need for his GMs to create a local vision, followed by his thoughts on the importance that MULs play in framing local visions.

… I have driven over 1,000 miles this week visiting 23 Mecca and Grosvenor clubs in Scotland, the North East and Yorkshire. I met so many passionate, enthusiastic colleagues that I could not do justice to them in this short blog. Apart from my usual focus on the Gamecard areas of the team, the customers and the results for investors, the main themes discussed with GMs were:

- What sort of assessment do GMs make of a club when they assume local leadership responsibility? My own preference is that GMs take time to understand how the club has developed over the past 5 years or so in terms of team satisfaction and turnover, active customer numbers, customer visits, NPS scores, and the key financial outcomes including revenue and profit. It is very difficult, in my view, to map out a plan for the future without a really good understanding of the past and present (and the three questions – what happened or is happening? why did this happen? and what should we do about it? – are key and useful questions);

- How might the local market develop in the next few years and what are our leisure competitors doing?;
- *What is the GM's local vision* (eg 'to be the leading community gaming based entertainment business in Dundee') and business plan for the club over the next three years?;
- How are Mecca GMs trying to learn from Grosvenor GMs and vice versa and are there opportunities for our brands to work together for mutual benefit?, and
- How can we engage GMs and their teams to play their part in building Mecca (which is so much more than a bingo business even though bingo is about 60 per cent of total revenue) and Grosvenor (which is much more than a roulette business even though roulette is about 55 per cent of total revenue) as leading gaming based entertainment brands? In other words how do we broaden the appeal of our (multi-channel) brands to attract and retain new customers without alienating existing customers? As we expand our range of gaming and non-gaming product, our under 35 year old customers are the fastest growing age group for both brands. This age group accounts for about 14 per cent of visits in Mecca and over 50 per cent of visits in the G Casinos.

Our businesses generally are in good shape with motivated teams and good standards, which allows us to look hard for ways to grab the limitless opportunities in our local markets and grow each brand every year in the years ahead....

4.2.2.2 Cross-portfolio involvement

Although setting a clear direction is an imperative it is also crucial that MULs collectively involve their direct reports in setting team goals in order to foster engagement and accountability. In the survey in Figure 4.3, HIPO MULs had a 6.9 per cent positive variance to their peer group with regard to the question 'my manager involves me in setting our team's goals'. Further research indicated that more experienced, confident MULs, understood that in order to achieve buy-in, rather than taking a top down approach, they had to encourage bottom-up involvement and participation in setting the direction of their area. Sometimes effective MULs had to achieve this in a wider context where there was a lack of formal or informal involvement mechanisms. To this extent they saw themselves as one MUL put it, as 'swimming against the grim tide of command and control'. Why do effective MULs involve their people in setting goals and how do they do it?

Effective MULs involved their people in goal setting and decision-making for a number of reasons. First, they wished to create a sense of collective responsibility, where their people, having been genuinely involved in setting goals, felt accountable for their execution and achievement. This enabled them to make their portfolios *self regulating*, where team members who were seen to be underperforming against agreed standards and metrics, became subject to pressure from within the group rather than from just the MUL. Second, cross-portfolio involvement was seen as a useful means of harnessing the ideas and energy of a wider pool of expertise and knowledge. MULs cannot know every detail regarding their operations; the people best placed to translate super-ordinate goals into a workable local vision are the front-line operators. They know what is feasible and operationally practicable given the resources and local context in which they operate. To this extent the effective MUL acts as a facilitator in shaping ideas and feedback into a workable plan. Third, involving the whole team dissipates cliques; integrating experienced 'old lags' with enthusiastic newcomers.

How do effective MULs involve their people in setting the strategic path for their portfolio? As previously stated, on many occasions MULs will feel that they are operating in an 'involvement vacuum' where their views and preferences are rarely considered by policy makers. Why should they operate any differently? In some organisations there might be a multiplicity of involvement and feedback mechanisms such as face-to-face two way feedback meetings with executives, problem solving groups, suggestion schemes, intranet forums, joint consultative meetings and other forms of representative 'voice' in unionised environments. However, this does not mean that such mechanisms lend any cohesion or focus at a local level. Effective MULs are more likely to construct and utilise their own channels of communication to effect consensus.

First, they set rules on desired and expected behaviours for involvement which are agreed by the group. Observed rules included 'people should listen with respect', 'contribute maturely', 'avoid negativity and blame', 'leaving' as one district rules of engagement stated 'egos outside the door'. Second, formal processes are either created, or existing mechanisms used, to facilitate involvement, such as:

- area meetings – effective MULs used face-to-face encounters, predominantly during monthly or six-weekly area meetings, to involve their teams in framing agreed goals. a variety of techniques were used such as cluster discussions, brainstorming and problem-solving, joint feedback sessions validated agreed goals.

- weekly conference calls – these sessions, primarily used as regular communications updates, also served as 'sounding board' mechanisms.

- on-line communication – use of e-mail, intranet and, in some instances, Facebook and Twitter, in order to harvest views and generate debate, was also used by effective MULs.

With regard to informal involvement processes, effective MULs encouraged their people to share ideas and thoughts on how the local vision of the portfolio could be enhanced and improved, useful in organisations where the super-ordinate direction changed dramatically, or in a few cases, frequently.

Given the constraints of perfect information, time and space, how do effective MULs involve their managers in setting a local vision? Generally they achieve alignment in team meetings at the beginning of the financial year where they:

1. share information on the company strategy and objectives

2. establish key priorities

3. define what success looks like, and

4. agree measurement, monitoring and feedback mechanisms.

Case Study 2 – Cross-Portfolio Involvement at Jewson

Tony Taylor is an Area Director responsible for 19 branches at Jewson, the UK's largest builders' merchants owned by St Gobain (France). With approximately 640 outlets it reached the pre-eminent position in its sector in the UK through its purchase of Build Centre from Wolseley in October 2011. Tony reflects upon how he involves his branch managers in goal attainment.

… I am measured against a balanced scorecard with 11 key metrics (including live accounts, sales, stock, shrinkage, health and safety etc); these are then broken down to site level scorecards. My overarching vision for the area given the state of the market – which I start my Area Meetings with and also sign off my e-mails – is the 3 Ps 'Progress, Progress, Progress'! The guys like it and buy into it. What I am looking for is for my unit managers to take ownership of their scorecard business objectives and make relative progress on the three or four things that are real gaps in their units. Just concentrating on three or four things at the beginning of the year at a district level isn't sensible for me because, first, the weightings and priorities of things change throughout the year, and, second, all the branches are in different places on their scorecards for different reasons. For instance one branch might be really up on generating and servicing live accounts but down against stocks.

Nevertheless, there are times when the company has a drive on certain metrics that supersede everything else in their importance. This is when we need a cross-portfolio drive which involves everyone engaging on 'what good looks like' for us and then helping one another to make it happen so everyone benefits …Take reducing over-aged stock. We have recently had a new Supply Chain Director appointed who has, quite rightfully, made it his priority to free up inventory space by shifting excess stock. In order to create the right behaviours, a notional charge was put into our P&Ls penalizing us for retaining over-aged stock – so the incentive to shift it became very high! As we have good reports that detail which stores have got 'over' and 'under' stocks on items it became imperative to shift stuff around the district to move it.

In order to solve the problem, I consulted with the branch managers and we decided on a certain plan of action. First, we carved up the area into four geographic quarters. Second, we all agreed that one branch manager would draw up an 'excess stock master plan'. Third, this person worked with the four quarters to devise means of identifying which saleable stock could be moved shifted to and moved on. So if a driver was out delivering near a certain branch boundary – could he transport saleable excess stock to a branch with depleted inventory? This has required a lot of trust, honesty (not shifting on damaged stock!) and teamwork. Basically, with the support and buy-in of the team he has 'cracked on with it', holding weekly conference calls chasing progress, sorting out the logistics. The net result of all this action has been a reduction of excess stock levels on my area by 15 per cent in the first period of action!

Another KPI we have concentrated on, involving the wider team, is live accounts. In some of the branches the sales executives work separately from branch management, reporting into a different line. As live accounts drive a lot of other lines on the P&L (product sales and average transaction values) it is important we involve and engage them in what we are trying to do at branch level. After all their goals are our goals! One thing that has come out of this is the identification of accounts that are opened but not used. As a team we have put a plan of action together with the sales guys of current initiatives to push live accounts forwards. This is a good example of my team networking with others in a quest to improve their performance ....

4.2.2.3 Portfolio 'talent matching'

Proactively matching talent within the portfolio, ensuring that the unit manager 'fits' with the individual site characteristics, is the most important role of the MUL. Indeed, Helen Webb, the HR and Logistics Director of Sainsbury's, estimates that the difference between a 'good' or 'bad' unit manager 'matching' can be up to 10 per cent of turnover. In leisure, where emotional and service attributes feature more highly, Simon Longbottom, MD of Greene King, estimates that this figure can be anything up to 30 per cent. What are the problems faced by MULs in this 'matching conundrum' and how do effective ones overcome them?

The main challenge posed by attempting to fit the right unit manager to the appropriate site lies in the sheer complexity of the exercise. Within their portfolio of sites MULs will have a variety of units with specific traits; some might be newly invested (posing particular problems in changes of customer mix and systems design), others will have larger/smaller sales/staff profiles and/or specific issues relating to safety, pilfering and non-standard layout and flows. *No one store or unit is completely identical to any other*: a number of contextual factors need to be taken into account when making appointments for optimal fit between manager and site. Other challenges include issues such as invisible, ineffective or poor employment branding and attraction policies, defective recruitment systems, lack of HRM dedicated support, relentlessly high rates of turnover in some sectors (such as hospitality), competitor poaching activity and the threat that predecessor MULs might seek, as one MUL put it, 'take all their best people with them'.

Given these constraints, how do effective MULs deploy talent within their portfolio? First, they gain a deep understanding of their sites and unit-specific idiosyncrasies. Second, they will ask themselves the question, are the right people in the right sites? Does the extant unit manager's skills and behavioural profile match the demands of this store? Third, in tandem with previous point, effective MULs will quickly build up their own personal talent bank, having appraised all the staff within their portfolio. Effective MULs create back-up plans and options (see support and development section below) to ensure they can react to voluntary or forced departures. In extremis, MULs will make temporary appointments or make use of relief managers to buy time whilst they appoint the right person. Fourth, and most importantly, effective MULs will proactively shape the *human architecture* within their portfolio in order to optimize talent 'fit'.

Rather than being reactive – waiting for vacancies to occur naturally – effective MULs are proactive in engineering moves across their portfolio. Many MULs use performance management techniques to 'move people out' of units where they are inappropriately matched, implicitly or explicitly threatening sanctions or punishment relating to any one of a myriad of compliance measures. One MUL described this as 'encouraging underperformers to read their own horoscope'. However, whilst such an approach might be effective in the short-term, it has a long-lasting effect on the MUL's level of trust and reputation amongst the 'survivors'. Effective MULs are more adept at *'proactive matching'*, using softer influencing and negotiating skills to, as one respondent put it, move people 'out or around with minimum collateral damage'. However such an approach takes a disproportionate amount of time, effort and planning, involving the application of highly sophisticated ER and behavioural skills; a fundamental reason why only a limited number of MULs choose this path of action.

The visible costs of making a bad appointment are poor sales and margins derived from poor service standards and systems application. Invisible costs to the MUL include the disproportionate amount of time devoted to 'fixing' the problem, neglecting other core functions and duties across the portfolio. But what do effective MULs generally look for when making important appointments? Alongside 'matching', which requires a combination of art and science, effective MULs interviewed for this book coalesced around three main areas:

1. Attitude – in order to ensure that they appoint unit managers with the right attitude, MULs will check the potential appointees through assessing prior performance, testing or a trial period observation. The key point is that potential unit managers have appropriate *needs and expectations* that will be fulfilled by the role. They are realistic about the constraints surrounding the position

but feel *intrinsically motivated* by the challenges and opportunities of leading a team of service providers.

2.   Aptitude – the level of capability and skills required for unit managers is contingent on size of unit, its range of products and the organisation's systems, standards and service concept. In general, however, generic requirements will include:

   – Numeracy; performance is measured through financial metrics and tracked through key data reports, therefore the requirement for numeracy is high.
   – Cognitive; ability to interpret and critically analyse data in order to take remedial action is also an important requirement.
   – Administrative; strong administrative skills in order to apply and monitor blueprinted systems and processes.
   – Team leadership; capability to select, motivate and lead service providers and the team, especially in units with a small management structure.
   – Customer service; good social and interpersonal skills backed up with a real passion for satisfying customer needs.
   – Technical/craft; perhaps less important because they can be acquired and learned, craft (such as food production in casual dining), merchanting (layout and display) and/or technical (volume and capacity management) skills are desirable attributes that enable greater efficiency and effectiveness.

3.   Team contribution – in addition to attitude and aptitude at an individual level the capacity of the unit manager to contribute to the wider team is commonly reviewed and considered by effective MULs. Questions they are seeking to address in this respect include:

   – will this appointment improve the balance of skills, capabilities and capabilities within my team?
   – will this appointment infuse the team with more energy and drive?

How does the effective MUL measure these factors prior to appointment? First, as most unit managers are promoted vertically within, or horizontally across, organisations, the MUL will have been able to calibrate or observe the potential of aspirant unit managers in order to minimize the risks of failure. Second, some organisations will have in place sophisticated development centre mechanisms that measure the capability of external and internal aspirant unit managers through a battery of tests, interviews and observed work simulation exercises. Effective MULs will seek information from a number of formal and informal sources to optimize chances of success.

Case Study 3 – Talent Matching at Sainsbury's

Tim Elliot (pseudonym) is the Regional Operations Manager for 21 units with Sainsbury's (150,000 colleagues and 1,000 stores). One of the UK's oldest multi-unit enterprises, it has undergone a successful transformation under its CEO Justin King, and was awarded the title 'Supermarket of the Year 2011' by the retail industry journal 'Retail Week'. Tim reflects upon the importance of optimising talent within the portfolio, particularly prior to a major refurbishment.

... To my mind fitting the right person to the site is one of the most important jobs I do. I have a range of units that vary in size from 30 to 60k sq ft, the amount of colleagues (200–500), size of management teams, range of demographic areas and locations – out of town, in town and suburban. Also the stores are in different phases of their investment cycles – one of my main tasks is to ensure that any major refurbishments maximize their investment and, in the case of new openings, the stores set off in the right direction, with the right culture and performance trajectory; once a culture in a store is set, it is very difficult to shift! I can give you three recent examples where I have talent matched to improve performance; one was a major refurbishment, the other where I changed the team around the GM to enhance her performance and the last one where I put a really good GM into a smaller, underperforming store.

In the first case, when I took over the patch a year and a half ago, I knew that one of my stores (which accounts for 10 per cent of the overall sales in my area) would be undergoing a multi-million pound investment, increasing its size by nearly 30 per cent to increase the general merchandise and clothing area. The store manager that was in place had been appointed by my predecessor, having followed in an extremely popular GM. This GM, unlike the one he followed in, lacked buy-in and followership in the store. Colleagues complained that he was rarely seen on the floor and seemed to 'hide away' in his office – staff pick up on messages from the GM pretty quickly; if the GM is in a bad mood or is invisible, morale throughout the store can change quite dramatically! Consequently standards were not where I wanted them to be, units were uncared for and random rubbish seemed scattered every time I came in. The mystery customer and availability scores of this store were not where I wanted them to be.

So what I did was bring his personal development review forwards and was completely honest with him; 'this is how the previous ROM viewed you, but I think you are in the 'underachieving' box'. I also followed up with lots of one-to-ones and 'visits with a purpose' to put him on the right track. The upshot was that he decided to leave the company and work for one of our competitors. This enabled me to appoint a GM from a store nearby who is a great leader to oversee the 36 week refurbishment cycle. He managed it with great success; sales disruption figures were managed to target and excellent mystery customer (+8 per cent) and availability (+1.5 per cent) scores were maintained throughout. The new GM fits the culture of the store, is visible, has great leadership skills and colleague satisfaction is very high! I dread to think what might have happened if the previous GM had handled this project!

In the second case, in another one of my stores the GM was convinced that just concentrating on the process would deliver the numbers. Her standards and service numbers were down, she was unhappy and was still talking to her ex-ROM. Again I marked her as an 'under achiever' in her review and made a number of 'visits with a purpose'. On one of these visits I said 'what do you need from me?' She surprised me when she said that she wanted a new management team; she had found it difficult to change the old culture in the store with the team she currently had in place. So we took her Deputy out (moving him to a different store) and put an experienced 'softer' new one in. This broke up the clique beneath her and the team (under a new 'Clough and Taylor') approach has blossomed. They have come from the bottom to fourth or fifth on their cost controls, standards and service. The balance of the management team is now great. She got a great review from me last time out.

In the last case I had a store that had become vacant with really poor metrics across the board. Usually you might put in one of your 'rising star' deputies but I decided it needed real experience. Turning it around would really improve my district figures. I convinced one of my experienced guys to move in – this was a great turnaround opportunity for him that would enhance his profile and reputation. On the face of it, it wasn't a great move for him but the turnaround has been immense – he is happy, the store has really added to the overall performance of my area and the move has been a real success! ...

4.2.2.4 Tailored learning and development

Another feature of effective MULs is the degree to which they foster commitment and engagement through tailoring training and development for their people with a view to improving their technical and behavioural capabilities. In the survey in Figure 4.3 HIPO MULs had the largest variance against their peers at

7.2 per cent with regard to the question 'my manager and I regularly discuss how I could improve through training, coaching or development'. Clearly this is a key commitment-led intervention deployed by effective MULs on an *individual*, one-to-one basis. Further research indicated that the success of this practice rested on the degree to which coaching and development was tailored to individual unit manager needs. In addition to this individual approach, however, the degree to which effective MULs utilised the resources of the whole portfolio as a form of *local* support and development to junior talent and 'rising stars' was also found to be important, improving the talent 'bench strength' of the portfolio.

Normative accounts of training and development stress the importance of the provision of company-led programmes, company commitment to this area usually being measured in total training spend per head or training time allocated per employee per annum. Most of the multi-unit enterprises examined during the course of this research laid claim to the provision of extensive training and development programmes backed up with extensive personal development review mechanisms. However, the economic and financial challenges imposed by the 2008 downturn had led some organisations to cut their training and development budgets (reducing courses and the number of HR training professionals), cutting the number of allocated training hours from the labour budget or adopting cheaper, albeit more impersonal, means of delivery (such as e-training and development). In spite of these pressures effective MULs remained committed to providing support and development, adopting creative approaches to provision within their portfolios.

Most MUL job descriptions prescribe this area as a main duty of the MUL. However, it is the degree to which MULs tailor this support, both for individuals and the portfolio, which stands out as the most important contributory factor to success. At an individual level, effective MULs did not use training courses as 'sweeties', as one HRD put it, but as serious performance-enhancing interventions. Effective MULs approached learning and development seriously, firstly gathering data on their people to assess relative strengths and weaknesses. This information was derived from previous performance and development assessments, observation, one-to-one personal development meetings and, where available, employee survey data and 360-degree appraisals. What interventions were required to improve performance? For those new in job role, technical courses (security, safety, blueprinted procedures etc) are most likely to be deployed to improve job capability; for those longer in role, behavioural courses dealing with enhancing leadership capability might be used. On a one-to-one basis during personal development reviews (usually kept separate from performance discussions) the effective MUL was also adept a listening and coaching rather than talking and telling. In addition to set piece development interactions, effective MULs constantly kept up development discussions through ad hoc problem-solving discussions about what had happened, what had been learnt and how things might be approached differently next time.

Effective MULs used all resources at their disposal within their portfolio to advance learning and development and, as previously stated, did not exclusively concentrate on unit managers. At a local level, effective MULs identified individuals and units that were exemplars in various areas such as administration, labour control, inventory management, margin control, availability, merchandising and service. These were designated as best practice and used to train staff across the portfolio. Staff either visited these houses to 'sit with Nellie' or workshops were designed to train a number of staff across the portfolio at these stores. In addition, it was notable that effective MULs took an active role in initiating, monitoring and reviewing learning and development interventions for key individuals and cohorts within their portfolios other than unit managers such as deputy and assistant managers, section leaders and supervisors. Often 'rising stars' were identified and rotated around best practice houses to learn new skills and behaviours. Such a practice enabled the effective MUL to build a talent bank of individuals in readiness for voluntary or 'forced' vacancies.

Alongside, what might be termed *vertical* views of learning and development, the effective MUL also took a *horizontal* view on learning and development, assessing generic skills gaps, particularly in relation to achieving specific portfolio objectives and goals. Sometimes company programmes were inappropriate, ineffective or untimely in addressing current business objectives and needs across the portfolio (especially with regard to service delivery or change management). Here the effective MUL might devise workshops at area meetings to address specific cross-portfolio learning and development gaps.

The benefits of being committed to learning and development went beyond just capability improvement across the portfolio. It also had a strong signalling effect. Effective MULs were not only demonstrating a physical, but also an emotional investment in their people. The messaging from their commitment was clearly that effective MULs cared about the success, well being and longer-term prospects of their people. It formed a strong psychological contract between the effective MULs and their staff, compensating, perhaps, for the other stresses and strains of the job. It also fostered a culture of continuous learning and improvement within the portfolio; a view that this was a good thing. One important point was that effective MULs provided time off and space for their people to learn, rarely cancelling or 'pulling people' off courses at the last minute. Thus, to recap, effective MULs generally effect the following support and development practices in order to generate commitment;

1.   create time and space to schedule meaningful discussions.

2.   'actively' listen rather than talk

3.   coach rather instruct

4.   link 'tailored' support and development interventions to impact commitment and performance.

Case Study 4 – Tailored Support and Development at Harvester Restaurants

Alfie Molinaro is a Retail Business Manager for 15 units in Harvester Restaurants, the UK's largest full-service pub restaurant chain. Having undergone a transformation since 2008, through improved local leadership and product positioning (driven by Operations Director Steve Cash) Harvester was the winner of the 2011 Peach-Coffer 'Brand Icon Evolution' Award. A multi-ward winning MUL, Alfie previously worked in chain retail. Here he reflects on his approaches to building technical and behavioural capability within his portfolio.

… I concentrate my developmental efforts in three areas; building capability at Kitchen Manager (KM) and Assistant Manager (AM) level, improving technical skills *and* behavioural skills amongst my GMs. In order to be successful, however, I have to use all the resources at my disposal to ensure I achieve all my objectives in these areas.

Building capability beneath GM level is absolutely crucial for both succession planning and 'bench strength' purposes. Every four weeks I hold alternate Kitchen Manager (KM) and Assistant Manager (AM) meetings which I chair with the assistance of a 'lead' GM where we focus upon where we are with their training and understanding. With regard to training, the KMs on the company's 'training links' or 'accredited chef' programmes and the AMs on the 'portfolio' or 'transitions' courses update me on their progress. As some

GMs might not be particularly diligent in training and might leave training manuals on the shelf to gather dust, I am passionate about demonstrating that I am absolutely committed to self-improvement and progression to the wider team. In terms of group understanding we might take a certain issue – such as food quality with the Kitchen Managers – and seek to understand where we are and how we might get better. Over the past year we have improved our scores by 7 per cent by analysing the customer survey data and complaints and putting in place group actions as a result. It is a good forum for the KMs to share best practice and, where necessary, seek out help. Most importantly, these development meetings show these key people that they are valued by me …I am interested in their progression and well-being and I get to know them. I think I get more back from them because if I am interested in them, they are likely to respond … by returning that interest in spades!

In terms of developing technical skills on my area I use my 'leads', 'champions' and 'houses of excellence' extensively. Although they are not formally rewarded for these positions it grants them a level of influence and status within my district and puts them on a potential development track for RBM. It benefits both me and them! Given the wide geographical spread of my district my three leads on the area assist some period review meetings – they have specific skills in labour productivity, stocks and risk and compliance systems and can give practical advice to GMs who need help. Their views are accepted because they have a great deal of credibility. One of my 'leads' actually mentors two GMs at present … I also have a few 'champions' who act as the 'go to' people on customer service, compliance training and audits. Take food safety audits – the champion for this area will actually do dummy compliance audits. His credibility stems from the fact that his house audit scores average 95 per cent, from a base position from when he arrived there of 45 per cent...Every third week in the period I meet with my leads and champions and we discuss gaps, progress and development required. This might entail a GM who is struggling on some aspect going for remedial technical training in a 'house of excellence' environment which is trusting and non-threatening. It a win-win, as it raises the technical capability of my GMs but also gives the 'champions' involved a sense of ownership and purpose.

I have to accept that sometimes, however, technical deficiencies stem from attitudinal or behavioural issues. Here I take total ownership of the situation through one-to-one coaching. For instance, two of my GMs at present are overly controlling, and although they have good P&Ls they have poor customer and employee engagement scores. I am currently teaching them how they can build a team in which they can foster trust and accountability, enabling them to delegate certain key tasks. They cannot be dictators and try and do everything themselves! As one of the managers is frequently mentioned in complaints by customers I am coaching her how to handle customer complaints differently! Another of my GMs is like a nodding dog saying 'yes, yes, yes' to everything but then failing to implement what has been agreed. I have coached him in the art of prioritisation and the virtue of saying 'no' at times! Also, once I took photographs of his merchandising and back-of-house areas and said 'impress me on my next visit!' When I returned a week later there was a massive transformation and we could visually compare 'before' and 'after' ... The sense of accomplishment and achievement they feel in making real behavioural change has increased their levels of confidence, self-esteem and effort – I know they are grateful for this direct coaching and honesty ... I am also pleased with the returns ....

4.2.2.5 Recognition and positive reinforcement

Another way in which effective MULs generate commitment is the degree to which they recognise and positively reinforce good performance and high levels of discretionary effort. In the survey in Figure 4.3, HIPO MULs had a positive variance of 6.7 per cent in comparison to their peers with regards to the question 'I feel as if I get fair recognition for a job well done'. Further qualitative research in this enterprise and elsewhere established that effective MULs were adept, whatever the prevailing climate, at creating emotional buy-in through planned and spontaneous recognition at all levels throughout their portfolio. What does this look like and why was it regarded as being important?

Effective MULs applied both formal and informal means of recognition and positive reinforcement. Often this recognition was tied to meeting explicit objectives within the portfolio (sales, standards, service etc). Channels of recognition included;

- Formal:

  - nominations for awards at district, regional or company level; in some instances, staff were nominated for national awards (staff member of the year, store of the year, manager of the year etc)
  - 'winner' or best practice citations in round-robin e-mails, newsletters, area meetings.

- Informal:

  - spontaneous phone calls to thank staff in person

- store visits, sometimes with notables (regional or operations director), specifically designed to thank staff in person
- handwritten letters expressing personal gratitude.

In addition it was remarkable how effective MULs also showed as one unit manager called it a 'personal touch outside of just work things', remembering birthdays, recognising notable events such as births and marriages and showing genuine compassion and pastoral care for staff during times of personal difficulty (granting time off without any quibbles).

Why was this so important in getting staff to commit? First, formal recognition mechanisms set the benchmark for what good looked like with regard to service, standards and systems application, motivating the collective to achieve higher levels of performance. Second, especially with regard to informal and spontaneous recognition, effective MULs signalled their appreciation and care for staff 'not just as numbers but also as human beings' as one unit manager put it. Unsolicited positive recognition in the form of a simple thank you was believed to have a profound effect by unit managers who, in many instances, were apt to feel isolated, distant and highly pressurized. It bolstered their sense of self-esteem and well-being, reinforcing their sense that what they were doing was positive and worthwhile. However, care was taken by effective MULs that they did not over-praise or build egos that would become disruptive in the longer term. Effective MULs did not want to be perceived as having favourites who constantly gained the accolades, ensuring, for instance, those that improved their *relative* performance were encouraged as much as those that achieved excellent *absolute* levels of performance. In this way they brought on the performance of the portfolio as a whole, rather than just its pockets of excellence.

Case Study 5 – Unit Manager Reflections on Recognition and Positive Reinforcement

Over the course of three academic years (2009–2012) nearly 200 unit managers from retail, hospitality and leisure organisations have attended Foundation and Post-Graduate degree courses in Multi-Unit Leadership and Strategy at Birmingham City Business School. Selected delegates on the modules 'Managing and Motivating People' and 'Leading Service and Change' provided the following responses (within focus group discussions) to the questions 'How does your Area Manager personally recognise you and/or your team's effort and performance? How does he/she demonstrate that he/she cares?:

'...Unlike some of the managers I've had before this one does send out sinister district e-mails praising a few and then dumping on the rest by *highlighting people at the bottom of league tables in red !*... actually what he does is recognises how far some people have come on certain measures and praises improvement as well as top performance ...' Unit Manager, Retail.

'My manager is very good picking the phone up to me and saying 'well done' particularly on Mondays after busy sessions over the weekend to give me a bit of a lift or after we've done something particularly good ... like great sales, mystery customer or safety visits ... unlike other managers I've had I don't hear his voice and think 'here's another bollocking! ... ' General Manager, Hospitality.

'What impresses me about my Area Manager is the way, when he comes into the store, he remembers everybody's names ... I'm sure he's written them down ... also he always has a quiet word with me to ask whose done something particularly well and then he says 'well done' to them ... ' Unit Manager, Leisure.

'Our Area Director held a competition for the most new accounts opened in a quarter ... what he did as a reward was to run the store for a day with some of the other store managers and gave me and my team a day out at the races which he wrote off against the District P&L ... You should have seen the amount of engagement and buy-in that created! ... ' Unit Manager, Merchanting.

'My Retail Business Manager is good at remembering our birthdays and always delivers a present ... a few bottles of wine or a tin of sweets at Christmas. It's a personal touch and we really appreciate it ... Actually, we would walk over hot coals for him! ... ' Unit Manager, Leisure.

'Our manager came to our charity fund raising day and dressed up like the rest of the staff and got stuck in ... our staff thought that was brilliant ...the pictures that were posted on Facebook were brilliant ... ' Unit Manager, Retail.

'In our store we have a staff member of the month award and our Regional Manager often comes to present it at Team Meetings or on the floor to the winner in person ... I don't know how he does it because I know he does it elsewhere across his district ... The returns he gets from this are massive in my view ... ' Unit Manager, Retail.

4.2.2.6 Openness, trust and promise fulfilment

A further feature of the way in which effective MULs generate commitment is the degree to which they appear to be more open and honest than their peers. Figure 4.3 shows that that HIPO MULs had a 4.2 per cent positive variance in comparison to their peers to the question 'my manager is open, respectful and honest with me'. What did this actually mean? Further research revealed that there were two main dimensions. First, MULs were perceived to be candid when interpreting the underlying meaning of certain initiatives and corporate communications for their staff. Second, they gained trust through protecting their people from punishment and sanctions but also 'following up on their promises', not as one unit manager put it, 'promising the world and then pissing off into the ether!'.

With regard to openness and honestyeffective MULs transacted transparently in two ways. First, they sought to be as 'open as they could be' about the underlying motives and messages of general corporate communications. When asked what things 'actually meant' they gave a balanced view of the underlying intent of the organisation. MULs would attempt to, as one put it, 'colour in communications', putting both sides of the argument, explaining that there might be additional facts and information driving decisions that needed to be taken into account. Second, in respect of interpersonal relations they were consistent as to when, as one unit manager put it 'yes meant yes, and no meant no!' Effective MULs were seen to be 'firm but fair'; giving honest answers to questions and acting with a high level of moral and ethical integrity.

Such behaviour had an impact on levels of trust, a state that was further reinforced through demonstrable actions such as *protection from punishment*. Effective MULs were judicious in their application of retribution, reserving such actions as the last resort. As Chapter 3 outlined, the inordinate number of compliance measures backed up with draconian sanctions within standardized multi-unit enterprises afforded managers ample opportunity to punish non-compliance. Effective MULs did not conspire with their staff to hide non-compliance in order to curry favour, rather they chose to punish extreme offences rather than as on effective MUL put it, 'apply the letter of the law in every instance'. Effective MULs discreetly held 'car park chats' or 'store room conversations' in which they took mild corrective action in preference to formal sanctions for minor misdemeanors. 'Nipping things in the bud', as one effective MUL put it, was deemed to be more effective than things getting out of hand and 'jumping on people'. Such behaviour not only created higher levels of trust between both parties (MUL and unit manager) but also a sense of indebtedness; many unit managers were grateful for the 'protection' afforded by their MUL's 'from the Centre'. In turn, both they and the MULs examined during the course of this research believed that this led to higher levels of commitment and effort at a local level (see Case Study 6b).

Trust was also formed through effective MULs 'delivering on their promises'. Chapter 2 referred to one view of the MUL role as 'fixers'; in this capacity MULs are the bridge between the Centre and unit in resolving a number of day-to-day operational issues. This is demonstrated most acutely, for instance, when an MUL takes over a new territory. Often they are presented with a list of grievances and problems that the previous MUL 'had promised to sort out'. MULs can establish instant credibility by fixing as many issues as possible (such as delivery timeslots, maintenance requests and backdated payroll queries). In some cases, given the rampant scepticism of their unit managers, effective MULs 'under promised but over delivered', letting their actions speak for themselves. In turn, a level of trust builds between the MUL and unit manager where they are not perceived, as one unit manager put it, as a 'man of straw'. Unit managers perceive (perhaps slightly inaccurately in a number of cases) that the MUL has far more power and influence than they do and believe that one of the main duties of the MUL is to resolve some of their daily irritations and frustrations. Effective MULs do not underestimate the amount of exchange acting upon promises affords them. Resolving issues for units affords them reciprocity; 'if I get this done for you, this is what I want you to do for me!'

Effective MULs are careful to maintain a professional distance between themselves and their staff to maintain trust. MULs who form inappropriate relations with staff, bad mouth their colleagues, gossip indiscreetly and share confidences are most likely to lose trust and respect. This behaviour will create the perception that the MUL is immature and cannot be relied upon whatever their protestations of allegiance and commitment to the recipient. Using managers, as one described it, as 'an emotional crutch', discussing personal problems and difficulties, also undermines authority, generating (in extremis) derision rather than sympathy. Effective MULs maintain a high level of self control in all their dealings with staff, reserving emoting to positive rather than negative issues.

In summary, effective MULs articulate their honesty and authenticity in the following manner:

1.   follow up on promises

2.   mean yes or mean no

3.   build indebtedness through 'protecting' subordinates

4.   avoid 'toilet talk'

5.   act themselves

6.   avoid mixed messaging.

Case Study 6a – Building Trust at Vacation Inns

Bill Stevens is a District Manager for 17 units at Vacation Inns (both pseudonyms) one of the fastest growing value hotel chains in the UK (470 hotels to date). Catering for business and short-stay travellers and holiday makers, Vacation Inns prides itself on its 'space fulfilment' booking systems and high standards of quality and service at affordable prices. A veteran of the leisure and hospitality sectors, Bill was headhunted for this role having been Regional Manager of the year in his previous organisation.

… On joining Vacation Inns I took over an area that been 'sweated' by the previous District Manager. Due to pressure from the top he had made sure his bottom line P&L looked great and he had smashed budget. However, what he had done to hit his figures was totally contrary to any long-term planning. My predecessor had taken out or reduced unit budgets for things like duvets, cutlery, laundry and kettles, 'skimming' the other management costs line by about 20 per cent. He also had put a stop to non-essential maintenance. To give you an idea of how ridiculous the situation was – on my tour of some of the sites I found that coffee sachets were being put in open teapots rather than the brand standard ramekins. Everything was totally driven for short-term profit. The brand standard scores and mystery guest scores on the district were shocking. Morale amongst the team was low … there was a lack of trust … people had been afraid to speak out in case he 'targeted' them for 'special treatment' … (*like what?*) like being put on report for any of the centrally based compliance, hygiene or due diligence scores …

What I did was put in place a longer term vision around service and standards but I had to get my boss to sign it off and my team to buy into it. I told my boss that I needed to give my team 'the tools to do the job' and that I needed his sign off to spend some money before we could move forwards. He agreed that I could spend a certain amount of money, over and above, on a period by period basis – really what for me was a series of non-negotiables. I then asked the team 'where are we?' and how are 'we are we going to get there?' on standards and service. I compiled a site per site list of the priority areas and said to the guys 'ok, I'll give you the resources in this order but in return ... your part of the bargain ... is to deliver better brand standards, superior customer interaction and sales'. I think some of them thought 'bollocks, he'll never do it!' but I was as good as my word and chased down a lot of the items for them, such as maintenance requests.

What happened was that over a six months period my net promoter score went up by 14 per cent and there was a step change in performance on the district. Obviously there were some gripes and issues I could not sort out and I had to level with them on the reasons why. But by doing as much as I possibly could and delivering on what I said I would do, my team responded in kind. To my mind that is one of the fundamental jobs of the District Manager; setting a direction and then delivering the resources to get the job done. Often there is a lot of talk from District Managers with no back up or carry through ... people then get disillusioned and demotivated. You have got to deliver on your promises to make sure that others fulfil their side of the bargain...

Case 6b – Fostering Indebtedness through Protection from Punishment

The quotes below are a selection of reflections garnered from interviews and focus groups with unit managers and MULs on the important role that protection from organisational sanctions and retribution has to play in fostering indebtedness, trust and discretionary effort;

'It is quite clear to us (Regional Operations Managers) that some of the rules and procedures fall into the 'business prevention' category but the Audit Team hammer the units if they don't comply when they come in and do their quarterly checks. What I do is tell my people to ignore some of the trivial box ticking and focus on what really matters – the customer. Anything that relates to selling more ... creating a good customer experience in a safe environment will do for me ... There have been times when I have gone to quite senior personnel to get some of these 'process jockeys' off my case ... My team know I stick up for them and am trying to so the right thing so (as a consequence) I think they trust me and therefore 'put more out' for me ... I really do'. Regional Operations Manager, Retail.

'...to a certain extent we are made to look like dicks on occasions because things hurtle down that we have no input into but can have quite bad effects ... my people can look at me sometimes and think what power does he have !... so the way in which I get people on-board is to cut a deal with them really ... 'you concentrate on what is really important and I'll do my best to act as a shield against all the crap '... 'if somebody comes in for you I promise I will protect you – they will have to sack me before you! '... it is this, what I call – as the guy in the Fokkers film put it – the 'circle of trust' that keeps the show on the road! .. .because my team knows that I will do everything to protect them from the Centre I can rely on them to do things for me 'quid pro quo". RBM, Hospitality.

'You can never be 100 per cent with anybody but I think I have a good relationship with my District Manager ... once I got a low score on my due diligence and was black rated on the BRAG (black, red, amber, green) Report... he could have disciplined me but appreciated the pressure I had been under through lack of staff ... (*how did you react to that?*) to be honest he knows that I will try my best for him because he has protected my back! ... Unit Manager, Leisure.

4.3 Summary

The commitment-based practices highlighted above triangulate with the aforementioned literature in several ways. First, the practices bear a close resemblance to the 'best practices' outlined in the HRM literature (Pfeffer 1998). This would indicate that whatever the contextual position and the ambient levels of HRM at an organisational level, effective MULs are adept at applying 'best practice' HRM at a local level (ie communication, involvement, training, selection etc). In short, effective MULs focus on employee *inputs* to achieve operational *outputs*, in spite of the fact that, as the previous chapter elucidated, they might operate in a compliance-led environment. Second, the practices accord with insights made by various models in leadership literature, especially situational leadership (contingent models of leadership) and emotional frameworks of leadership. Effective MULs adapt their leadership styles to different states of follower readiness, are experts in devolving key activities (more of that in the next chapter) and exhibit high levels of emotional intelligence (EI). Third, by instinctively recognising the linkages outlined in the service operations literature, they display high cognitive appreciation of the critical dependencies between the employee-centred practices and service excellence.

As a consequence of deploying local practices that drove high levels of commitment, effective MULs are able, due to high levels of cooperation, to effectively leverage scarce talent and knowledge *horizontally* across their portfolio. As one MUL commented:

> ...*by getting the team to work together more effectively and getting them to recognise themselves that they are a team rather than an individual collection of units means that I can get access to and move people to plug gaps quickly so that things don't fall over ... the guys really do understand that it benefits them all if we share because one day they will have a pressing need that they need help on ...*

According to social exchange theory obligations are generated between parties in a state of interdependence, where 'people reciprocate to those who benefit them' and 'general social indebtedness' is shaped, forming the basis of a community that can be kept in balance over time and across people (Cropanzano and Mitchell 2005). A theme that runs through all the case studies presented above is not only the extent to which effective MULs deploy commitment-based practices but their reasons for doing so; namely, their use of such interventions as a form of 'currency' exchange that elicits reciprocity.

Reference is made within the case study accounts to achieving 'buy in' and 'engagement', with respondents recognising themselves that the practices are form of social exchange designed to stimulate accountability and discretionary effort. To this extent, in keeping with the observations made by Cohen and Bradford (1989), the practices outlined above can be re-framed. Commitment techniques can be seen as an elevated form of exchange in which MULs bargained for control by *exchanging inspiration, positional, relationship and personal-related currencies of exchange*. Thus, 'local visioning' and 'cross portfolio involvement' practices can be seen as generating *mutual goal attainment*; talent matching and openness, trust and promise fulfilment can be conceived as a form of *free market exchange* through the exercise of positional patronage, promissory speed and protection from punishment; and recognition and support and development can be viewed as forms of *compensated costs* where treats, public recognition, the investment of emotional capital and the transmission of portable skills for advancement are traded for increased discretionary effort.

5

Ensuring Control

The previous chapter discussed the means by which effective MULs sought to generate commitment through providing a clear local vision, site 'talent matching', tailored support and development, positive reinforcement techniques, promissory speed and protection from punishment. The fact remains, however, that in standardised multi-unit contexts the MUL must ensure rigorous conformity to certain pre-set processes and standards; a position that is made all the more difficult (as outlined in Chapter 3) by random, ad hoc and insensitive behaviour from the Centre which threatens to undermine their levels of authority and follower connectedness .

As was previously argued, the origins of the MUL role lie in its 'checking' and 'policing' function for organisations – ensuring that geographically dispersed units adhere to the operational blueprint. This means that in addition to motivating their staff through commitment-based practices, MULs must also sensitively address how they ensure control to ensure optimal productivity, service delivery and product consistency. Increasing *psychological* attachment to the goals of the district makes applying control easier for the MUL, however, given the aforementioned ambiguities and complexities of the operational space in which they operate, how do effective MULs address the *sociological* aspects of the commitment-control paradox; achieving order and conformity in a complex and ambiguous space which constantly threatens to undermine their levels of positional power and influence?

This chapter will first consider the subject of control, looking at general academic commentaries on the phenomenon, followed by elucidating three main streams of inquiry relating to control; traditional management theory, broad management literature and the 'critical management' perspective. Chapter 3 presented a major discourse on the reality and effects of compliance regimes in many multi-unit enterprises; these academic perspectives provide some explanation for the structural and organisational preference for control, whatever the prevailing rhetoric. But how do MULs manage to exert control effectively at a local level in such complex, ambiguous and (in some instances) chaotic circumstances? The following section will argue that they gain control through a number of mechanisms and techniques such as *Pareto prioritisation, social network optimisation, distributive delegation, sanctioned autonomy* and permitting *added value deviance.*

5.1 Understanding Control

The term organisation in itself implies a structural form whose central purpose is to control and coordinate activities to ensure the maximum efficiency and effectiveness of human endeavour. Characteristic of most organisations is therefore the underlying purpose of control; the assumption being that the imposition of consistency and order will produce measurable and dependable outcomes. According to Tannenbaum:

> *Organisations require a certain amount of conformity...It is the function of control to bring conformance to organizational requirements and the achievement of the ultimate purposes of the organization ... (1968: 3).*

In normative terms the prescription of processes, tasks, roles and reward systems are designed to simultaneously achieve alignment and control. As managers seek certainty of outcomes, the imposition of a series of interventions that facilitate control is seen to be preferable to its diametric alternative; anarchy (Dunford 1992).

In ideal conditions effective control systems have a number of defining characteristics. First, they are simple, visible and easily understood by all workers within the organisation. Second, they are aligned with the structure, culture and vital activities of the organisation, connecting with key strategic objectives and functional decision centres. Third, extant control systems should be designed to signal deviation, malfunction and adverse performance quickly and clearly to decision-makers in order to facilitate remedial action. Fourth, and most importantly, such control systems – whilst being dependable – should be adaptable and subject to continuous improvement and review (Huczynski and Buchanan 2004: 836).

It is acknowledged, however, that levels and types of control are contingent upon a number of intervening variables. Organisational maturity, economic conditions, industry, culture and leadership have all been cited by commentators as having an effect on the form and nature of control. For instance, Child's (1988) four typologies of control – ranging from loose to tight, are heavily influenced by sector and nature of work processes (ie variable or repetitive). Professional organisations (such as solicitors and management accountants) are characterised by *loose* and fluid 'cultural control' systems due to the variety of their work. Small owner businesses, on the other hand, have high levels of 'personalised central control' where the proprietor keeps a very *tight* control on tasks and activities. Within multi-unit enterprises, contingent variables relating to control will (in addition to aforementioned factors such as maturity, economic conditions etc) include the degree of branding (ie 'hard' or 'soft') and/or the level of customisation and localisation.

How desirable or beneficial is control? From an *individual* perspective, research has found that in *certain circumstances* workers actually accede to control systems, a state that Lawler (1976) ascribes to three reasons. First, most workers actually welcome feedback on job performance; second, they prefer some semblance of task structure and order – as opposed to disorganisation – in order to calibrate their performance; third, in situations where pay is contingent on performance, workers are apt to accept control systems as a *cost* that can be outweighed by the financial *benefits* accruing from the coordinated organisation of their effort and labour.

At the *organisational* level, control is deemed beneficial from a scientific management perspective because discipline and order can be applied in order to ensure that tasks are executed on time, to standard, for predictable and measurable outcomes. Thus control involving all the foundations of modern management – objective setting, planning, organising, directing, monitoring and reviewing – is desirable in order to direct the right behaviours to optimise organisational performance. However, whilst scientific management, exemplified through work processes such as Fordism, has merits in terms of its emphasis upon central coordination and measurement of standardised and repetitive tasks, it falls short due to its lack of worker autonomy and contribution to the decision-making process, with all its attendant negative effects.

Critics of control regimes have four principal objections to both its desirability and sustainability. First, from an ethical and moral standpoint, excessive control runs counter to the principles of Western liberal democracy. Second, as previously surfaced earlier in the book, as control is fundamentally defined as regulating behaviour and, as such, rewards compliant behaviour whilst punishing misdemeanours, it can create fear and stress (Argyris 1964). Third, from a Human Relations perspective it is actually an inefficient means of raising productivity and discretionary effort. As organisations are as much about informal groups as individual relationships, behaviours are not optimised through excessive controls. Indeed, for eminent industrial sociologists such as Watson (2002), because organisations are essentially a construction of complex webs of informal human interactions only *limited* control can ever be achieved over work behaviour through control systems. In reality a large proportion of work and behavioural control is achieved through informal negotiation, persuasion and manipulation rather than formal rules and procedures. Control regimes neglect the social needs, expectations and aspirations of workers; high levels can therefore result in negative outcomes such as conflict, resistance and/or deviance affecting performance (LaNuez and Jermier 1994). Fourth, excessive control can negatively affect accountability, innovation, independent thinking and risk-taking as worker 'drones', worried about job security, 'keep silent before their superiors...obeying orders from above' in preference to being 'self-managing team members' who accept responsibility and accountability for results (Cloke and Goldsmith 2002: 5)

Importantly, some scholars claim that control is far more insidious and embedded as a prime managerial objective than is generally acknowledged (Braverman 1974). Thus, in order to further our understanding of the area, it is now necessary to examine three literature streams which adopt an organisational perspective on how control should be/is exerted within firms; traditional managerial control theory that takes a normative view of management, managerial literature examining the role, process and paradoxes of management and finally, the critical management perspective that views managers as 'actor control agents' largely pursuing self-interested courses of action. This will be followed by a consideration of how effective MULs actually exert local control in practice.

5.1.1 MANAGERIAL CONTROL THEORY

The founding father of management theory, Max Weber, conceptualised managerial bureaucracy as a preferred state to charismatic solus 'divine right' leadership that had characterised Western society until the mid nineteenth century. Professional managers were detached, dispassionate functionaries who operated according to rational rather than emotional principles. With the rise of mass production industries, Weber's work was advanced by Fayol (1916) who conceived of managers as professional administrators and Taylor

(1916) who proposed the work study method that, by measuring time and task through 'scientific management', could lead to the constant improvement of the 'efficient frontier' of production. As stated in the previous chapter, such theories were superseded by 'human relations' and 'socio-technical' studies that examined the people factor in production processes, ultimately leading to the HRM stream of research that purports to prove linkages between 'bundles of HRM' high performance work practices and performance outcomes (Huselid 1995).

5.1.2 MANAGERIAL LITERATURE

Different streams of management literature have emerged over the past century, taking different perspectives on what the most important function of the manager actually is, including; control (Taylor 1916), planning (Selznick 1957), muddling through (Lindblom 1959), decision-making (Simon 1969), logical incrementalism (Quinn 1980), doing (Peters 1980), thinking and analysis (Porter 1987) and the application of 'management practice' (Mintzberg 2009).

5.1.2.1 Role of managers

Two views have been influential in conceptualising the role of managers. First, Mintzberg (1973), who saw effective management as being contingent on formal authority and status before managers could perform a number of roles, including interpersonal roles (figurehead, leader and liaison), informational roles (monitor, disseminator and spokesperson) and decisional roles (entrepreneur, disturbance handler, resource allocator and negotiator). Second, Quinn et al (1990) who listed eight managerial roles with mediating variables of internal/external and flexibility and control, including rational goals, internal process, human relations and open systems; faced by opposite 'competing values' of participation, openness, productivity and accomplishment.

5.1.2.2 Process and distributed delegation

It is the *process* of management, however, that proves most problematic. According to Mintzberg (2009) managers are confronted with personal, organisational and external dimensions before they enact four processes around thinking, information, people, and action. Importantly he conceived management as an inter-linked process:

> *... managing takes place on three planes – from conceptual to the*
> *concrete: with information through people, and to action directly ...*
> *(2009: 69).*

Management was also conceived as a delegative process (Carlson 1951), in which tasks were distributed by managers to followers according to fit and ability. More recently a stream of management scholarship, distributed leadership (DL), has conceived effective management as a collective social process that emerges through the interactions of multiple actors (Uhl-Bien 2006). A useful definition is provided by Bennett et al;

> *Distributed leadership is not something 'done' by an individual to*
> *others, or a set of individual actions through which people contribute to*
> *a group or organization ... [it] is a group activity that works through*
> *and within relationships, rather than in individual action ... (2003: 3).*

In part it is a 'post-heroic' conception of leadership; a reaction to a perceived over-emphasis on the attributes and behaviours of individual leaders, exemplified by the trait, style, situational and transformational theories outlined in the previous chapter. DL extends beyond individual agency to collective managerial responsibility and expertise; appropriate given the contemporaneous challenges that face most organisations. Given the rise in cross-functional team working, increasing speed of service delivery, greater availability of management information and greater job complexity, leader-centric approaches offers a misguided sense of order and control. DL is a far more appropriate managerial approach given the new paradigm (Pearce and Conger 2003).

On one level DL as a concept can be seen as a natural extension of other 'democratic' theories of leadership and management that have been prevalent over the past 60 years including leadership diffusion (Benne and Sheats 1948), informal leadership within groups (Heinicke and Bales 1953), group leadership (Gibb 1954), distributive influence and power leadership (Dahl 1961), executive leadership and the informal organisation (Barnard 1968), emergent leadership (Beck 1981), collective leadership (Denis et al 2001) and shared leadership (Pearce and Conger 2003). Whilst it draws from many of these perspectives (Gronn 2002) delegated or dispersed leadership is underpinned by three fundamental concepts (Bennett et al 2003):

- collective property – leadership is an emergent property of a group or network of interacting individuals

- open borders – there is an openness to the boundaries of leadership

- expertise – varieties of expertise are distributed across the many, not the few.

In this respect it can be seen as 'a dynamic, interactive influence process among individuals in groups for which the objective is to lead one another to the achievement of group or organizational goals or both' (Pearce and Conger 2003: 1).

Defining how DL functions in practice has proved more problematic although some notable frameworks (many related to school management) have emerged from empirical studies over recent times (Gronn 2002, MacBeath et al 2004, Leithwood et al 2006, Spillane 2006). Of these frameworks MacBeath et al (2004) provide some useful definitions:

- formal distribution – where leadership activities are intentionally delegated or devolved

- pragmatic distribution – where leadership roles and responsibilities are negotiated and divided between different actors

- strategic distribution – where new people, with particular skills, knowledge and/or access to resources, are brought in to meet a particular leadership need

- incremental distribution – where people acquire leadership responsibilities progressively as they gain experience

- opportunistic distribution- where people willingly take on additional responsibilities over and above those typically required for their job in an ad hoc manner

- cultural distribution – where leadership is naturally assumed by members of an organisation/group and shared organically between individuals.

Although MacBeath et al do not specifically state which form of DL is most successful, arguing that different approaches need to fit with circumstance, Leithwood et al (1997 and 2006) make it clear that formal, pragmatic or opportunistic distribution (or as they term it planful and spontaneous) are most likely to contribute to short-term success. On this basis it is worth postulating that strategic, incremental and cultural distribution have a greater contribution to make to long-term success.

5.1.2.3 Paradoxes of management

One feature of the management literature is the degree to which many writers (most notably Drucker 1955, 1989) acknowledge the essential contradictions between what they are asked and expected to do and the reality of managing purposefully in a chaotic environment. Aram (1978), commenting on the dilemmas of management, stated that managers strove:

> ... to be an individualist and a collectivist, a commander and a counsellor, a dispassionate official and a passionate human associate, a group member and a individual conscience, a supporter of tradition and an agent of social change ... (1978: 119).

Kotter (1982) recognises intractable issues that managers face including time, pace and high pressure, leading to what Handy (1994) termed 'the age of paradox' – the pursuance of goals that were at odds with either resource availability or capability. Developing this theme, Mintzberg (2009) lists thirteen seemingly irreconcilable conundrums of management where:

> ... every way a manager turns there seems to be some paradox or enigma lurking ... (2009: 157).

One of the main conundrums is 'the syndrome of superficiality' where managers ponder 'how to get in deep when there is so much pressure to get it done' (2009: 159)

5.1.3 CRITICAL MANAGEMENT THEORY

Finally, the radically based 'critical' management literature is rooted in Marxian and post-modernist interpretations of capitalism; both taking a rather sceptical view of both the causes and nature of control. Both genres are apt to label commitment-based HRM as 'rhetoric'; a devious unitarist discourse to serve more efficiently the interests of deceitful self-interested, self-serving agents of capital. This section will consider contemporary Marxian and post-modern perspectives, followed by empirical evidence from more mainstream studies that seem, in part, to validate their position.

To Fox (1974), the employment relationship between workers and organisations is defined according to three main frames of reference; unitarist, pluralist and radical. *Unitarist* regimes are defined by their one-sided managerial approach with direct communication mechanisms conveying management's agenda, whilst *pluralist* ones were characterised by balance within the employment relationship between organised representation, management, workers and the law. In his *radical* framework, the employment relationship goes beyond both these frameworks into the realms of outright inequality between the various actors within the employment relationship. Developing this theme, contemporary scholars arguing from a Marxian perspective (for example, Armstrong 1987a and Kelly 1999) use as their starting point that capitalist societies continue to be characterised by constant class struggle. This struggle is caused by inequalities in the distribution of wealth and the skewed ownership of production causing alienation and exploitation.

To radical scholars, there remain irreconcilable aims between the owner/shareholders (represented by their managerial agents) and workers (employees). Managerial agents seek to drive 'surplus value' on behalf of their owner/shareholders through techniques such as cost cutting and control, whilst employees seek better wages and conditions. There are two outcomes to this; first, hierarchically, highly incentivised agents of capital within the firm such as senior directors and certain co-opted parties occupy a privileged position in the firm where they manipulate, deceive and control according to their own self-interest (Armstrong 1987b). Secondly, industrial conflict, employee resistance and sabotage *not* cooperation, is deemed inevitable (and desirable) due to the opposing objectives of both classes (Kelly 1999).

In a similar vein, post-modernists strongly contest unitarist perspectives of the mainstream commitment-based HRM approach. They argue that in capitalist societies the construction of certain types of discourses built into the language of enterprise, work and employment draws workers into a set of meanings and understandings that validates the unequal position that they hold in the industrial process (Townley 1994; Legge 1995a,b, 2005). This connection of meaning and understanding to the way people construct their personal identities and notions of work is exemplified in techniques used by

HRM. Such techniques, post-modernists argue, have focused on developing cultures, symbols and language as means of manipulating and controlling the behaviour and thinking of employees. Positive meanings of status and recognition are attached to notions such as teamwork (on management's terms), while negative meanings are attached to recalcitrant behaviour and thinking that aligns itself with alternative sources of authority such as trade unions.

Legge, in addition to arguing that HRM is a socially constructed phenomenon – a language and discourse that has its origins in individualist 'Thatcherite' Britain and 'Reaganite' United States of the 1980s – is also sceptical about many of the surveys (many derived from research in the US) that reputedly prove the effectiveness of commitment-based HRM:

> *Not only then, is there a lack of agreement about what are the key 'high commitment/performance' practices, but little consensus on the appropriate level of specificity in operationalising these concepts … If there is a question-mark over the validity of the data in these studies, their reliability (and, hence, generalizability) is also suspect … the majority of American studies are cross-sectional rather than longitudinal and, hence, as intimated above, while causality maybe inferred from correlation, technically it is not tested … As is evident from the forgoing analysis, much of the research on HR 'high commitment/performance' practices and organisational performance is at best confused and, at worst, conceptually and methodologically deeply flawed … Thus there are advocates for an increasing focus on within-industry studies … business level studies … (2001: 25–32).*

In her view it is only through penetrating the HRM discourse through thorough in-depth qualitative research that scholars will be able to understand the meaning and, hence, reality of HRM in modern times. While it is convenient to dismiss the work of critical scholars on the grounds of complicated abstraction and political posturing (Harley and Handy 2004) strong empirical evidence seems to validate elements of their position, with several studies showing that 'in the real world', in spite of the 'rhetoric', deployment of commitment-based HRM practices is at best patchy, at worst, non-existant (Storey 1992, Purcell and Ahlstrand 1994, Gratton et al 1999).

Storey (1992), in his two year case study-based research into 15 organisations designed to assess 'modern developments' in the management and execution of HRM, argued that firms previously described as 'standard moderns' ten years before his study could now be described as 'pragmatist opportunists'; the decline of collective bargaining had heralded the rise of 'rhetoric HR' with managerial unitarist, rather than pluralist, intentions. He found no movement towards integrated commitment-centred 'good' HRM, finding instead piecemeal 'soft' HRM initiatives which masked delayering and downsizing approaches to achieve organisational redesign. A reason for this was elucidated in the seminal work on HRM's input into strategic processes in UK MNCs, where Purcell and Ahlstrand (1994) concluded that HRM professionals – the supposed champions of commitment-based employment practices – were neutered. Lacking a compelling commercial narrative they fulfilled a 'second or third order' position within the strategic decision-making process, with the authors commenting 'HRM, whatever the rhetoric is now a third order activity in organisations' (1994: 80). Their study, conducted over an eleven year period in nine industry sectors through case-study based research at multi-level (corporate, divisional and SBU level), found that that firms were moving their styles from a pluralistic 'bargained constitutional' models to individualistic and directive models of management.

The relative lack of good, soft, best practice or commitment-based HRM in organisations was further borne out by the 1998 UK Workplace Employee Relations Survey (Cully et al 1999). In spite of the plethora of US studies that had purported to demonstrate a positive correlation between 'good' HRM practices and positive performance very few firms in the UK seemed to deploy a significant number of these practices. Its conclusions on its data relating to the usage of 'high performance (or involvement or commitment) work systems' in the UK was bleak:

> For most employers, it might be best to characterise their approach as one of retaining control *and doing what they could to contain costs* ... *the diffusion of High Commitment practices was not especially widespread ... just 14% of all workplaces had a majority in place ... (1999: 295).*

Likewise Gratton et al (1999) in what they described as 'one of the most open and honest evaluations of what HRM means in large, complex companies', during their in-depth examination of seven 'leading edge' companies – some of which were multi-unit enterprises – found that:

> ... *our study has shown the* tensions and contradictions between a
> rhetoric of high commitment and developmental humanism and
> a reality experienced by employees of tight strategic direction
> *towards organisational goals ... (1999: 212).*

Gratton et al found that a disconnection between deployed HRM practices and
corporate strategy existed due to 'slip up' where organisations made HRM
'rhetoric' complex and ambiguous. In particular, compensation systems had
'unreasonable stretch gaps' expressed through unrealistic financial targets
which juxtaposed internal HRM rhetoric preaching fairness and equity.

5.2 How do Effective MULs Exert Control?

Thus far, this book has argued that due to the structure, form and purpose
of the standardised multi-unit organisation there is inevitably a major focus
on compliance and control due to geographical dispersion and the need for
the Centre to impose order. The MUL plays a key role in monitoring and
implementing many of these controls and initiatives, acting as a conduit
between the Head Office and their units. At times, however given the vast
number of measures, tasks and ad hoc requests, MULs face information
overload combined with a real fear of punishment and retribution if they fail
to fulfil central dictats. This can result in immobilising levels of fear, stress
and dissatisfaction. Couple this with the fact that they could be operating, as
has been referred to above, in regimes that deploy 'rhetoric' type HRM and
where their senior executives might be playing power games in their privileged
position as 'hired guns' or, to put it more prosaically – 'agents' rather than
'stewards' of the business – then MULs are faced with seemingly intractable
and insurmountable obstacles in exerting meaningful, sustainable control in
some multi-unit contexts. How are MULs able to perform effectively in such
hostile conditions?

Although many commentators assume that prevailing company cultural
climate, leadership and HRM practices frame general organisational
performance, it is the contention of this book, based on empirical observation
and evidence, that MULs can still make a significant difference to outcomes at
unit level. As has been previously argued, each unit will have its own particular
micro-market, local labour supply characteristics and unique sub-culture based
on previous local management styles and approaches. Add to this observation
the fact that in *uniformly* challenging contexts some MULs outperform others,

it becomes self-evident that those who demonstrate better performance over a sustained period are doing something more effectively than their peers. The previous chapters alluded to the specific commitment-based practices that they were apt to deploy. However, another feature is the degree to which effective MULs are able not only to generate commitment but also to ensure effective control.

The following section will argue that effective MULs are able to facilitate control – adherence to measurement, rules, procedures and acceptance of initiatives – through a number of means such as *Pareto-type prioritisation, social network optimisation, distributed delegation, sanctioned autonomy* and permitting *added value deviance*. These mechanisms will now be considered in turn.

5.2.1 LOCAL CONTROL MECHANISMS

5.2.1.1 Pareto portfolio prioritisation

Effective MULs harvest information from a wide network to triangulate formal objectives against gaps and requirements of their portfolio. In effect they have a filtering capability for calibrating, given all available information, where and what needs to be concentrated upon in the portfolio in order to improve performance. In general, effective MULs increase the validity and reliability of this process by engaging their teams in prioritising goals and associated actions. They also understand that in order to achieve their objectives, improving a small number of unit or personnel malfunctions in the portfolio will generate a disproportionate performance dividend. Also resolving breakdowns in one failing unit will usually increase performance in other areas, given their interlinked nature. Pareto prioritisation therefore encompasses *formulating* portfolio objectives and where to *concentrate* effort and resources within the portfolio for optimal outcomes.

The reason why prioritisation is conceptualised in terms of Pareto analysis is rooted in relevance of the theory to the process of MUL filtering. According to the Pareto principle 80 per cent of most problems in organisations will be rooted in 20 per cent of the operation. Commonly expressed in diagrammatic terms as a histogram, a Pareto chart is commonly used to view the origins of an issue in order of importance from the most to the least significant, thereby graphically demonstrating the 80/20 rule. The challenge for the MUL is to disaggregate the key priorities from the myriad of objectives flowing from the organisational level, identify the input linkages that are the causal drivers of these goals, understand where the input opportunities lie in the portfolio to close performance gaps and then concentrate relentlessly on these areas *across the portfolio* and *within specific targeted units* to improve delivery.

One of the main issues that MULs have, however, is balancing the tension between fixed (annual) objectives around improving enforcement of the standard operational blueprint and the requirement to constantly take on board changes and ad hoc initiatives. How do effective MULs deal with this conundrum? The answer is that they will relentlessly focus on improving priority input drivers but they will increase their capacity by delegating certain responsibilities and functions to key members of their team; this will be dealt in the next section. Thus, in summary, effective MULs prioritise in the following manner:

1.   identify key priorities

2.   understand key input drivers

3.   conduct gap analysis within portfolio

4.   involve team in formulating action plan

5.   concentrate on 80/20 wins

6.   delegate responsibility.

Case Study 7 – Prioritising Objectives and Resources at Lloyds Bank

Nick Andrews was a Regional Director at Lloyds-TSB responsible for 10 Area Directors covering 120 branches until 2009. Lloyds-TSB, the UK's largest personal account bank, is acknowledged as having entered the recession in good shape, having applied sound banking practices, avoiding any value destructive acquisitions. Its 'spur of the moment' takeover of HBOS, at the behest of the British government, was a disaster; leading to the government taking a 41 per cent share. Nick reflects on some of the prioritising behaviours of his Area Directors prior to this calamitous decision.

... In High Street banking there are two main dynamics; sales and service. It is imperative to open new accounts and then ethically 'push' lending or saving products and maintain 'pull' through excellent call centre and branch service.

What Lloyds were particularly good at was focusing the Area Directors and their branch managers on key objectives on a quarterly basis. The incentive scheme effectively allocated points to certain products and the weighting of these points would change according to the strategic objectives of the bank. For instance, in one quarter a lot of points (that would result in incentive payments) might be awarded to deposit products, in another quarter it might be the amount of mortgage referrals. What the really effective Area Directors did was to constantly appraise and then re-order the priorities and resources of their Districts in order to hit Company objectives.

The way in which successful Area Directors operated was to, first, understand how the scorecard was weighted, second, communicate out key priorities and, third, put a plan together with their branch managers to align resources accordingly. The business allowed a process called 'change control' whereby Area Directors could re-cut the budget amongst their branches on an ongoing basis. As they were granted an FTE (full time equivalent) staffing budget for their areas they could redeploy people around their patches, according to priority needs, without disadvantaging individual branches. Hence, sales staff from one branch in an area that did well in loans rather than deposits could be switched to a branch that did well in that area and cost budgets would be flexed accordingly so that nobody was penalised. To give an example, once there was a push on new accounts and in one district the Area Director redeployed sales staff to branches situated in areas where there were a lot of new Polish migrants with extremely positive credit profiles. He was extremely successful in exceeding his new account opening targets and everybody benefited!

Of course there was also the day-to-day operational element and each branch had to maintain a 'minimum coverage' to conform to the brand standard. But it was the exploitation of this 'localised flexibility' that was they key to Area Director success. Through 'control change' the Area Director could not only re-shape branch cost bases, he could also move targets around the area; upweighting or changing targets by branch. This 'redistributive' approach gave a degree of adaptability to the best Area Directors which they maximised to the full. It is important to say, however, that the best Area Directors were not just short-term hedonists; out for their own personal gain and attempting to test every rule to its limits. In order to get this level of flexibility they had to keep people onside by bargaining, contracting and applying a high degree of fairness … in order to generate resource swapping. For those that really put themselves out for the team they might grant one-off prizes such as a trip to the Grand Prix, for instance … But essentially they were able to keep discipline and control by prioritising and focusing upon the key metrics; making sure everybody shared the spoils of success …The less able Area Directors always seemed to misread the priorities, inefficiently use their resources and lose control of the 'locker room' as a result …

5.2.1.2 Social network optimisation

As stated, in order to prioritise effectively MULs are adept at understanding boundaries and utilising available resources within the multi-unit enterprise. To this end MULs cultivate a wide social network which helps them first, to execute operational imperatives and second, to provide them with intelligence and information about tolerances to understand which controls are important and which are not.

To organisational network theorists, firms are social structures comprised of workers (called 'nodes') which are linked (or 'tied') by specific types of interdependencies such as friendship, common interest, relationships, knowledge or financial exchange (Freeman 2006). These networks, which can be very complex – operating horizontally or vertically (upwards or downwards) – are crucial in the affecting the way in which issues and problems are solved, enterprises are operated and the extent to which employees are able to successfully achieve their goals and objectives. The nodes to which any employee is linked can be termed social contacts, which can be measured in terms of value or the social capital derived from these connections. In multi-unit enterprises, the local network's nodes can be highly dispersed and connections hampered by distance. In order to leverage social capital, effective MULs must therefore be discerning and focused in their identification of social contacts that are key enablers to their role.

Thus, in order to optimise operational efficiency, effective MULs locate and leverage *'enabling social contacts'* throughout the multi-unit enterprise. In practical terms this involves identifying key people who can help them in their day-to-day execution of the role such as administrators in key support functions such as supply chain, payroll, recruitment, training, maintenance and promotions. As their role often involves smoothing out operational problems and troubleshooting on behalf of their units, effective MULs identify the key contacts (who are not commonly direct reports) who can help resolve specific blockages or friction points. Effective MULs are expert in creating bonds and relationships whereby they derive at least the same or greater level of *internal service* than their counterparts. Given problems of space and distance this is time consuming activity but one which is ultimately highly beneficial in terms of net outcomes. In general the means by which successful MULs go about creating and leveraging a valuable 'enabling' social network are as follows:

1.   identify key operational support staff enablers

2.   create relationships based on exchange; friendship, financial or goal fulfilment

3.   understand formal and informal rules of engagement

4.   leverage support for portfolio (speed, quality, flexibility, dependability etc.)

5.   sustain relationships through continued exchange.

In addition, effective MULs create and sustain *'insight networks'* that can help them locate truth, meaning and knowledge within the organisation. These networks can operate horizontally amongst their peer group or upwards amongst the strategic population of the firm. Such relationships help MULs understand, beyond formal narratives of what constitutes acceptable behaviour and conformance, what the implied or informal rules, procedures or codes of the organisation actually are. As has previously been stated, MULs are confronted by a myriad of measures and controls but which ones are really important, to whom and why? What are the real boundaries and tolerances; ie which breaches really attract sanctions and/or punishment? It is only through creating a wide network that the MUL can collate and process information that generates understanding as to what constitutes an effective platform for action. To this end, the means by which effective MULs activate and sustain an 'insight' social network are as follows:

1.   locate actors that have high 'truth' value

2.   create relationships based on exchange

3.   build network through mechanisms such as;

      – participating in working parties
      – volunteering for trials and best practice initiatives

4.   understand 'reality' of controls and objectives

5.   interpret information and formulate plan of action based on insights.

The data and information gained from social networks, when added to the formal objectives, goals and measures of the organisation, can then act as a foundation for prioritising goals within the portfolio.

Case Study 8 – Enabling Networks at Greene King

Daniel Wilkinson is a Regional Manager responsible for 48 units with Greene King Pub Partnerships (1,200 pubs). A member of the British Franchise Association, Greene King Pub Partnerships run a 'soft franchise' model for their pub tenants that includes a mandatory product range, bespoke standards/service training and 'retail eyes' mystery customer programme. Previously an Area Manager for Lidl, Daniel was awarded the Area Manager 'Rising Star' prize at the 2011 ALMR Awards.

… Given my large span of control there is no way I could do my job unless I enlisted the help of everyone around me. If I took everything onto my own plate in order to do the role I would fold. It is absolutely critical to create and sustain cross-functional relationships. Support functions that are respected will act for specific Regional Managers – politeness and a lack of 'them and us' approach really does get me further. I suppose, in a way, it's about manipulating relationships to your own advantage. The specific Head Office functions I call on are as follows;

- *Credit Control* – In order to get them to help you, you need to know their parameters. They will go the extra mile if they have confidence in you. They will be supportive through your track record – they will trust you to make the right calls and will act quickly for you if they have commercial confidence in you.
- *Financial Shared Services* – These guys tell you what you can and can't do at unit level – inventory, write offs, money back to franchisees. It is essential that they close down my actions. In order to make it a two way process I do them a favour by giving them the heads up on what might be coming down the line and do my best to resolve any inaccuracies for them.
- *Business Analysts* – At times information on specific data can be slow or inappropriate. To me this is a key relationship – in the past I have brought a bottle of wine in for analysts that have pulled me down really useful exception reports on volumes, purchases and trends.
- *Operations Administration* – Now these are really key people as I am out on the road for so long. The two admin. people assigned to my area also cover other patches; what I aim to do is *make my agenda their agenda*. I create good relations by calling in and spending time at Head Office. It makes a huge

difference in driving my profit and performance. They help with things like dealing with new franchisees coming in, closing off old utilities accounts, business rates appeals, following up on e-mails for me and getting hold of the data I need. Basically execution is guaranteed through this relationship.

- *Property and Maintenance* – Unfortunately I didn't have a permanent surveyor for a while so I instructed and worked with outside agencies to work with us on large projects according to our specifications. But there is no doubt that in order to get essential maintenance works done this is a key contact at Head Office. You need to get your jobs to the top of their action lists!
- *Recruitment and Training* – I make sure I am totally plugged into what the R&T team are doing. Can I get the best franchisees? Who's available? What courses will benefit my franchisees?

What else helps me? The fact is that most Regional Managers operate pretty independently on a day-to-day basis. I make sure I keep in touch with what's going through cross networking. It is particularly important where I might split a town with a colleague in terms of geography. Perhaps I can share approaches to solving problems with colleagues? I am generally on the phone to them out of hours, perhaps when I am driving. Also some Regional Managers are useful because they are really switched onto the company issues. They spot what the next issues are and what is coming around the corner. Being plugged into the grapevine is essential – you can anticipate things – you know what you need to react to next! ...

5.2.1.3 Distributed delegation

A key attribute of effective MULs is their ability to *improve their span of control* by delegating important objectives, tasks and functions to individual team members. To this extent they are archetypal *distributed leaders* (see 5.1.2.2 above). Given time and spatial constraints allied to the scope and breadth of their role, they succeed by successfully distributing ownership of key tasks and objectives, leveraging the human capital that they have at their disposal. Delegation, however, involves trust and the ability to 'let go', something that many MULs newly promoted into the role from unit manager, find notoriously difficult. As previously stated, at first unit managers tend to try and run their district as a series of independent units; in effect trying to manage and control each specific store as they had done so themselves in the past. This leads to high levels of overload and stress and can be a principal reason why some MULs fail in their transition from unit to district level.

Delegation, the opposite of micro-management, is the assignment or deputation of responsibility and authority to a designated individual (usually a manager to a direct report) to expedite specific tasks. It must be stressed, however, that the manager remains accountable for the performance outcomes. Delegation cannot be used a means of shifting problems or abandoning culpability (see previous references to distributed delegation). To this extent *strategic* and *cultural*, rather than *pragmatic* or *ad hoc*, forms of distributed delegation are likely to be far more successful within multi-unit enterprises. The benefits, both strategic and cultural, of delegation lie in the fact that first, as the process empowers a degree of independent decision-making it can have a positive motivational effect on 'matched' individuals who are granted a degree of influence that they might hitherto been lacking. Second, delegation can have associated payoffs such as saving time and money, and bolstering capability within the portfolio. Done badly, however, delegation can have negative consequences such as stress and frustration on the part of the individual deputed to execute the specific activities, and confusion amongst the wider team.

In order to overcome these issues effective MULs successfully delegate by addressing five important questions:

1.   Impact – which activities and objectives can be overseen more effectively by subordinates?

2.   Development – which delegated responsibilities afford the most appropriate development opportunities?

3.   Fit – who would benefit most from assuming responsibility and/ or who has the right skills to implement the assigned tasks most effectively?

4.   Communication – how will the act of delegation be communicated to the wider team in order to achieve buy-in and consent?

5.   Review – how will tasks and activities be monitored and controlled to effect optimal outcomes?

Overall, a review of the empirical data for this research suggests that effective MULs delegate successfully when they follow six important steps:

1.   Clarity – objectives are clear and appropriate structures are put in place to support execution.

2.   Agreement – understanding, acceptance and buy-in to the delegated activity's 'charter' or terms of reference, detailing boundaries of authority and responsibility.

3.   Support – provision of sufficient resources, training and associated communication.

4.   Review – regular up-date and review procedures.

5.   Independence – autonomy within agreed guidelines.

6.   Recognition – appropriate recognition mechanisms to acknowledge effort and contribution.

Case Study 9 – Delegation and Follow Up at Ramada Encore

Kelly Grimes is the Operations Director of eight units for a multiple franchisee operating a group of Ramada Encore hotels in the UK. A new entrant into the UK value hotel sector, Ramada has given a high degree of flexibility to their franchisees to develop the brand beyond their core operating principles. Kelly was previously with Holiday Inn and Hilton.

... There is absolutely no way that I could do everything myself given the geography I have to cover. In my view the sign of a good manager is a clean desk. What I have to do is delegate but make sure I follow up to ensure that things are done on time, to specification. Two main examples spring to mind. The first one was part of a cost reduction drive – I got the team to come up with ideas as to how we could do things more efficiently and effectively. One of my GMs at Crewe came up with the idea of e-billing, a process that would replace sending out paper invoices. I let him drive this project with his reception manager, consulting with reception managers across the Company. A new procedure was then tested, set up and then put out as a standard around all the hotels. In all it saved us approximately £10k a year, but the point was it was a cost saving project that was driven entirely by the GM and his reception manager. The second example was updating the SOP (Standard Operating Procedures) manual for the front of house standards and systems. I gave this project to one of my GMs who had great experience in this area and she revamped the manual. This then became the standard operating blueprint that had to be followed in all the other hotels. Not only did this improve the system but also increased her levels of confidence and made her feel that she was making a valuable contribution to influencing and improving our estate through the use of her skills and knowledge. Other examples include delegating out a breakfast project and a liquor initiative. Here I got GMs to lead their formulation and implementation.

But *delegating is the easy part* – it is the following up and chasing that is most important. My GMs often say that I 'don't forget anything' and I suppose I am very well organised administratively. In my e-mail system I have a colour coded section for each GM and every time I send an 'action' e-mail I copy myself in and then file it in their box. Also I operate what we call 'Kelly's book'. Everything that I have asked the GM to do is written in my A5 note book which is divided up into hotel sections. This includes anything that I've asked them to do, things they've agreed to do and reminders for me on questions to be asked. By the same token each unit has their own book in which they write down what they've been asked to do or asked me to do. In some of the units these books go down the chain. The point is this – I have a process in place where I constantly monitor progress and delivery. But the GMs can do the same with me – they can chase me on progress ... so it's not all one way!

Although I prefer to chase things up through face-to-face meetings I rely a lot on e-mail and the telephone. Because I drive a lot it is easy for me to pick up the phone between hotels. Although we talk about the usual things like revenue, costs, customers, staff I am always tracking progress on certain things I have asked them to do. After the conversation I will follow up with an 'action' e-mail. Is it overly controlling? I don't think so, my GMs know I am well organised and that action will flow both ways. Delegation without follow up, given all the other tasks the GMs have to do, is a waste of time ...

5.2.1.4 Sanctioned autonomy

The word autonomy is derived from ancient Greek meaning 'one who gives oneself their own law'. In organisational terms it is related to sanctioning space or freedom for individuals to make un-coerced decisions. Moral philosophers such as Kant (1985) describe autonomy as encapsulating the 'essence of human dignity' allowing rational individuals to make unfettered choices unrestricted by law or higher authorities. It is regarded as a desirable state by behavioural social scientists because self-determination is seen to promote increased effort, motivation and commitment. The principal issue with autonomy is where it should start and end. Unlicensed autonomy in the absence of rational moral behaviour can lead to anarchy and disorganisation; the very antithesis of what organisations are designed to achieve – order, control and dependability. The question therefore, in multi-unit enterprises, is what should be the tolerable balance between autonomy and control? How much discretion shouldbe vested in individuals without threatening the integrity and function of the organisation?

The section above referred to the positive effects of delegation in not only solving span of control issues but also motivating subordinates through involvement in decision-making and wider responsibilities. In addition, however, effective MULs will also leverage other mechanisms to encourage autonomous behaviour. Either the business model of the enterprise or unit-level roles will permit *'corridors of autonomy'* to be exploited by the effective MUL. With regard to the business model, some multi-unit enterprises will allow local decision-making and/or micro-market customisation with regard to store-specific promotions and/or local buying. In some 'soft' brands up to 30 per cent of the product ranges of stores can be determined locally in response to competitor activity and/or in response to idiosyncratic local needs. In this context the latitude for autonomous behaviour is high, with potentially powerful returns for the organisation. Ironically perhaps, this release from the restrictions of central control (albeit in a sanctioned and prescribed manner) actually assists in gaining consent for compliance in other areas. Less control can paradoxically lead to the organisation's ability to exert more order.

The other 'corridors of autonomy' open to exploitation by MULs include aspects of unit-level roles and responsibilities. Effective MULs will encourage unit managers to show imagination and ingenuity around certain processes such as layout, staff selection, training and development. By posing the question 'how can you (within reason!) do this process more imaginatively with better outcomes?' MULs challenge their teams to be creative and innovative. Also, establishing links with worthwhile local charities and encouraging teams to think of ingenious ways to raise money will not only serve to embed businesses in their local communities but will also serve the dual purpose of creating a feeling of independence, identity and worth within the Unit team.

Within standardised multi-unit business models there are many ways, therefore, by which the effective MUL can sanction and encourage a degree of autonomy. The pay-off from this is that by granting a degree of latitude and independent decision-making the MUL is, in effect, exchanging a degree of freedom in return for control and compliance in other areas. Best practice tips as to how MULs are able to grant autonomy are therefore as follows:

1.   identify viable 'corridors of autonomy' that will add to rather than subtract from business performance

2.   sanction autonomous behaviours in exchange for conformance in other areas

3.   review impact and effects of independence.

Case Study 10 – Service Provider Autonomy at Pasta House

Jeremy Hyde is the Director of Service Development at Pasta House UK (all pseudonyms), owned by a major international casual dining operator. Over the past five years the brand has undergone a transformation, broadening its offer and extending its format into bespoke takeaway stores. Since 2010 Jeremy has been leading a service change project designed to increase the emotional connection of the brand with consumers.

... Over the past year what we have tried to do is develop a brand personality through our staff and redesigned service cycle. In order to do this we have had to grant some latitude to our Area Managers and Unit Managers to encourage their staff to display some autonomous behaviours within certain boundaries; a prime objective of our new service excellence programme (SEP). The SEP was born out of the insight, after rigorous research (that went beyond 'rational excuses' into subconscious feelings about the brand), that Pasta House was seen as 'safe', its customers conceiving its personality as a 'large, inert TV addict!' The only emotion it stimulated was 'refuelling' (feeling empty to feeling full) – there was a complete absence of bonding and fun. Clearly, we needed to effect a service transformation.

Our research led us to design the 'true essence' of the brand around three central principles 'embracing, uninhibited and light-hearted'. Every aspect of the brand template; asset design, food development, promotion and, most crucially, service had to mirror these key principles. With help from service experts we designed a five step service cycle for staff that would stimulate positive customer feelings – the descriptors for which were; 'embrace a friend' (welcome), 'discover the desire' (establish customer needs), 'showtime' (simultaneous delivery), 'feel the fun' (check back) and 'smiling send off' (quick cheque). The challenges of embedding this service concept were formidable; it would require a change in behaviours throughout the operational line. The way in which we achieved this was to give the operators the challenge; how would you deliver this? It had very positive results.

The way we sold this in was by enabling the three Area Managers that were on the original pilot to contextualise the change through encouraging individuality at store level, albeit there had to be consistency between the elements ... By allowing two-way feedback we were trying to release people, 'engendering the spirit of worthwhile work' ... The Area Managers acted as 'train the trainers', so they had high degrees of credibility (especially at 'stump speech time') and owned it, not allowing standards to slip. But they were also able to innovate from the bottom up inputting into the training materials ... The Area Managers actively encouraged freedom of expression amongst staff in the way in which they interacted with customers. They also encouraged ideas such as 'food WOW' and 'service WOW' comments back of house. New team incentive schemes devised by staff such as a group meals out – should they achieve certain service targets over the quarter – were signed off by the Area Managers...What the Area Managers were doing was fostering intellectual curiosity amongst the service teams, getting them to come forward ideas – releasing ownership and creativity.

An important element in its success was making one member of staff a 'self-selected' expert on a specific element of the service concept. This was not only designed for improvement purposes but as way of us saying 'you are important, your views count' – a position that we believe leads to even more effort and commitment. This enabled other stores adopting the SEP in a measured roll-out plan to refer to these nominated individuals and also Head Office to 'listen' to front-line implementers ... A shift in behaviour meant that the right shift leadership practices could be reviewed with regard to cover turns at peak but also task allocation during non-peak periods. Although specialised jobs need execution by specialists at peak, multi-tasking was now taken up enthusiastically in down-time periods; demarcations were broken down ... What we have found is that new people have learnt the principles and behaviours underpinning the 5-step cycle faster than the older guys who have had to 'unlearn' old behaviours ... What is the net result of allowing Area Managers to encourage autonomous behaviours within certain boundaries? In the stores where SEP was introduced sales have been significantly above core business growth, net promoter scores are up 10 per cent+ and 'guest complaints per cheque' are down 35 per cent ...

5.2.1.5 Added value deviance

The techniques referred to above can act as a transactional exchange device to ensure more general conformance. The common denominator is that they are generally sanctioned by the organisation at large and fall within the formal boundaries of permitted behaviour. Research shows, however, that on occasions effective MULs will consent or turn a blind eye to breaches of company standards, rules and procedures if they believe that either the 'law is an ass' or that there are better ways of doing things. This behaviour can be termed added value deviance because whilst such behaviour might be deemed illegal by the organisation, it might actually serve to improve the performance of operations and, again, act as an exchange for compliant behaviour in other regards.

The term deviance, in a sociological context, refers to behaviours that undermine cultural and social norms and/or formal rules. According to sociologists, norms are specific behavioural standards codifying predictable patterns of permitted behaviour. Often these are translated into laws and formal rules, the deviation from which elicits punishment or retribution. A major issue with norms and rules, however, is that, while being pragmatic, they fail the rationality test. Over time, rules might morph into a reflection of the self-serving interests of the dominant group, becoming completely irrational and illogical to other groups within the system. In the case of multi-unit enterprises units might be well ahead of technocrats in the Centre in terms of what the customer expects and what might give them competitive advantage within local micro-markets. At times, explicit approval will be given to 'bend the rules' by senior personnel, with one CEO stating in the author's presence during the course of this research that he didn't 'expect (his) leaders to ask for *permission*, only *forgiveness*!' More frequently the operational line will covertly conspire to give tacit approval to breaches that add manifest value; such as the deployment of social media at Unit level as a direct local marketing device or the employment of extra staff on the area – trainers and recruiters – that are 'hidden' at Unit level P&Ls to circumvent central headcount restrictions.

It is important to state, however, that added value deviance will only flourish under two conditions. First, it is only operable or sustainable within 'circles of trust' where units feel that they are protected by higher authorities who will protect them against punishment. Second, a strict code of morality and ethics must apply. Short-termist, self-interested 'blatant cheating' will have harmful long-term side effects. There are many instances within multi-unit enterprises when MULs have instituted policies in their own interests that, as one area director succinctly put it, 'have blown up the machine'.

In summary, deviance can also assist the effective MUL in asserting control as it can act as a form of exchange. It will only be effective, however, if the following general rules are followed:

1.   rule breaking is added value *not* value destructive

2.   trust enfolds the process removing fear of retribution

3.   actors are bound by a sense of morality and ethical behaviour.

Case Study 11 – Spirit Planogram Deviance at Spar

David Thompson is an Area Manager of 12 managed stores at a regional franchise company of the symbol convenience group Spar (346 stores). Spar were one of the first movers in standardised convenience retail in the UK, although its business model has been challenged recently by the movement of the major supermarket groups into the convenience sector. David was Spar Area Manager of the Year in his regional company in 2009.

... One of the main areas of focus in this role over the past few years has been to react to the threat posed by the big supermarket multiples moving into our territory. A Tesco Express opening nearby can have a dramatic effect on sales in a single store; therefore we have to do things differently and quicker to respond. We have to shout service, quality and value. On occasions the 'Centre' can be slightly behind the curve and we have to do things at a local level, prove that they work and then feed them back up the line. Asking for permission at times is a risk because they might say no ... so we just do it ... without sabotaging the entire operation...making sure everything is legally permissible, obviously! ... What it also does is keep my guys onside – if they see that I am pushing the boundaries they know that I am striving for us to get better and they imitate my behaviour. They just don't accept that 'nothing can be done'. Obviously I keep my Regional Director completely in the loop when we 'kick off', just in case!

Take behind-the-counter spirits planograms for instance. We know that spirits, as a category within our stores, have been in decline for some time. This area is (rightly) very strictly regulated from a licensing point of view with normally a three metre run in which we can display spirits on vertical shelving. Our Trading Team determines the layout of this space by sending out a standard template planogram, detailing which products should be displayed where. The problem is that many of the worst selling brands (such as liqueurs and schnapps) are in the 'eye line hotspots', with little space being allocated to promotional lines on vodka and whiskey. What would happen if we reconfigured the space? ... *I quietly decided to do my own trial* in one of my stores to see if I could increase sales in this area.

What I did with the Store Manager, who was totally onboard, was to move half- and quarter- size bottle key lines into the hotspots and increase the number of facings for the promotional offers. This had two results. First of all our spirits margins went up because they are higher on smaller spirit SKUs. Second, our sales went up significantly on the promotional lines, as our cash-strapped customers opted for some excellent deals that we hadn't been shouting about properly until then! As a combined result both margin and sales increased – that's what I call a result!

Where do I go from here? Well I've proved it works; now me and my boss have to sell it to the Trading Team internally! ...'

5.3 Summary

This chapter began by analysing the meaning of control and then moved onto its referencing within different streams of the management literature. There is a sociological bias to many of these tracts, involving conceptualisations of structure, agency, power and authority. However, the argument is then made that, far from 'imposing controls' in a mechanistic, one-dimensional manner effective, MULs exert control first through understanding priorities, boundaries and enablers (through social network optimisation) and then apply control-based practices judiciously through enabling networks, distributed delegation and making allowances for (and encouraging) deviant and autonomous behaviour. Like the previous chapter, the prism through which such practice interventions can be viewed is social exchange. The narratives within the case studies suggest that effective MULs use structure and agency for their own purposes; where they have bargained through *mutual goal attainment* (by means of Pareto prioritisation and distributed delegation), *free market exchange* (added value deviance), *compensated costs* (sanctioned autonomy) and *uncovering hidden value* (insight and enabling networks). This book will now turn to implementing change, a process that is familiar to most MULs who have operated in the multi-unit enterprise environment over recent times!

6

Implementing Change

The third function of an effective MUL, alongside the intertwined activities of generating commitment and ensuring control, is implementing change. As previously stated, disruptive forces faced by the multi-unit enterprise have accelerated the nature and pace of change in many firms and sectors in recent times. At a strategic level, policy makers have had to react to the challenges wrought by economic instability, technological innovation and altered consumer behaviour by attempting to adjust many facets of their business model and value chain to new environmental paradigms. These policy makers have, in turn, been reliant on the operational line to enact and implement transformational changes, with MULS – positioned between the Centre and unit – being charged with efficient and effective execution of a plethora of centrally-driven initiatives at unit level. To a certain extent, the calamitous economic environment has provided a 'burning platform' creating organisational climates that are receptive and conducive to change, assisting the role of the MUL in this process. However, as the organisational behaviour literature relating to change elucidates, the function of creating, implementing and sustaining both transformational and incremental forms of change is a complex process that requires a highly sophisticated and sensitive approach.

This chapter will first outline the literature relating to change, furthering our understanding of best practice approaches and their effect in overcoming barriers to change within organisations. However, it is the contention of this chapter that while transformational change might be transmitted top-downwards, incremental change is often adeptly applied locally by MULs. Given the flexibility that some business models afford units in terms of micro-market customisation and, due to estate issues (ie differences in site sizes and layouts), effective MULs are exceptionally adept at making micro-process improvements throughout their portfolio that, in *social exchange* terms, leads to the uncovering of *significant hidden value* with mutual benefits accruing for both the MUL and recipient unit. Hence, alongside the change literature, texts relating to operational process improvement and innovation will also be considered. The second part of this chapter will then consider what effective MULs do to implement change by illustrating how they *shape mindsets, upsell benefits* and expedite through *portfolio change champions*. Following this, consideration will be given to how effective MULs sanction *patch ups and workarounds* to poorly conceived initiatives, effect *continuous micro-process improvement* and ensure *best practice portfolio diffusion* across their units.

6.1 Understanding Change

Change is a constant feature of organisational life, generally triggered by external forces. Macro pressures such as the economic environment, globalisation, regulatory intervention, commodity scarcity, unremitting technological development, changing composition of the external labour market and consumer expectations for quality and affordability have increased the pace with which organisations have had to evolve their business models in order to maintain efficiency and competitiveness (Carnall 2007). In response to these challenges many organisations have had to embark on organisational change programmes promulgated by existing or, more likely, new leadership, with numerous goals including behavioural modification, increased organisational flexibility, enhanced people capability and the introduction of new technology or work practices. However, the process of conceiving and implementing change is ridden with problems, not least the levels of resistance and inertia to change in most organisations. The succeeding sections will now consider common barriers to change before moving on to means by which commentators suggest that firms create readiness for change and ideal forms of transformational and incremental change processes.

6.1.1 BARRIERS TO CHANGE

In the literature relating to change one of the main themes is the degree to which the middle of the organisation represents a real barrier to change (Lee and Lawrence 1985, Orgland 1997). Given technology-enabled changes to patterns of organisation over the past 30 years, with delayering initiatives reducing the numbers of middle managers (the survivors being expected to fulfil more tasks and duties) the role of today's middle manager is acknowledged as having increased in complexity, effort and workload (Burnes 2004). Added to which many middle managers have, through e-business enablers, been relocated out of offices into 'working from home environments', the psychological burden of work, without supportive social structures, has become intolerably stressful for some (in the case of MULs, especially ex-Unit Managers who are new to the role who feel displacement through a lack of social interaction). To this cohort, change has become a byword for extra work, eliciting a high degree of dissatisfaction, scepticism and resistance. Managers are apt to behave reactively rather proactively to change because of the negative consequences for their work life balance and perceived threats to their security and status.

Thus at an *individual level*, although organisations exhort workers to embrace change, there are strong psychological reasons why people resist. First, there is the dimension of 'future shock' where 'amongst many (managers) there is an uneasy mood – a suspicion that change is out of control' (Toffler 1970: 27). Wave after wave of change couched in positivistic managerialist rhetoric is juxtaposed against its reality of disruption and chaos for many people in the middle and lower tiers of the organisation (Newman et al 1995). Second, most individuals, rather than embracing change, are fearful of its disruption to their identity and well-being (Carnall 2007: 121). Change upsets routine and habit, often leading to restrictions in freedom and autonomy. Individuals are often psychologically attached to the past 'when things were better' and experience a sense of disorientating loss in a future state that they find hard to believe will bring improvement and progress. From a transactional perspective there is also the fear that destabilisation will bring costs such as reduced financial incentives and increased sanctions.

At an *organisational level* cultural barriers such as embedded norms and values and accepted ways of behaviour also act as blockages (Collins 2001). Organisations have generally grown through being successful in addressing markets in specific ways in the past. The strategy, structure and processes of the organisation, supported by belief in the 'way in which we do things around here' have been sufficient for success in the past, act as a formidable barrier to change. There are also vested interests in maintaining stability; people have insufficient skills and capabilities to do what is required in the new world. Where their power, status or influence is likely to be undermined or threatened by change they are apt to fall back on previous structure, contract and agency in order to protect their position. A natural consequence of this level of countervailing force to change is that policy makers are often left with little choice other than 'change the people on the bus' in order to enact their change agenda.

6.1.2 CREATING THE CLIMATE FOR CHANGE

Lewin's (1951) classic text relating to planned organisational change and behaviour modification advocates that managers can only facilitate successful change if they transition people through three stages. First, the organisation needs to be *unfrozen*; the forces that maintain behaviour in their current form should be reduced before any progress can be expected to be made. This might involve extensive communication and development to increase 'change readiness' or, in extremis, removing impediments through wholesale people changes. Second, the organisation needs to be *moved* where – in conjunction with new attitudes and behaviours – new policies, structures and norms are introduced to the organisation. Third, changes in behaviour and policies need to be *refrozen* and reinforced through the new supporting practices and structures. Critics of this approach cite the difficulties that managers have in transitioning organisations in such a deterministic and prescribed manner given time and resource constraints. Also, such an approach infers that change is a planned 'big event' rather than – as it usually is – an ad hoc, organic, incremental process.

The notion that one of the principal functions of managers is to facilitate preparedness for change is compelling. A major issue, however, relates to the fact that many managers lack the necessary skills to manage change and that many remain 'behind the curve' in terms of mindset and disposition (Higgs and Rowland 2001). Crainer (1998) identifies seven skills that managers require for managing change, including the ability to manage conflict, strong interpersonal skills, project management capability, high levels of leadership and flexibility, the capacity to manage processes and the ability to manage 'self' and one's own development. To Drucker (1989), however, 'change leadership' is not only about managing change; it is about creating a mindset that moves beyond managing the change cycle. As change is unavoidable, change leaders should seek to 'be ahead' of the game not only anticipating and embracing change but also actively engaged in framing change policies of the future. Like other commentators (such as Higgs and Rowland 1995, 2001), he argues that change leaders should be careful not to upset the organisation's core values and that there is a need to balance both change and continuity in successful change projects.

6.1.3 TRANSFORMATIONAL AND INCREMENTAL APPROACHES

A caricature of the change literature is that it can be sub-divided into two main approaches; transformational versus incremental or breakthrough versus organic. Although the truth is that most organisations must pursue both paths to ensure success, treating them as different constructs is useful for the purposes of this book due to their origins within the organisation. Transformational change tends to be top-down whilst incremental change has both top-down and bottom-up inclusive dimensions. These will be considered in turn.

6.1.3.1 Transformational change

Implicit in the description of this approach to change is the type of leadership style that is deemed to make major change both successful and sustainable. As the people factor is the most important variable in affecting whether or not a change initiative succeeds and most change is derived from policy makers at the apex of the organisation, leaders need to demonstrate transformational characteristics such as explaining 'the why' in order to 'take people with them' and establishing effective contingent structures and processes (Gardner 2004). Hooper and Potter (1999), in their empirical research of 25 CEO's, identified a number of critical success factors for change leaders, including effective communication, inclusiveness and involvement, leaders themselves setting a good personal example and 'self pacing' to avoid stress.

One of the most influential contributions to effecting high performance change within organisations is provided by Kotter and Cohen (2002). In their eight step model of change implementation they elucidate the key elements required for lasting transformational change:

- create a sense of urgency – inculcate process with a sense of pace and dynamism

- build a guiding team – ensure actors have skills, credibility and organisational connections

- create visions – sensible, clear and uplifting representation of the 'to be state'

- communicate – widely broadcast the goals and strategy to induce commitment

- empower action – remove obstacles that impinge achievement

- produce short-term wins – provide the process with credibility, attracting further resources and momentum

- don't let up – consolidate early changes and create 'wave after wave' of changes

- make change stick – nurture a new culture and embed group norms of behaviour and shared values.

Again, their approach can be criticised for its determinism and also a presupposition that policy makers first have the capability to apply such an approach, and second, they are concentrating their efforts on the right areas and know what they are doing! However, its concept of pace and short-term wins to galvanise the organisation have merit in organisations where levels of inertia and resistance are high.

In addition to notions of transformational change – focusing upon leadership style – the breakthrough approach, which focuses on major process innovation and improvement has also gained advocacy in recent times. Slack et al (2009) define breakthrough improvement such as business process redesign (BPR) as:

> ... the fundamental rethinking and radical redesign of business processes to achieve dramatic improvements in measures of performance such as cost, quality, service and speed ... (2009: 428).

The major principles underpinning breakthrough process improvement are three-fold;

- operational flow – rethink the business in a cross functional manner, organising work around the natural flow of 'transformed inputs' such as information, materials or customers;

- process stage reduction – cut out non-value added 'activity and decision' stages achieving process objectives of less cost and greater sales, service, speed, quality, dependability, flexibility and safety;

- control and action – ensure decision points in the process are located where the work is performed.

Such an approach can seem compelling; indeed many organisations invite third party consultants in to their firms in order to assist them in reframing their structures and processes in order to fit with exigent strategy and competitive forces. Issues, however, revolve around the politics of the change process and the re-design of 'transforming inputs' such as technology, buildings/facilities and staff that are key enablers to business process improvement. If proposed changes are ineffectively communicated, those involved are not consulted and commensurate technical and physical resources are not deployed behind such programmes, they will invariably fail.

Other means of effecting change, if resistance within the core organisation is too high or it lacks the capacity for radical transformation, is to create or buy structures that sit outside the dominant organisational entity (Galbraith 1997, Christensen and Overdorf 2000). Some firms have been exceptionally successful at creating a 'disruptive space' in which they permit independent agents and structures to evolve, decoupled from the existing architecture. Such units are granted the autonomy and resources to develop new norms, processes and values outside the constraints of the 'dominant space'. As long as these are ring fenced against interventions from vested interests and political dominant coalition within the core, these 'spin outs' can flourish using the resources of the parent. Reverse diffusion might take place, where knowledge, ideas and concepts from this new structure permeate back into the main business. Alternatively, organisations might buy a firm whose processes, capabilities and values more effectively fit new commercial realities and requirements. Although expensive, this approach can be a fast track route to achieving more quickly in months what would otherwise have taken years to effect.

6.1.3.2 Incremental approach

Unlike the transformational approach to change, the incremental path stresses the merits of constant improvement as a means of effecting successful and sustainable change (Johnston and Clarke 2008, Slack et al 2009). In this change paradigm the virtues of micro-process improvement as a means of enhancing operational capability are seen as essential in order for firms to maintain competitive advantage. In this sense change is not viewed as a 'big bang' one-off event but an everyday way of life for businesses. It can be viewed in two ways; top-down or bottom-up. These will now be considered in turn.

Top-down

Firms wishing to embed continuous improvement as a feature of their operation have had recourse to a number of frameworks over the past 30 years. Originating from the Japanese 'kaizen' quality approach that was perceived by many Western commentators to lie at the root of their commercial success from the 1960s onwards, several quality frameworks were conceived either by third party agencies or individual firms themselves in order to foster a continuous improvement mentality. Generic frameworks that have proved particularly popular include TQM (Total Quality Management), EFQM (European Framework for Quality Management), Deming and Six Sigma; the first two stressing *content* (what to address), the latter concentrating on *process* (how to address it). Internally, firms have constructed balanced scorecards as a means of balancing soft inputs with hard outcomes in order to achieve and maintain measurable incremental progress.

In the case of generic frameworks, EFQM provides a diagnostic model with five interlinked enabling inputs (leadership, people, policy and strategy, partnership and resources and processes) which lead to outputs (people results, customer results, society results and performance). Firms using this model can calibrate where they are and make incremental improvements to identified input areas in order, theoretically, to increase results and performance. By contrast, Deming and Six Sigma concentrate on the process of change – the former with its 'plan, do, check, act' route map, the latter stressing a 'define, measure, analyse, improve, control' methodology. In house balanced framework models such as the Tesco Wheel (which has measures attached to customer, people, operations and finance) have also been used by organisations as continuous improvement tools.

The availability of these frameworks does not mean that they are widely used within service environments nor, even where they are applied, that they have any change making or improvement impact (Van Looy et al 2003). In manufacturing environments where processes are continuous, the product is tangible with defined allocated resources, and people and plant layout are generally concentrated in one location, applying techniques such as EFQM or Six Sigma – especially with regard to implementing concepts such as lean synchronisation – have had a fair amount of success. Firms are able to expand the 'efficient frontier' of their operations by trading off and resolving issues such as variety or volume versus cost. In 'service shop' environments (Lashley and Taylor 1998), however, operational outputs are largely intangible; complicated by the fact that process flows (ie customer ordering) are intermittent.

Controlling all the inputs that feed into service outputs is a complex business, not least due to primacy of the people factor and the dispersed nature of service outlets. It is for these reasons that coordinating and implementing top-down continuous improvement initiatives in service contexts is far more problematic and challenging than in production contexts.

Bottom-up

Improvement interventions such as TQM place importance upon the ability of self-managed teams to generate performance improvements at the micro-level of the organisation. Such an approach envisages groups of workers operating in a semi-autonomous environments contributing ideas as to how to make the operation more efficient and effective, formulating best practices which can be disseminated throughout the rest of the organisation. However, many incremental improvement approaches such as TQM have fallen into disuse and been discredited by lack of management support and their 'stop-start' nature within some contexts. The question therefore remains how change is diffused from the bottom to the top of organisations?

Although a number of bottom-up frameworks abound in the knowledge and innovation literatures, a model pertinent to this book – given its bottom-up change generating features – is advanced by Hamel (2000) based on his empirical research at IBM. In 'Waking Up IBM' Hamel identifies seven steps that 'start small but end big' in generating bottom-up change:

- establish a point of view – create a credible, coherent, compelling and commercial POV based on hard data;

- write a manifesto – infect others with your ideas. Capture their imagination with a picture of how you can resolve their discomfort;

- create a coalition – assemble a group of colleagues who share your vision and passion. Present yourselves as a coordinated group speaking in a coordinated voice;

- pick your targets – go after the suits. Find some that are searching for new ideas and, if necessary, bend your ideals a bit to fit their goals;

- co-opt and neutralise – disarm and co-opt adversaries rather than humiliating and demeaning them. Reciprocity wins converts; ranting leaves you isolated and powerless;

- find a translator – find someone who can build a bridge between you and the people in power. Senior staffers and newly appointed executives are often good translator candidates – they're usually hungry for an agenda they can call their own;

- win small, win early, win often – demonstrate your ideas actually work; start small. As your record of wins grows longer, you'll find it easier to make the transition from an isolated initiative to an integral part of the business.

The utility of this framework is that Hamel, based on his research in IBM, conceives of large-scale change being initially generated from a number of small-scale initiatives. Its realism – surfacing power and politics as a constraint that needs to dealt with effectively – provides a valuable insight into how managers can effect improvement within organisations.

6.2 How do Effective MULs Implement Change?

Reference has already been made to specific issues confronting MULs; not least their wide span of control of dispersed sites and precarious situational position between the Centre and units. The sections above provide some understanding of the way in which change occurs within organisations and the mechanisms that managers may deploy to successfully execute it both from a transformational and incremental point of view. But what are the specific idiosyncrasies of change within multi-unit enterprises, and how do effective MULs institute performance enhancing change?

6.2.1 CHANGE WITHIN MULTI-UNIT ENTERPRISES

During the course of research for this book a consistent picture emerged relating to the nature and characteristics of change within multi-unit enterprises. These can be grouped around five main insights;

- 'Crippling initiativitis' – most multi-unit organisations suffered from what one respondent called 'crippling initiativitis' where wave after wave of ad hoc, uncoordinated initiatives 'rained down' upon the units.

- Central bias – most change initiatives were generated from the top with little involvement from those down the organisation expected to implement the changes.

- Third party reliance – with large transformational programmes, organisations seemed to lack the self-confidence to do it themselves, preferring to place their faith in third party change 'experts' or consultants who were co-opted by the Centre to redesign processes or structures.

- 'Hard' initiatives rule – given the economic environment and the focus of many organisations upon cost, most change initiatives focussed on 'hard' rather than 'soft' operational drivers. Hence new technology applications designed to improve labour productivity, stock control and shrinkage were more common improvement initiatives than those focussing on customer service.

- 'Soft' initiatives 'drowned out' – 'Soft' interventions focussing on people and service largely died or were postponed in order to accommodate the focus on cost saving changes.

It is within this broad context that MULs were expected to enact change. The literature outlined above referred to the necessity for organisations to explain, communicate and involve people in change in order to ensure its success and sustainability. Yet research for this book consistently found that many multi-unit enterprises failed to adhere to any of the best practice principles advocated by experts in this area. Even when they did, respondents felt that they were paying lip-service in order to provide, in the words of one interviewee 'window dressing to the whole charade'. The economic burning platform argument was used as a universal justification for many changes, although staff remained sceptical as to whether 'cutting costs to victory' rather than a sales and product-led approach, constituted a long-term, sustainable strategy.

Nevertheless some MULs were able to function effectively within this adverse context, producing exceptional performance results in the midst of this challenging environment. How did they enact change and what techniques did they deploy in order to survive in such adverse circumstances?

6.2.2 EFFECTIVE MULS AND CHANGE

Previous chapters detailing how effective MULs generate commitment and ensure control emphasised the significance of exercising social exchange in order to optimise the portfolio. While this remains true with regard to implementing effective change within the portfolio, especially in terms of *shaping mindsets, upselling benefits* and nominating *portfolio change champions,* there are also practical interventions that MULs can make to facilitate change. Effective MULs engage in identifying successful *patch-ups and workarounds* to ameliorate badly conceived initiatives from the Centre but also stimulate *micro-process improvement* and *portfolio best practice diffusion.* These mechanisms and attributes will be considered in turn.

6.2.2.1 Shaping mindsets

Given the adverse change context in which they inhabit – where they are called upon to explain and implement successive and overlapping change initiatives – MULs must first address their own mindset or state of preparedness before second, addressing the mindsets of those around them. With regard to self, extensive resilience and mental toughness testing amongst 68 high performing MULs from six retail and leisure organisations placed on a development programme over the period October 2009 until November 2011 showed that they possessed above-average levels of emotional control compared to the survey mean. Follow-up qualitative data revealed that these MULs possessed a number of characteristics that proved useful during times of turbulent change and disruption:

1. 'I make a difference' – effective MULs use imagery that enables them to see that they are capable of making a real difference;

2. 'What I do matters' – work is not regarded as superfluous but is believed by respondents to really matter. This had the effect of bolstering both their sense of identity and self-worth;

3. Control the controllables – effective MULs recognised the difference between the things that could be controlled by them, the factors that they could influence and the things outside their control. They rarely tried to control the uncontrollables, choosing instead to focus on what they could, rather than couldn't, positively influence.

These findings would indicate that effective MULs are able to cope with change by having high levels of self-esteem and the 'sense making' capability to understand that obsessing about things that were outside their control depleted their levels of energy and positive output.

In turn, effective MULs who display these characteristics influence their followers' mindsets; advocating and expecting high levels of maturity and emotional control during disorientating and threatening circumstances. As a starting point, effective MULs make clear the position faced by the enterprise and the reality that change is a given if it is to prosper or, indeed, survive. Stasis is not an option. The fact that some initiatives might seem badly worked out or poorly implemented should not diminish the rationale underpinning the necessity for change. However, effective MULs not only shape the mindset of their teams by constantly restating that change is an everyday necessity but also that their ability to control the agenda for top-down initiatives is naturally impaired. Team members should focus upon what they can control and, as above, be mindful of the importance of the job that they do within the organisation, instilling themselves with belief that what they do really matters. Should this fail, in the case of some individuals, then effective MULs are apt to review whether or not they have 'the right people on the bus'. Carrying people who wilfully disrupt change initiatives and the equilibrium of the team has to be addressed in order that the majority can flourish positively without negativism from within acting as a constant impediment.

In summary, effective MULs set the *conditions* for change management amongst their team through the following mechanisms;

1. review and address your own mindset

2. review change readiness of the team

3. ingrain 'constant refreshment and change' message

4. focus team members on the controllables

5. reinforce their sense of contribution and importance

6. address wilful saboteurs and constant blockers.

Case Study 12 – Shaping Mindsets at Haagen Dazs International

Clive Chesser was International Operations Manager for Haagen Dazs (owned by General Mills), responsible for the operations of 680 café stores in 56 countries; one third company owned, two thirds run by joint ventures, master and individual franchisees. Here he recalls designing, piloting and rolling out a branded service experience and the importance of co-opting the pivotal cohort of MULs in the organisation, the Shop Directors (responsible for ca. 25–50 units).

… It had become clear to us that the in-store Haagen Dazs service experience was not delivering the emotional connection that befitted a brand based around 'indulgence'; there was a mismatch between what the brand stood for in grocery channels and what consumers said that they experienced in our store cafes. In many ways it was worse in mature brand lifecycle markets (such as France, Spain, UK and US) than elsewhere, although developing markets required attention due to cultural issues. In light of this I transferred my P&L responsibilities and spent a year driving a transformational 'brand service experience' project with the help of a multi-national consultancy firm specialising in service delivery.

The process I went through during this project – having interpreted the original research (showing a mismatch between grocery and in-store perceptions) – was as follows. First, I constructed a major stakeholder map comprising internal (Regional VPs, Store Directors, support functions; HR and Marketing) and external stakeholders (master/individual franchisees, and joint venture partners). Then I went out and sold the project, flying around the world selling the 'why' we needed a new service concept around territories in Asia, South America, Middle East and Europe. There was more resistance to the idea of revamping service in markets such as China (positional power factors) and France (brand life cycle) where, culturally, they were not necessarily attuned to the benefits of such a project. In Japan I needed 'four yesses' before I got a real yes! Third, having got broad support and money we engaged consultants and really dug deep to understand the customer journey and the various service touch points. What staff behaviours did we want at each touch point to deliver a memorable customer experience that would match and/or exceed expectations? Fourth, we constructed a model for a pilot in four territories; this was comprised of a completely new service concept 'bringing the brand to life' backed up by intensive interactive training programmes. In the pilot countries all levels – Store Directors, franchisees, store managers and frontline staff were inducted; Haagen Dazs HR were pivotal in this exercise. Also the consultants were very clever in tailoring the touch points and behavioural training to impact them to local nuances; although the overall measures for the pilot – enhanced sales, customer loyalty and customer satisfaction – remained the same for all.

In terms of Store Director (MUL) buy-in, getting the main interfaces of the company-owned stores and/or franchisees on-board was crucial. Some saw it as extra cost and time for, potentially, very little benefit. I was fortunate that in one of the pilot territories in particular – Spain (which accounted for 10 per cent of the estate) – the Store Director was totally enlightened and on-board; even if initially, his franchisees were not. Our Mystery Customer data in Spain had indicated that service delivery was very patchy; hideous in some stores, better in others. It was one of the most inconsistent markets in Europe. The Store Director had a great attitude to change and believed that putting more form, shape and structure behind the service systems would really add value. He embraced the project and got his franchisees onside by holding meetings, conferences and by persuading them this was the right thing to do. We trained out the new 12 step programme with desired behaviours in a 'train the trainer' fashion – top to bottom. So ... making people feel welcome, bringing the brand to life through offering free samples, demonstrating product knowledge, identifying needs, speedy service, fun check backs etc. We awarded 'star moment' incentives to staff for great customer feedback. It was a massive success.

Overall the pilot was a huge success with sales increasing by 13 per cent and loyal customers (those likely to repurchase and recommend) increasing from 30 per cent to 43 per cent. Another consultancy engaged purely to measure outputs also reported very positive variances on ROI, other customer satisfaction indices, employee engagement and retention. During roll-out the success of the new service concept continued. Each training and implementation package was customised for the local market (what was permissible in Saudi Arabia for instance was different to Brazil). However, the customer measures remained the same across the world; allowing like-for-like-comparisons. Where the Store Directors were either culturally or personally tuned into the programme, it was a major success as they influenced their franchisees or store managers positively. As a major transformational change programme the role of the Store Directors in getting *their* heads right, and *then influencing and achieving buy-in down* the line was absolutely crucial ...

6.2.2.2 Benefit 'upselling'

After addressing self and team mindset, setting the foundations for change management, the effective MUL judges every change initiative in terms of cost-benefit analysis. That is to say, effective MULs actively seek to understand and communicate the benefits of change, weighing up the extent to which these benefits act as a positive exchange for the implied or real costs for their people. For instance, some inventory process changes might be complex to understand

and operate at first, due to new electronic procedures, but in time they reduce overall workload by automating what had previously done through form filling or over the telephone.

Generally, MULs have to overcome two major hurdles when selling in change. First, there is a natural reluctance to adopt new procedures and initiatives because unlearning old habits and procedures and learning new ones is time consuming – an unwelcome distraction from the pressures of day-to-day business. Changing ingrained behaviour is virtually impossible unless unit managers, in particular, buy into the effort and concentration that is required to adopt new practices, otherwise they will continue doing what they have always done in the past. Second, because many new initiatives have been 'oversold' in the past, with the benefits case being inflated against actuality, unit managers are apt to react cynically to any great claims for greater efficiency and effectiveness. The effective MUL overcomes such hurdles by first granting time and space (see below) for people to properly understand how to adopt new changes and second, being honest and not seeking, as one respondent described, 'to overly polish the turd'.

It is important to re-emphasise that during the selling in of new changes, benefits should not be oversold and the costs (time and effort) realistically expressed. At times the MUL will have to counter rather overblown benefits statements from the Centre concerning the virtues of some new initiatives, countering their assertions with more 'grounded' reasons why a change might be beneficial. Also, given that the Centre tends to underplay personal costs, the degree of realism that the effective MUL brings to play in this area can only add to his/her credibility and degree of authority within the team.

In summary, effective MULs upsell benefits in a balanced manner through the following means:

1.   make a cost benefit analysis of change

2.   present realistic summation of benefits (ie efficiency) and personal costs (ie time and effort)

3.   provide time and space for people to 'unlearn' and 'learn'.

Case Study 13 – Upselling Breakfast at Greggs

Clive Clinton was an Area Manager of 15 stores at Greggs, a fast growing bakery and sandwich chain (famous for its sausage rolls), currently with over 1,700 units in the UK. Recently Gregg's growth has been driven by a combination of both format and product extension under the energetic leadership of CEO, Ken McMeiken, previously a senior executive at Tesco and Sainsbury's. The introduction of a formal breakfast offer in the shoulder session before its main 12–2pm lunchtime trading event (which had accounted for 80 per cent of sales) has been heralded as a major success. In this case Clive reflects on how a breakfast initiative was instigated a corporate level and how he helped sustain its success at a local level.

'When the new CEO arrived he instigated a strategic review of our operations which commissioned a detailed customer and competitor research report. Out of this came five or six major change initiatives – which was quite a lot to handle simultaneously. But of all the initiatives perhaps the most successful was a sales initiative – the introduction of a breakfast offer – which addressed a major gap in our product portfolio and a serious customer need.

At a corporate level the change was handled in a textbook manner; it was piloted, trialled and communicated internally, each site was surveyed for equipment needs, all operations staff were taken into the centre to sample products and trained how to make it and two staff from each shop were trained at the training centre or larger stores. Prior to 'D-DAY' there was a Friday briefing, orders and standards were sent out with military precision. All the ingredients, POS and kit were in store ready for the Monday launch. In the first week staff were allowed to sample the product and hand out tastings to customers; it was well received in terms of both quality and price. Over the next few months the company reviewed its efficiency and effectiveness, innovating to increase speed such as two thin sausages instead of one and staff putting sauce on the rolls for customers.

Although generally successful, breakfast performance varied on a store by store and district by district basis. One of the main issues was labour allocation sign off. Although there were already staff in the shops in the morning making sandwiches for the busy lunchtime session, the production and service process for breakfasts (filling bain maries with cooked sausage and bacon, buttering rolls, serving coffee etc) was very labour intensive. The question was how many extra hours would managers need to support the sales uplift? Gregg's labour scheduling 'black box' (predicted hours based on task timings) gave us an indication what was allowable based on forecast sales but ultimately it was chicken and egg; did we proactively deploy staff first to generate sales, or build in staff hours reactively as sales rose; possibly endangering service levels along the way?

In order to make sure the initiative succeeded on my District I made sure that *I gave my managers the staffing hours* to do it properly from the start. I also reacted quickly to requests from managers for more staff hours in stores that were doing exceptionally well. I understood that in order for this to be a success managers had to have the right amount of staff to do it well. I think my managers appreciated this and reacted in a very positive committed manner. Also I didn't let up in terms of monitoring and then motivating my managers. We had a regular conference call every Monday morning where we would review everybody's figures; I would give out cake and flowers to the top three performers and discreetly highlight where improvements could be made. At Team Meetings we shared best practice on things like 'being set up for success' to deliver breakfast and 'how to overcome staff scheduling issues'. I think that this initiative was a success because of its great central design and fulfilment of a distinct customer need but also through good local implementation ... '

6.2.2.3 Portfolio change champions

In relation to helping team members to 'unlearn' past behaviours and practices and adopt new ones, effective MULs do two things; they master the change brief themselves and co-opt champions within the portfolio to 'train out' the changes. The previous chapter considered how effective MULs delegate specific control functions with defined responsibilities and feedback mechanisms; the process of transmitting change is similar, albeit there will be a defined start and finish point to the process. The important point is that, given the breadth and complexity of their roles, MULs cannot possibly succeed in implementing change unless, first, *they* understand its detail and nuances and second, they get their people to do so as well.

In terms of the former aspect – mastery of the detail in order to establish credibility – effective MULs will, as one respondent put it, ask questions and 'kick the tyres' of any new initiative. They will acquaint themselves not only with the reasons *why*, as outlined above, but also the *what* and *how*. They will effectively address questions such as;

- what is this change designed to do?

- what impact will it have on operations?

- how is it different from what has gone before?

- how does it work?

Ideally they will put themselves in a position where they are sufficiently knowledgeable to train the changes on themselves. In this way they can lead by example, demonstrating to their people that, as another respondent succinctly put it, 'we can walk a mile in their shoes'.

With regard to co-opting champions, smart MULs who have already delegated certain key functions within the portfolio to nominated team members will identify overlap, assigning additional change responsibilities to the same individuals, ensuring optimal alignment and expertise. Thus, the nominated team member responsible for labour productivity systems will also be assigned responsibility for understanding and 'training out' upgrades or major changes. In major 'one off' change projects that are either too large, or fail to overlap with existing delegate responsibilities, effective MULs will co-opt a number of 'cluster change champions' who they will utilise in ensuring that knowledge and skills are transferred as quickly as possible. Clusters within the portfolio will generally be identified on a geographic basis, allowing nominated champions to train out efficiently in units that are based nearby.

In summary, in order to effect the successful transfer of change effective MULs adopt the following techniques:

1. understand 'what' and 'how' of change

2. ideally, learn how to 'train out' the changes ('train the trainers')

3. identify overlaps with current delegated responsibilities in the portfolio

4. assign 'training out' to delegate experts or nominated 'cluster' champions.

Case Study 14 – Designated 'Leads' at Sainsbury's

Simon Jones (pseudonym) is the Regional Operations Manager for 21 units with Sainsbury's (150,000 colleagues and 1,000 stores – 2/3 supermarket, 1/3 convenience). One of the UK's oldest multi-unit enterprises, it has undergone a successful transformation under its CEO, Justin King and was awarded the title 'Supermarket of the Year 2011' by the retail industry journal 'Retail Week'. Simon reflects upon the importance delegating change projects to nominated 'portfolio holders' in order to spread ownership and expertise.

… One of the most important things I learnt on becoming a ROM was not to try and directly manage every unit but to lead my GMs to manage their stores even better. But, given the amount of change going on within the organisation, what I also had to do was distribute responsibility across the portfolio. Why did I do this? First, I could not possibly oversee every change initiative directly because of time and expertise constraints. Second, I wanted to drive accountability down to store level and improve the capability of my store managers.

The way I have achieved what I call 'diffusion' is to take the scorecard and ask my team who would like to 'lead' or become 'portfolio holders' on a specific element. This led to managers coming forwards to 'lead' on availability, mystery customer, talent development, cost control, labour productivity etc. It was important that they put their hands up – it might have fitted their skills area or, in some cases, provided the opportunity for further development. What these 'leads' then do is send out briefs and e-mails to their colleagues on developments, changes and initiatives in the areas that they oversaw. They also provide capability workshops in their stores to educate other store managers and their teams on the 'what, how and why' of their specialism. At Regional Meetings they also had the opportunity to request agenda time to brief out changes in their area and/or train initiatives on. The question remains how I monitor and keep control of this complex web?

As an element of their annual assessment is made around 'personal contribution' levels I can keep a check on the degree to which my 'leads' have effectively discharged their duties – particularly with regard to keeping up-to-date with changes. This 'personal contribution' assessment is linked to incentives so there is quite a high motivational factor here where my store managers will be actively demonstrating to me that they have effectively led the areas they are responsible for. Take my 'Talent Lead'; there is a lot of change within the portfolio with new systems and vacancies – what this 'lead' did was put together a really good talent matrix and development programme, based on his intimate knowledge of the area and work with the HR Business Partner, which has kept abreast of change in the Region. In recognition of the work he had done I gave him 100 per cent pay out due to his 'personal contribution'.

The way I chase progress is through personal development reviews or ad hoc discussions through my 'visits with a purpose'. Where are we with the implementation of such-and-such change? What are the blockages? What can I do to help? Most large companies are averse to change, so what I find myself doing is acting as an intermediary and facilitator for my leads to help them drive things through – getting them the resources (manpower and cash) to make things happen. Is this approach successful? In my experience, it follows the 'third, third, third' principle ... The top 1/3rd are brilliant – they have bought in totally and see the benefit of their position ... they can make a difference ... it also puts them on the radar if their contribution is noted elsewhere (which I make sure of!) ...This means that for the really high profile areas within the company or the area's most susceptible to change, if you the right attitude and skills you can really get things done ...

6.2.2.4 'Patch ups' and 'workarounds'

Reference has previously been made to the fact that given the distance of the Centre from the units, its failure to use (or listen to) operator expertise in the conception of new change initiatives, coupled with its lack of insight into the minutiae of unit operations (due to few operators transitioning into jobs 'in the Centre'), many change initiatives in multi-unit enterprises might be ill-conceived or badly thought out. The MUL now has a choice; does he accept the change initiative lock, stock and barrel or seek to make (legal) alterations that make the initiatives more workable? For sure, many MULs, fearing sanctions from the centre for non-compliance will adopt the former route, passively accepting what they 'have been told to do'. Braver, more self-confident MULs (a state usually born through experience) will, however, not accept the status quo, either suggesting modifications to the Centre immediately to enhance chances of the initiative's success or make adaptations themselves following consultation with their teams. In this sense they are acting in the same manner that was referred to in the previous chapter; sanctioning added value deviant behaviour for high performance purposes. The main difference in this instance is that within the context of change they are, as one respondent put it, 'permanently on watch to actively divert sewage from the Centre!'

In the first instance, effective MULs will to make modifications by 'patching up' the deficiencies of the change initiative. This means that having understood the detail of the change initiative and consulted with their nominated champions or team, they will sanction improvements that will add value to the efficiency and effectiveness of the initiative. These modifications can apply both to the *content* and *process* of the change programme. With regard to content, effective MULs might give permission for alterations that make the initiative more impactful; such as in one organisation, allowing unit managers to add additional training slides to a new induction package to engage new joiners more effectively. In terms of process, effective MULs might speed up or slow down the timetable of certain initiatives and the manner in which they are rolled out. In doing so they will have taken into account factors such as capacity or 'bandwidth' and the relative priority of certain initiatives in relation to others promulgated by the Centre. At times, the MUL might not be acting unilaterally but will be acting in sync with what already might have been agreed at area level after discussion with the regional director and their peers.

In exceptional circumstances, effective MULs will 'work around' certain initiatives because of, in the words of one highly eloquent respondent, 'their asinine and crapulous mechanics'. This is not to say that they fully reject the concepts and aims underpinning the initiative. 'Workarounds' fulfil the main intentions or *ends* of the initiative without any resort to the *means* suggested by the policy designers. This is a highly dangerous strategy that, in the hands of inexperienced or over-exited operators, can foster and embed bad behaviour. Living solely by the dictum that 'the ends justify the means' can lead to chaos and anarchy in standardised multi-unit contexts. Nonetheless, there are instances where, after mature and rational consideration, implementing a 'work around' strategy can pay dividends. Usually, effective MULs will gain permission from higher authorities before embarking on such a course of action in order to eliminate penalty or punishment. Sometimes, as the case below illustrates, they do not.

In summary, effective MULs will judiciously apply 'patch ups' and 'work arounds' to change initiatives generated from the centre, following the steps below:

1. locate the *content* and/or *process* deficiencies of the change initiative

2. add value through the application of 'patch ups'

3. 'work around' defective initiatives with other means to achieve the same end

4.   ensure support systems are in place to prevent penalty or punishment.

Case Study 15 – Display 'Patch-Ups' at JewelerCo US

Brad Schultz is VP Regional Operations of 26 stores for JewelerCo (both pseudonyms) in the United States. JewelerCo is one of the largest jewellers in the US, having grown by aggressive acquisition of regional operators, and has a premium brand and mid-market brand. Brad, who works for the premium operation, was originally a Regional Manager for one of the companies acquired by JCo in 2006. He was Regional VP of the year for JCo in 2010. Here he reflects on a major change programme involving display changes and the local action that was taken to facilitate its success.

... In the past any changes to the displays were rolled out geographically, usually for specific ranges say watches, gifting and/or diamonds. What the company decided to do this time – and you can understand given the way trading is – was to trial a complete display change in 10 stores, see if it worked and then go for a 'same-time' roll out throughout the country to catch Xmas trading in four months' time. The trial had been a success and we were told that the average sales uplift between the trials and control stores were $1,400 per week – that's a lot of dollars across the company!

What happened was we were called to a company conference with a load of our store managers and the SVP Marketing explained the concept and told us how it was going to be rolled out. It was going to be complex. For a start within premium, each store has a different configuration and we have segmented our formats into nine different range offers according to the local market. At Head Office they know the dimensions, counter runs and segmentation types; it was down to them to get the stuff commissioned and shipped out. As I understand it the stuff was made in China where they had special plastic injection tools and mouldings, magnet for prices and special material. It was shipped in containers to a warehouse where packages were made up for each store (on average 40 packages per store) and then on a certain date they were released on to us. Our store teams had to take the new displays out of the packages and replace the old displays – in evenings and over the weekend. In my Region the store managers and their teams were really hot for this – they had been given enough hours to do the work and really wanted to do something that would grow revenues.

Overall the programme was a success but, inevitably there were things we had to do at a local level to make it so. As Regional VP my job is to oversee the implementation and make sure it happens. What sort of things did I do?

> Well, some of the stores needed more hours than the company had allocated so I granted them straight away ... Some display units were the wrong size, had parts missing or didn't arrive at all so I authorised retention of old units whilst others were re-ordered. Also we had to improvise ... in some of the units there weren't any price magnets so we had to find solutions around ticketing items in a stylish way (pins, hang-offs, bows). In some cases there were blemishes on the material – did we cover it up or keep the old units? Again we took a decision based on what the customer could see and how it might affect the brand perception. In some of the stores we had high end Swiss watch concessions – it was important that in these places we not only didn't compromise our brand but also that of important partners. We worked around any problems ... local decisions were made according to local needs, but with my managers usually checking with me. Overall I'd say the roll-out was 95 per cent there but we dealt with the other 5 per cent to make sure it worked. Our 'sats' (customer satisfaction) scores actually went up over the change-over period! But that's our job – don't moan, find solutions, make it happen! ...

6.2.2.5 Continuous process improvement

In addition to the above, where effective MULs transmit, implement and adapt changes from other parties, they also effect continuous process improvements within their units and across their portfolio. The definition of a process, in a service context, is the efficient movement of customers, materials and information from one stage to another where added value activities occur, fulfilling overarching objectives of speed, cost, quality, dependability, flexibility and safety (Slack et al 2009). It is the role of the effective MUL, either through rational diagnosis, or (in some cases) instinct, to ensure that all processes work optimally to satisfy these objectives.

As has been previously stated, in most multi-unit enterprises, because estate building is bounded by constraints such as site availability and evolving size and scale requirements, few units within portfolios are replicated *exactly* in terms of footprint or location. Idiosyncrasies relating to layout, position, trading patterns, customer demographics and local labour market dynamics will apply to most units led by the MUL. This represents an opportunity for the effective MUL, who has a significant influence on adapting processes to fit local conditions. Additionally, in multi-unit firms, where a degree of customisation is permitted, MULs have the capacity to flex the product and promotional offer to fit local demands.

With regard to leveraging the unique characteristics of the site, effective MULs will acquaint themselves with the salient differences of each unit, posing a number of questions:

- Location – How good is this location? How visible is it? What is its footfall? How can we attract more attention?

- Car parking – What is the car parking capacity? How safe and secure is it? Is it used solely by our customers; are other users or staff appropriating the best spaces?

- BOH layout – What is the delivery access? What is the storage capacity? What are the office and staff room dimensions? How are the the services (ie plant and kitchens) configured? How can these features and flows be improved?

- FOH layout – What is the size and layout of the unit? What is the customer flow? What are the blockages?

- Service cycle – What is the customer journey from entry to exit? How smooth is the experience? How do service providers frame the *emotional* experience? What are the *functional* blockages (ie epos sites and shelf, rack and counter access and positioning)?

- Sensory experience – What *senses* are stimulated positively by the visit? How effective are the *emotional* stimulants?

- Product and promotion – Does the range address the local market? Are the promotional mechanics fit for purpose?

Information for these questions is garnered through the digestion of all empirical data relating to the site and also, importantly, on-site field investigation and observation. Effective MULs are adept at *listening* and *watching*; processing what is actually happening to *customers* on-site in order to estimate what type of process improvements need to be made. Site visits are not only conducted during non-peak trading hours, but also during peak sessions when units are operating at an optimal level. This enables them to assess which transforming input processes underpinning the questions above – such as staff, technology and facilities – need to be tweaked and adjusted to improve capacity, throughput, rhythm and *customer service*.

One of the benefits of having a multi-unit portfolio is that it affords the MUL the opportunity to experiment and learn from mistakes. Digesting the reasons for failure in one site is of great assistance when applying solutions in others. In this way the role is quite exceptional; the fact that MULs have a dispersed portfolio of units enables them to take risks in one unit without affecting the operations of their other sites. Thus, adjustments to processes that have failed in one site can be contained and rectified without contaminating the rest of the portfolio. Where micro-process change and innovation works, the effective MUL is in a position to replicate best practice across the portfolio with the necessary evidence to elicit support and buy-in from team members. This will be explored below.

In summary, the effective MUL is not merely the passive recipient of change but has a significant role to play in improving unit and portfolio process effectiveness applying the following techniques:

1. assess the process efficiency and effectiveness of each unit

2. identify improvements, eliminating blockages and rate limiters that degrade the customer experienc

3. address process input drivers (ie staff, facilities, technology and machinery) to effect change

4. be prepared to fail and learn but contain errors to single sites

5. apply best practice throughout the portfolio.

Case Study 16 – Optimising Capacity at Nicholsons

Nolan Spratt is the Retail Business Manager of 14 sites for Nicholsons (94 units), a high street premium branded pub chain which caters for the professional and tourist market, offering quality drinks and dining in an authentic pub environment. All of the sites have a long pub heritage, many retaining features dating back to the eighteenth and nineteenth centuries. Nolan, Nicholsons RBM of the Year in 2011, previously worked in supermarket retail.

… One of the major challenges of my role is to optimise capacity utilisation given the constrained nature of many of my sites – many of are listed as they date back hundreds of years. To do this I need to make the most of what I've got in terms of available space, trading time and product execution speed. If you take space, in the White Lion at Covent Garden we were limited by the amount of tables and chairs that we could put in the dining area. So we hit the layout! At the time of a minor refurbishment spend I got heavily involved to ensure we reconfigured the space more effectively. They weren't going to do anything on furniture but I insisted we changed the shapes of the tables and chairs and put 'two tops' side by side. This increased the capacity by 13 per cent and was one of the main factors in us growing meal volumes at the site by 23 per cent in 2010/11. This outlet is now my highest taking food site per square foot.

We also have done various initiatives on utilising capacity in shoulder periods (ie 12–1pm and 3–5pm) around our main trading sessions. The way we have done this is to proactively fill these timeslots by going out and getting people. Previously it was probably our natural English reserve that prevented us from putting staff out on the street with our menus attracting people in; particularly when tourists didn't seem to mind. To give you an example, in the Argyll Arms, by allocating specific staff hours to staff to do 'street PR', we were able to significantly increase our trade in non-peak sessions through more 'twos' and 'fours'. Last week we added 184 parties through these means – we know because the duty manager pressed an exception key on the tills every time we netted prospected business. Obviously you need the right staff to do it. But as it's been such a huge success we're scheduling in labour to do this in the next financial year across the piece and I think it will go some way to contributing to my growth target … The guys have really bought into this concept of continually trying to innovate and improve everything if they can see it unlocks value; increasing sales improves their P&Ls – nice at bonus time!

The third thing we have looked to continuously improve to ensure we get maximum cover turn is combining simplicity and quality in our menus. Previously the brand had items such as a club sandwich on the menu which was like 'throwing a hand grenade in the kitchen!' – production of all the component parts slowed down the whole kitchen. What we did in a couple of my sites was to cut the number of mains down from 16 to 10, starters from 7 to 4 and deserts from 6 to 3 items. Of course we retained all of the top selling lines; fish and chips, for instance, was 30 per cent of food sales. We didn't blow up what menu development and Marketing were telling us to do but we did remove items from the menus unilaterally. But now we have proved that it works – volumes and sales are up significantly – this approach is being rolled out across my District and the brand.

The last thing we did to improve capacity utlisation was to tweak the service cycles. Previously the brand standard at busy peak times had been to offer coffees and deserts. Counter-intuitively perhaps, we stopped offering them in peak 1–3pm session, only responding willingly if customers asked. However, from 3 to 5pm we actively upsold! This meant that at peak we increased our throughput of customers to maximise cash sales whilst in quieter times we encouraged grazing so that we could maximise margin ...

6.2.2.6 Portfolio best practice diffusion

When process improvements have been generated in segments of the portfolio how are they effectively transmitted to other units? The literature on best practice and innovation highlights the issues with transferring explicit and, in particular, tacit knowledge (Nonaka and Takeuchi 1995). In multi-unit contexts the problem is amplified by the barriers of time, distance and space, making the role of the MUL pivotal with regard to ensuring that best practice is not only generated and captured but also disseminated to maximum effect. To this end effective MULs act as transfusion mechanisms; facilitating the process of knowledge sharing across the portfolio. In addition they act as important actors within the regional structure, sharing ideas and insights with colleagues in order to foster progress.

Within the portfolio, the main problem that MULs face in effecting best practice diffusion is 'knowledge hoarding'; the belief by certain team members that the 'superior' methods they have 'invented' are proprietorial. As units are under pressure for constant growth and high performance – being assessed by all manner of metrics and league tables – it is understandable that innovators feel that they should retain any form of knowledge-based forms of competitive advantage in-house. In order to solve this, previous chapters have referred to the importance of fostering exchange within the portfolio where people and knowledge are traded according to conventions of reciprocity and reward. In addition to this, however, effective MULs will diffuse best practice through other methods such as social capital; providing trusting and safe environments where knowledge can be shared. Hence, effective MULs will encourage site visits, cross-site placements and time during area meetings that focuses exclusively on diffusing best practice. In order to overcome the 'not invented here' syndrome, effective MULs ensure that everyone feels that they are making a contribution, a technique made easier due to the unique aspects of each site and, consequently, the means by which each team member has adjusted their operation accordingly.

Additionally effective MULs will exchange best practice ideas with colleagues. They will make time to go on 'trade visits' with peers in order to harvest new approaches and insights. If their regional director is sufficiently competent, they can act as an additional best practice transfusion mechanism, providing guidance and advice on the efficacy and effectiveness of certain methods. Effective MULs also tend to absorb lessons from competitor visits and, in some instances, sate their curiosity by reading widely and attending (where possible) thought provoking developmental and training courses, seminars and conferences. Learning from these sources can then be transmitted across the portfolio, engaging team members through their contemporaneous nature.

In summary, effective MULs facilitate the transfusion of best practice not only through personal direction but also through approaches such as:

1.   encouraging portfolio social exchange and reciprocity

2.   establishing mechanisms such as site visits, people placements and discussion forums

3.   going outside the portfolio to harness new ideas.

Case Study 17 – Joint Problem Solving at Grosvenor Casinos

Paul Benton is an Operations Director for Grosvenor Casinos, directly responsible for 27 units which are sub-divided into northern and southern regions. Currently undergoing a significant re-branding into a 'G' template, Paul is responsible for Grosvenor's pre-conversion estate. Grosvenor is owned by Rank Plc which also runs Mecca Bingo. Paul was previously a Unit Manager and then Area Manager at Mecca.

... Best practice can be a bit like 'showing off' – some people resist being told that what somebody else does is better than what they do! – therefore I like to frame this as joint problem solving instead ...The approach that I take given the different sizes and locations and of sites and the differing skills and perspectives of my GMs is that there is a lot to be gained from acting as a facilitator to spread good ideas and solve common problems. What I try to do is restrict the day-to-day to my weekly conference calls with my guys and use the regional and joint area meetings to add value through development and insight sharing. For these monthly meetings I get my guys to drive the agenda and try and focus on two or three areas where we can get everybody involved, collaboratively working together. In one of my last meetings we also looked at a '4 Step Change Process' as a means of understanding how you lead change.

In terms of best practice sharing we will often meet at different units and the team will all adopt different customer roles – high roller, hen party visitors or a lone person on their first visit, for instance. They will go from outside the building, through reception, into the different trading areas and conveniences. They will then reconvene and make post-it note presentations on what they've seen and what their specific customer journey has felt like (from the perspective of their adopted role). The problem that GMs of specific units have is that, understandably, they end up missing a lot because of familiarity – this helps break that cycle. The combined expertise of the team acts a great best practice feedback loop for the GM of the Unit being scrutinised. I must stress that it is done maturely and sympathetically; we have certain rules about how people should conduct themselves. The net result is that not only does the Unit get some great ideas but also the participants become more sensitised to product, standards and service from the perspective of different customer groups.

What I also hold sometimes at meeting are 'can't crack it sessions' which enables people to 'show off their dirty washing'. What it allows GMs to do is talk about problems they might have encountered from an employee relations point of view or systems and standards implementation. It is another way of approaching best practice discussions, in my view, because sometimes best practice can perceived as bragging! If you can create an open, honest and trustful environment where people can speak up with confidence in a close knit environment, people can get a lot out of it. There will always be somebody in the room that has solved a particular problem successfully, in a particular way. Interestingly, these discussions can be of great value – particularly to those that have been sitting on a festering problem but haven't had the confidence to able to speak up.

How do I generate a culture that enables best practice sharing and joint problem solving? Basically I try and mix it up to keep the interest and commitment going. Once we had a team meeting where we played extreme poker one mile beneath ground in an ex-coal mine in South Wales! Often we'll combine area meetings with things like charity fund raising nights and one offs such as cocktail training in a proper cocktail bar. What I am doing is creating a real bond between people through shared experiences. Trust builds and then the GMs swap ideas and share solutions without any encouragement from me. Some will even advance big ideas up the chain; one GM is presenting to the MD and FD soon about a new festival designed around different card games aimed at a specific consumer group. What it shows me is that my GMs are prepared to go into their teams for ideas, share ideas across and go upwards if they think they have something that can really bend the curve …

6.3 Summary

This chapter highlights that effective MULs deploy a number of practices in order to facilitate transformational change implementation and generate micro-process incremental improvement at a local level. The techniques used to ease the implementation of organisationally driven transformational change – shaping mindsets and benefit upselling – accord with the general academic literature on transformational change elucidated at the beginning of the chapter. It can also be framed in *social exchange* terms as a form of *compensated costs* where the costs of an initiative (time, focus and effort) are offset against personal or wider organisational benefits. Likewise, the appointment of designated change champions and 'patch up' and 'workarounds' are insights that suggest that effective MULs not only require a high level of confidence, adaptability and imagination to make certain change initiatives function properly, but also imagination to engage in *free market exchange* with regards to delegated responsibilities and permission to innovate. Also, effective MULs, either through prior expertise, tacit intuition or cognitive reasoning, are extremely adept at *uncovering hidden value*; stimulating significant process enhancements at local level by their own interventions or sharing best practice and/or joint problem solving across the portfolio. Thus, effective MULs are not the passive recipients of change. High performing MULs actively initiate, guide and shape interventions to ensure they that improve the idiosyncratic characteristics of their individual sites and portfolio. To this extent they also they require high amounts of energy and persistence in order to ensure seamless exchange and flawless execution, attributes that will be considered amongst a range of other personal characteristics in the next chapter.

Characteristics

7

Personal Characteristics

The previous chapters elucidated the context within which MULs operate and their primary activities and practices. But what are the attributes or characteristics of effective MULs? What competencies and associated behaviours are required for the effective discharge of this highly complex and ambiguous role? Prior chapters on commitment, control and change briefly surfaced various characteristics attributable to effective MULs in the summary sections, but a proper consideration of this dimension is now required at this juncture for two reasons. First, it enables us to complete an integrated framework of the effective MUL, an overview that has been hitherto lacking within this field. Second, it provides a useful framework for practitioners with regard to MUL selection, appraisal and development. An absence of such a template in this book would have left the reader wiser with regard to what effective MULs do, but less certain as to which personal characteristics are enabling factors, making for an incomplete picture.

Many multi-unit enterprises included in the research for this book possessed a range of leadership competencies that they used to measure their MULs for appraisal and development purposes, which they *believed* contributed to superior performance. In a few cases these competencies had been designed through inductive methodology (albeit for their managers generally rather than MULs specifically) and most models were adaptations from generic ones provided by consultants, bringing into question their relevance and performance linkages. Clearly there is a gap in most multi-unit enterprises for context-specific MUL competency frameworks and measurement.

Since McClelland's (1973) seminal work in which he argued that competence required testing alongside intelligence, academics have sought to define the behavioural competencies required by effective managers, including functional, ethical, cognitive, motivational and emotional dimensions (Cheetham and Chivers 1998). Within academia the subject of competency development and measurement is a knotted problem, with varying views as to what a competency actually is. A useful definition of a competency is provided by Klemp:

> ... *an underlying characteristic of a person which results in effective and/or superior performance in a job ... (1980).*

A number of problems with the field remain since its inception, including the extrapolation of generic managerial models that lack context specificity and, most importantly, a lack of clarity on what actually constitutes managerial effectiveness.

With regard to MULs, some research has been completed into various behavioural determinants of area management effectiveness with regard to competencies (Boak and Coolican 2001), key success factors (DiPietro et al 2007), attributes and attitudes (Muller and Campbell 1995) and opinions and practices (Umbreit and Smith 1991). Useful as these studies are, they are hampered by a few key issues, not least the fact that many are single case studies based purely on quantitative evidence, and are principally concentrated on the US fast food industry.

The qualitative and quantitative data that underpins this book has been drawn from a number of actors and cohorts from within multi-unit enterprises. An important aspect of this enquiry was not only to establish what effective MULs did but also their enabling characteristics. This involved data collection from three main areas

1. MULs; critical incident interviews, focus groups and observation of high performing MULs

2. senior managers; in depth interviews with line managers, HRDs, operations directors and MDs as to what constituted effective MUL

3. unit managers; in depth interviews, focus groups and unit-level engagement survey analysis of local leadership effectiveness.

Following content analysis, codification and triangulation of the data, three broad themes or 'characteristics' clusters emerged around the areas of *expertise*, *emotional intelligence* and *energy*; represented as the 3Es in the effective MUL conceptual framework, outlined in the first chapter. There were a number of dimensions attached to each area; expertise incorporating *knowledge, judgement* and *confidence and adaptability*; emotional intelligence including *self knowledge and mental toughness, social awareness and authenticity* and *relationship and conflict management*; energy including *stamina, executional edge* and *passion*. These will now be considered in turn.

7.1 Expertise

Expertise – the skills and knowledge applied in an impactful manner within the area management practice domain – is the first characteristic of the effective MUL. Intriguingly, few corporate, consultancy or academic-based models list domain expertise as a generic leadership competency possibly due to a presupposition that it already exists or, more likely, it is dealt with from a KPI performance measurement perspective. From a general academic view there are two main approaches to understanding expertise; first, the *communities of practice* and second, the *individual expert capacity* view. The former sees expertise as a socially constructed phenomenon where narratives and bias for action are shaped by groups, enabling members to codify, transfer and enact expertise within specific domains (Goldman 1999). Problems pointed out by this domain relate to the emergence of 'groupthink' and isometric convergence that stifles original thinking (Janis 1972). The latter defines expertise as an innate characteristic of individuals which is formed as a result of absorptive capacity, environmental context and continuous and deliberate practice (Chase and Simon 1973, Ericsson 2000). Achieving expertise in certain fields or domains has been estimated by some commentators to involve 10,000 hours or a period of five years of complete immersion (Gladwell 2006). The acquisition of expertise confers status, enabling organisational actors to exercise power and influence (French and Raven 1968).

With specific reference to effective MULs, expertise manifested itself along three behavioural dimensions; *knowledge, judgement* and *confidence and adaptability,* the former being instrumental in the latter characteristics.

7.1.1 KNOWLEDGE

The first characteristic of effective MULs is domain knowledge of area management; a distinctive role due to its wide span of control, positional ambiguity and spatial complexity. In the academic literature, knowledge is a familiarity or understanding of something such as information or skills that is gained through experiential or taught processes (Polanyi 1962). Within organisations, knowledge manifests itself in both explicit and tacit form (Nonaka and Takeuchi 1995). *Explicit knowledge* is expressed formally, being transferred through mechanisms such as written instruction and/or verbal communication. By contrast, *tacit knowledge* is difficult to transfer as it comprises informal habits and cultural idiosyncrasies that people and organisations are often unaware they possess or how it provides inimitable added value. Dissemination of this form of knowledge requires a high degree of trust-based personal contact and interaction. The process of transforming tacit knowledge into an explicit form is regarded as possible in some instances, through codification, articulation or specification.

With regard to area management, explicit knowledge required by organisations from MULs usually involves 'hard factors' such as:

- margin management (stock and shrinkage)

- labour cost control

- rostering and shift optimisation

- volume throughput and capacity utilisation/management

- quality standards and systems adherence

- customer complaint resolution

- training compliance.

As discussed in Chapter 3, applied knowledge of these areas is usually measured through performance reviews, league tables and regular manager-subordinate discussions. Effective MULs will be successful in comparison with their peers in the achievement of many of these company-set objectives, but it is not their explicit knowledge of 'what matters' that counts, rather their tacit knowledge 'how to do it' that separates them from the norm.

In particular, effective MULs possess extensive tacit knowledge with regard to how to mediate wide span of control issues through mechanisms such as:

- portfolio optimisation through social exchange

- distributive delegation

- social network optimisation.

Thus, given the number of measures and tasks, coupled with the problems of time, distance and space, effective MULs are adept at achieving their goals at a unit and district level through exchange processes, delegating out core tasks with defined responsibilities and utilising internal and external networks to provide assistance and support for objective fulfilment. As previously stated, unit managers promoted to MUL status usually take a long time to realise that as they cannot, as one respondent put it, 'manage every individual unit'; they have to build tacit knowledge of how they can positively influence unit operations when they are absent (which is for the vast majority of the time) and ensure that key functions and initiatives are carried out across the portfolio to maximum effect through using extant resources. This is principally achieved through binding understandings and generating a high degree of *reciprocity* through the application of exchange-based currencies (see Conclusion).

How is this tacit knowledge developed? In some organisations nascent MULs are given 'starter' or 'strawberry' districts that are smaller and easier to manage in order to enable them to acquire appropriate skills and techniques. Often companies buddy new MULs with 'old lags' who act as mentors and guides into the 'dark arts' of area management. Some firms have significant induction programmes that combine taught programmes (P&L management, employee relations, company standards and procedures etc) with time out in the field with experienced operators. Other techniques include developing MULs out of 'sister' field roles such as stocktaking, compliance and merchandising. In the main, however, many companies underestimate the training and development required for effective MUL and launch new recruits straight into the role with very little support other than the coaching and input expected to be provided by the direct line manager.

7.1.2 JUDGEMENT

Explicit and tacit knowledge endows MULs with information, skills and technical ability but, in addition, effective MULs must exercise sound judgement to make the right decisions in order to optimise performance. It is important to state that the exercise and evidence of sound judgement is not only essential in terms of performance, it also has a reputational dimension; conferring a high degree of credibility and legitimacy upon effective MULs amongst their superiors, peers and, most importantly, unit managers.

To academics, judgement is viewed in two ways; first, as a *cognitive capability* to effectively evaluate evidence prior to making a decision and, second, the capacity for *wisdom and discernment* (Tichy and Bennis 2007; Nonaka and Takeuchi 2011). With regard to the former, the possession of key cognitive capabilities which enable managers to make connections and linkages, disaggregating data and information to provide valuable insights, is an essential feature of effective leaders. This capacity for the acquisition and effective application of knowledge is seen as being dependant on specific cognitive processes such as perception, association and reasoning. With regard to the wisdom and discernment, as Nonanka and Takeuchi note:

> ... *our studies show the use of explicit and tacit knowledge isn't enough ... [successful leaders] draw on a third, often forgotten kind of knowledge, called practical wisdom ... (2011: 60).*

Practical wisdom or an ability to apply adjudication or discernment is regarded by Tichy and Bennis (2007) as being particularly important for leaders with regard to three specific domains – people, strategy and crisis – with people being highlighted by them as the most important 'judgement call'. In addition, Tichy and Bennis argue that judgement doesn't occur in a single moment, rather it grows out of a process that involves three phases; preparation, the call itself and execution.

With regard to cognitive reasoning, the ability to apply association and reasoning is crucial with regard to the plethora of data and tasks to which the MUL is exposed. In particular, effective MULs must demonstrate superior cognitive capability with regard to two essential areas:

- connecting inputs into P&L outputs

- Pareto prioritisation of measures, tasks, issues and initiatives.

In the case of district and unit P&Ls, MULs are presented with a voluminous amount of information. How do they discriminate between the most significant data sets and indicators and, more importantly, focus upon what do they need to do to improve performance? The answer is that they apply a high level of cognitive reasoning to a series of problematics arising from the P&L. Effective

MULs are adept (due to their explicit and tacit knowledge) at *asking the right questions*, locating patterns of dysfunctionality and/or opportunity, with appropriate interventions at hand to, as one respondent stated, 'move the P&L in the right direction'. These cognitive skills also apply to the prioritisation of measures, tasks and initiatives. Although effective MULs involve their teams and local cluster champions in prioritising and resolving certain challenges, the fact that accountability ultimately resides with them renders their ability to ensure that the right things are being focused upon, at the right time, by the right people through a complex process of association and reasoning as absolutely critical.

With respect to practical wisdom, discernment or adjudication, effective MULs are adept with regard to the following areas:

- portfolio talent matching

- taking calculated risks

- process improvement

- balancing the commitment/control paradox.

The process of selecting the right people is crucial in multi-unit enterprises with the right unit manager being estimated to add 10 per cent in sales in *functionally-led* retail environments and up to 30 per cent in *emotionally-connective* leisure. Thus, fitting the appropriate manager to a vacant unit with inimitable local market dynamics (from both a labour and customer point of view) that melds and *complements* the district team is a non-trivial matter of judgement that is developed over a period of time. Also, judging when risk-taking or process improvement is either permissible or desirable is another core skill of effective MULs. Weighing up the extent to which allowing such behaviour will be performance additive or destructive is an inexact science, a skill that effective MULs also develop over time. Finally, practical wisdom with regard to how to balance the commitment/control paradox, discussed in previous chapters, is a key requirement of effective MULs. Judging when to act in a 'soft' or a 'hard' manner according to situational requirements is a matter of adjudication borne of significant experience.

How do effective MULs develop judgement? On the one hand cognitive faculties can be viewed as an innate characteristic of humans; something that can be assessed through mechanics such as numerical or verbal reasoning tests. Some companies therefore include a battery of tests in their MUL selection processes that test candidate association, perception and reasoning abilities. In role, line managers can assess the degree to which the MUL applies sound judgement and reasoning by analysing the outcome of decision-making patterns. With regard to practical wisdom, learning from more experienced operators and time on the job add to MUL's abilities to 'make the right calls'. In the view of some respondents the unfettered ability to make and learn from mistakes was seen as one of the main determinants of improving judgement.

7.1.3 CONFIDENCE AND ADAPTABILITY

The third dimension of expertise is confidence and adaptability, characteristics which, in part, are derived from the possession of knowledge and judgement. It is important because the very process of local leadership – where MULs are directly and indirectly responsible for hundreds of employees – requires them to feel and inspire confidence concurrently adapting their style to situational demands. In psychological testing, confidence is typically measured in two ways; *confidence in abilities* and *interpersonal confidence*. The former calibrates self assurance and belief; the feeling that individuals have that they genuinely possess the capability and adaptability to deal with most situations and challenges. The latter measures the degree to which people feel comfortable in groups and social situations and are able to play a significant role when dealing with other people. In the academic literature confidence is portrayed as a leadership trait denoting transformational connotations, having an 'inspirational' and 'transformative' effect upon followers (Burns 1978). It should, however, manifest itself in a genuine and authentic manner, as false or naive confidence will elicit cynicism, despondency and disillusionment.

Personal confidence and adaptability within effective MULs is typically manifested from both a perceptual and behavioural perspective:

- perception that they;

    - understand the domain and business
    - can adapt to deal with most situations and challenges
    - their actions will have positive outcomes

- ability to take charge and lead a team.

Self-perception plays a large part in bolstering feelings of self-confidence and adaptability. In part this perception is framed by the views of others but, from a psychological perspective, it is derived from self appraisal of capability (see EI below). Interestingly, 'confidence in one's abilities' seems, on the basis of MTQ48 tests carried out on the Diploma of Multi-Unit Leadership at BCBS, to be higher amongst men than women. Female MULs tended to more critical of their own performance and required more reassurance (and mentoring) than their male counterparts. The relevance and implications of such a finding are avenues that future researchers can pursue, although one hypothesis that might be drawn from such a finding is such lack of self assurance might be one of the main limiting factors in promotion to regional director. This might provide some insight into why so few females make it to senior line positions in multi-unit enterprises.

Interpersonal confidence is portrayed by effective MULs in a number of ways, the most significant of which are:

- assured communication (verbal and non-verbal)

- presence, body language and disposition

- ability to 'take on board' criticism and challenge.

Unit managers respond to MULs who are deft communicators and convey a sense of presence and know-how. However, this is insufficient; self-confident MULs should have the ability to 'take on board' criticism and challenge, adapting their approach accordingly. New MULs tend to mask their inexperience behind 'false confidence' and extremely inflexible behaviour; ignoring contrary views and perspectives. It is crucial that MULs reach a stage where they are sufficiently mature and self-confident to acknowledge the views of others, adapting their style and behaviour to circumstances, if they are to advance their own performance.

How is confidence and adaptability developed? Clearly possession of knowledge and application of sound judgement adds to feelings of personal confidence. However, it is the validation of these characteristics through others combined with self perception that leads to greater self assurance. From a practical point of view interpersonal confidence and adaptability can be developed through 'on the job experience' and a number of training interventions such as presentation, influencing, negotiation, meeting and situational leadership skills. However, confidence and adaptability is also the outcome of greater emotional understanding and insight, a dimension that will be explored in the EI section below.

Case Study 18 – MUL Hospitality Expertise Requirements

Kevin Todd is the President and CEO of Rosinter Restaurants, Russia's largest casual dining chain (approximately 400 units and 6 brands operating in 10 countries). Previously he was Executive Managing Director of Premium Brands at Mitchells and Butlers, the UK's leading casual dining group. Premium Brands has 643 units over nine brands with 44 MULs in the UK and Germany.

… There is little doubt in my mind that successful MULs firstly get the 'nut and bolts' of the job, understanding the critical importance of volume and capacity management – it is a fundamental part of the skill set. What I mean by this is that they understand product demand patterns and service requirements and can see what needs to be supplied in terms of resources, staff, tasking and what I term general 'capability and readiness'. But how do they achieve this? They achieve it through what I call 'formal' and 'informal' contracting. This is where they need to apply judgement and discretion. Formal contracting is clear direction and 'telling' which works for new and inexperienced Unit managers. Informal contracting occurs when trust has been built up, where they gain commitment from their GMs from implicit understandings. Fundamentally they do not bully but contract on a trust-based level. This is learnt over quite a period of time.

From a judgement point of view great MULs are good team builders who know how to balance an appropriate team to the context. Blending experience with youth and different personalities and talents is an art not a science. Also great MULs, in my view, create stories and rituals around the team – a vibe is created amongst a group of people that goes beyond just 'management'. It's interesting that when I go out (with my MULs) I can feel the imprint of a certain MUL on their area. You can see it in the way the places are set up, the standards and above all the behaviour of the staff. It is perceptible the degree to which great MULs have a positive effect on unit operations through their local leadership and behaviour! The best MULs are also adaptable – when they move brands or come in from different companies they know that a certain style fits the culture and operation … A further insight is that great MULs create great unit managers and that they are not afraid to surround themselves with challenging, talented people. They have the self-confidence to handle good people and get the best out of them for the unit and the team rather than employing mediocrity …

Case Study 19 – Developing MUL Expertise at St Gobain

Amanda Dodd is the Head of Learning and Development at St Gobain Building Distribution, the owner of the largest Builders Merchants chain in the UK (over 700 outlets with brands such as Jewson, Minsters and Grahams). Here she reflects on the approach she adopts when training and developing effective MULs.

…Our research and insight indicates that our best Area Directors optimise the people and skills in their area to maximise the opportunity that the area presents. But they don't 'do the doing themselves'; they are expert at observing and reflecting on what is going on at Unit and team level and then delegating and instigating improvements. They have to 'remove themselves, step back, stop the doing, let go!' – take a helicopter view from above in order to see the wider challenges in context and, in particular, see it from an area perspective. The way in which we train our Area Directors, the majority of whom come from Unit level (usually the larger, high performing units) is two-fold. First, we have a standard training programme that addresses 'the bare bones' of the job; standards, processes, policies, procedures, best practice – what we call the 'one size fits all' approach. Second, we are context specific in developing individual needs and skills, where we take the direct opposite of a 'broad brush' approach. Here the training interventions will be more bespoke and tailored for maximum impact.

In terms of this tailored approach what we do is look at the strengths and weaknesses (skills and behaviour) of each prospective Area Director prior to them taking up position. Do they have people skills but lack process and finance skills for instance or vice versa? To gain this knowledge you can obviously put them through an assessment centre process (which we do) but generally you have to invest time in them; you can't make assumptions. It is also useful to observe them when they are in role and get quality feedback from peers, HR, their Regional Director and teams. Also I have regular contact with new appointees and ask; how are you doing, where are you at? I make visits to see them operating in their environments, go out with them for a day on their patches. What I do is help them develop an understanding between what they think they need and what they might really need! To achieve this level of insight you need to create trusting relationships based on the foundation that we want them to succeed.

Once gaps have been established we can recommend development options from a menu of training interventions. We have many Corporate courses at St Gobain including negotiation, sales, leadership, operational management, service and marketing etc. In many instances, however, what we do is put new Area Directors with experienced mentors and 'buddies' who will be able to compensate for their gaps. We also have a number of accredited in-house coaches that we use or external coaches that really understand our people, processes and market...Let me give you an example of two recent promotions to Area Director that have gone particularly well. Both of these individuals were identified through our people planning review some time ago and we were able to get them 75 per cent ready for the role prior to their appointment. They were sent on courses that addressed particular needs and placed on a Corporate post-graduate programme which raised their cognitive capacity (ability to make linkages and critically reflect) to another level. Then when placed into role they were given specific coaching and experienced senior mentoring that helped accelerate their capability. One individual had issues with time management in his new role and was given tools to plan and execute both short term and long term objectives.

Both of these Area Directors are performing extremely successfully after nearly a year in role but I believe that their success, and others like them, is down to us in HR having the networks and trust of the organisation. In my role you have to know personalities and 'who might fit who'. You have to make time to do that and invest a lot of time in really getting to know your people. Placing a new Area Director with the wrong mentor can be hugely damaging ...

Case Study 20 – Developing MUL Expertise at Sainsbury's

Helen Webb is the Retail and Logistics HR Director at Sainsbury's (150,000 employees, over 1,000 stores). Since the appointment of Justin King as CEO in 2005, Sainsbury's has doubled its profits and consistently grown its share of the UK market through product innovation, format extensions and a focus on operational excellence (availability, quality and service). Helen previously held senior HR positions at Morrisons, Asda, Aviva and M&S. In 2010 the HR team was recognised by the HR Excellence Awards as the 'HR Team of the Year'.

... My main observation – born of long experience analysing the performance of Regional Operations Managers in a range of organisations – is that the most successful MULs have a real expertise judging the 'what, who and when' of *objective and task prioritisation*. In retail at present this is compounded by the speed and pace of change which means that effective MULs have to do the day job (keeping the shops clean, legal, enforcing standards, POS, range and price changes etc) whilst simultaneously prioritising emerging initiatives and priorities. Sometimes organisations do not necessarily prioritise on their behalf (data, information or objectives) therefore effective MULs have to decide (with the consent of their stakeholders) what the three or four real hard deliverables are. This requires a high level of courage and judgement; they must be able to trust their judgement enough to know what the right areas might be. Through judgement-based expertise and taking decisive action they will get it right most of the time and they will be able to build up a reputation that, when things might go awry, protects them…Allied to this effective MULs are adept at delegating to 'lead' unit managers (for instance on stock loss, wastage or charity and PR initiatives) … I think that when people from the Centre are appointed to these roles they are surprised at the pace and intensity that Regional Operators work at and the levels of resilience and judgement they have to display on a day-to-day basis!

At Sainsbury's we have a well-developed three stage programme for Regional Operations Managers (who generally have 25 stores) which we have refined over the past five years. First, there is the Development Centre selection process where talent that has been identified as having ROM potential is subject to a range of psychometric and aptitude testing coupled with an intensive review of their performance profile. Second, those that have been successfully screened undergo a Development Centre where we use a range of instruments (case studies, group exercises and tests) to measure levels of motivation, *range of influence in the business and their decision making ability*. Given the stress and pressure of the role we also use a specific tool to measure psychological balance and ability to perform under pressure. We are currently looking at this resilience measure which we are coming to understand might have more importance in predicting future performance than we had thought before. Third, when managers are signed off for the role we have a range of tools that we deploy for development purposes; a range of courses, coaching programmes and mentoring facilities. The success of the programme is evidenced through the fact that we have a very high retention rate amongst this population (we've only lost 1 out of 32 in the last couple of years) in spite of the fact that our competitors have tried to poach some of them.

Although we have very positive engagement scores within Sainsbury's (based on industry comparators) there is also very strong evidence that there is a strong correlation between ROM local leadership, Unit engagement and scorecard performance at store level. Stripping it back it becomes clear that those ROMs that are able to articulate a powerful *'local vision'* are more effective in mobilising their people. What these ROMs do is agreeing with their people that out of the entire jigsaw 'our key parts are x, y and z'. They also get people to concentrate on things at local level that move on the strategic priorities. For instance generating a large local 'noise' through PR has an impact both on community and sales (through consumer awareness and trust and bolstering colleague pride and commitment) …

7.2 Emotional Intelligence

Given the importance of the human dimension of multi-unit enterprises with its heavy operational reliance on labour, it is unsurprising that the second major characteristic of effective MULs is emotional intelligence (EI); defined generally within the academic literature as an ability, skill or perceived ability to identify, assess and control the emotions of oneself, others and groups. There are two main models academics have constructed in an attempt conceptualise and measure EI; the ability (Mayer et al 2001, 2003) and the 'mixed' or trait model (Goleman 1998). The former is constructed around the notion that emotions are used by individuals to make sense of and deal with their complex, ambiguous social environments. This model argues that humans vary in their ability to process, understand and absorb information of an emotional disposition. Mayer et al claim that EI can be understood and measured by assessing four types of abilities; perceiving emotions, using emotions, understanding emotions and managing emotions.

The 'mixed' or trait model (Goleman 1998) conceives EI as a set of competencies and skills that shape leadership performance. This model is based around four principal items; self-awareness, self-management, social awareness and relationship management. Within each of these constructs Goleman proposes a number of emotional competencies that can, in his view, be learned and developed in order to produce exceptional leadership performance. Although both approaches have been criticised for their 'pseudo' psychology and lack of face validity, their utility for conceptualising intelligence in an emotional as opposed to a purely intellectual dimension has gained in credence over the past 15 years.

7.2.1 SELF AWARENESS AND MENTAL TOUGHNESS

The combination of 'knowing oneself' and exercising personal control through high levels of mental toughness is an important feature of effective MULs. Due to the workload and associated pressures and stresses of the role, effective MULs need to acquire a degree of self-knowledge and discipline with regard to how they react to certain situations, demonstrating a fair amount of, as one MUL respondent put it, 'manners and grace under immense provocation'. In the academic literature *self awareness* includes accurate self reflection and assessment, whilst self control is expressed through attributes such as emotional self management, transparency, adaptability, initiative and optimism (Goleman 1998). The concept of *mental toughness* within business managers is derived from the health psychology 'hardiness' (Kobasa 1979) and the sports psychology literatures (Nicholls et al 2008). Researchers working in the organisational mental toughness domain maintain that constructs such as emotional and life control, personal commitment, viewing challenge as an opportunity, interpersonal confidence and confidence in one's own abilities have a strong association with age, organisational seniority and genetic make-up, but that they can also be acquired through experience (Marchant et al 2009). The acquisition of mental toughness traits, however, is dependent on high levels of self-awareness (Clough and Strycharczyk 2008).

Effective MULs demonstrated the following behaviours with regard to self awareness and mental toughness:

- heightened self awareness through;

    - honest reflection
    - desire for improvement
    - ability to listen to feedback

- exhibited mental toughness through;

    - adapting to different challenges and circumstances
    - emotional self control under pressure
    - balanced view of success and failure
    - confidence in one's own abilities.

Two points need to be made about these features of effective MULs. First, there is a connection between three areas; individuals gained at least partial knowledge of self before they were able to exercise deliberate self management and mental toughness. How do effective MULs develop these attributes? Some MULs will enter the role having developed many of these characteristics through prior experience, socialisation and imitative development. Various tools such as psychometric testing (MTQ 48) and 360 degree appraisals can accelerate self knowledge around mental toughness, but ultimately it is the ability of individuals to openly take on board insights, modifying behaviour accordingly, that marks out effective MULs.

7.2.2 SOCIAL AWARENESS AND AUTHENTICITY

MULs operate in a highly social context where it is necessary to exercise high levels of social awareness of others (staff, peers and customers) and extant networks, whilst maintaining a transparent and authentic modus vivendi. With regard to *awareness of others*, this would typically denominate, from a psychological perspective, a capacity to empathise with others through listening and seeking to understand *ally goals* and expectations. More significantly, perhaps, it also includes the ability, once insights have been processed, to control, guide and shape the behaviours of others in a transparent manner (Goleman 1998). Transparency, otherwise labelled *authenticity* by other commentators (George et al 2007) is an important dimension as:

> ... *people trust you when you are genuine and authentic, not a replica of someone else ... authentic leaders demonstrate a passion for their purpose, practice their values consistently, and lead others with their hearts as well as their heads. They establish long-term meaningful relationships and have the self-discipline to get results. They know who they are ... (2007: 129).*

According to George et al, authentic leaders have a number of attributes including; an ability to learn from their life story, knowledge of their authentic self, sound values and principles, a balance between extrinsic and intrinsic motivation, a grounded personality and an ability to 'temper their need for public acclaim'. In addition, from a sociological standpoint, social awareness includes an appreciation of the importance of social networks, understanding prime linkages and interdependencies within organisations (Freeman 2006). Chapter 4 elucidated how effective MULs sought to leverage 'enabling networks' (such as support staff) and 'insight networks' (such as policy makers) in order to optimise their performance.

With regard to awareness of others; in order to shape and control emotions, effective MULs displayed the following attributes:

- ability to 'read the motives of others' (staff, peers and customers)

- display empathy; listening and processing skills

- ability to ask the right questions

- coaching and guiding capability to meet own/ally goals

- acting authentically through;

  - being themselves
  - having sound values, morals and ethics
  - mature behaviour.

This ability to read the emotional state of others was a skill more evident in female rather than male MULs during the course of this research. The ability to sense, understand and respond to the emotions of others did not come naturally to a number of output focused male MULs. In addition the tendency of some MULs to 'talk at' their people and customers rather to listen and empathise was a major inhibiting factor in gaining control of the emotions of others. Where effective MULs spent time and patience understanding the views and concerns of their charges before applying leadership and coaching techniques, they stood a far greater chance of successfully influencing desired outcomes. Some features stand out within authentic behaviour, none more so than having sound values, morals and ethics. MULs who were able to demonstrate that they were not just in it for themselves but were exercising stewardship in the furtherance of both the district, subordinates and customers were more likely to be successful than those with a short-term, agency perspective which promoted fear and distrust.

In terms of understanding and leveraging social networks, effective MULs acted in the words of one respondent as 'explorers and prospectors ... seeking maximum intelligence and resource from the organisation'. To this end those who optimised social networks behaved in the following fashion:

- created horizontal and vertical 'insight' and 'enabling' networks through;

  - spending time at the Centre (either job role or networking)
  - telephoning and meeting peers
  - volunteering for project work and task forces.

It is the natural inclination of many MULs to 'go native', disassociating themselves from the rest of the wider organisation in the misplaced belief that it is 'out to get them' or because, in the words of one MUL, 'the rest of them (the Centre) are a bunch of idiots'. Such a position is not only immature and ultimately self-defeating; it also has a negative impact on performance by closing off access to valuable information and potential support mechanisms.

How do effective MULs develop the skills outlined above? Again, many of the traits will have been acquired through previous life experience, although there are some interventions that can be deployed in order to foster these attributes. Training MULs to listen and apply coaching techniques in a simulated role play environment can teach participants good practice. Also accompanied trade visits with regional directors or peers, where behaviour is observed with staff and customers and scrutinised for the purposes of improvement, is another popular method. Again – as in the case of self knowledge – MULs need to have reached a state of readiness to change their ways (possibly to a more authentic approach) so as to 'unlearn' past behaviours in order to embed new ones. In the case of fostering social networks, old attitudes and prejudices towards others and the Centre need to be discarded and views concerning the utility and desirability of networking need to be reframed. Getting MULs to spend time working at the Centre in a project capacity or in a defined job role is an effective way of both broadening networks and also creating understanding of other individuals' pressures and perspectives.

7.2.3 RELATIONSHIP MANAGEMENT AND CONFLICT RESOLUTION

In addition to social awareness and optimising social networks, effective MULs are adept at fostering and maintaining good relationships whilst minimising conflict. Relationship management is typically expressed as the ability to develop others, provide inspirational leadership, act as a change catalyst and collaborate in a team environment (Goleman 1998). However, this can only be achieved if boundary tensions are neutralised and competing interests are managed effectively. In academic terms, conflict is typically depicted as arising when there are differences between the interests of two or more stakeholders. In such situations, the more influential and powerful group usually gains precedence over others to protect its own interests (Sims 1991). Although conflict is often inevitable, even desirable, in order to implement change and/ or assert control, it is acknowledged that conflict resolution is necessary prior to generating positive performance (Morris and McDonald 1995). Successful managers minimise conflict through first, recognising competing interests and second, seeking consensus – aligning competing interests towards achievement of a common objective. This can be achieved through intrinsic approaches such as a compelling vision or extrinsic means such as integrated reward mechanisms.

How do effective MULs foster good relationships and minimise conflict? The sections above referred to authentic behaviour, operating with sound values, morals and ethics and establishing wide social networks. In addition, however, from a practical point of view, effective MULs minimise conflict through:

- transparency and honesty during dealings (limiting game play)

- involving others in solutions

- creating 'win-win' situations through social exchange.

Effective MULs are able to deal with ambiguity. They understand that most organisations are riven by competing interests and that they can only control the 'controllables'. In the absence of having the power and influence to prevent conflict between the operational line and, for instance, parts of the technocracy such as Property or Marketing, they focus upon getting the very best outcomes possible in difficult situations. Within their own orbit of control, they use the techniques and methods outlined above, the most significant weapon being creating 'win-win' outcomes through the process of social exchange. Thus, effective MULs will bargain, transact and negotiate with individuals and their districts to minimise conflict and/or debilitating levels of interference.

How do effective MULs develop conflict management skills? Many of the techniques outlined above can be taught and learned either through simulation exercises and/or field-based observation and feedback. The psychological disposition of the MUL is crucial, as is the extent to which he/she is willing to expend energy and effort in order to effect optimal outcomes. This important dimension will now be dealt with in the section below.

Case Study 21 – Psychologist's Reflections on MULs and Emotional Intelligence

Dr Nollaig Heffernan, Chartered Psychologist, is an expert in mental toughness amongst leaders and elite athletes. Designer of the ILM 72 psychometric test, she teaches at the EHL (Ecole Hotelier Lausanne), is a visiting lecturer on the MSc in Multi-Unit Leadership at BCBS and is employed as a consultant and coach by many major international corporations. Dr Heffernan has assessed and coached numerous cohorts of Multi-Unit Leaders with the aid of the MTQ48 personality profiling questionnaire.

(On Self Awareness and Resilience) ... The often excessively stressful nature of the MUL's job means it is essential that MULs understand their response to critical situations, their limitations and their overall well-being so that are resilient enough to optimise in their roles. A misconception of one's ability can have severe consequences on event outcomes and will almost certainly be detrimental to the reputation of the MUL on which their unit managers build trust. Development of self-awareness is high risk as it exposes us to our weaknesses. Effective MULs however consider such insight as an opportunity for improvement rather than crippling negativity and actively seek methods of self-development ... A further strength of an effective MUL is the ability to ask how they could have performed better in a given situation and what they need to improve to enhance future performance. This proactive attitude is often the most outstanding characteristic of the effective MUL ... Developing self-awareness firstly requires a willingness to put aside our often false self-perceptions. This is not always an inflated notion of our abilities but on the contrary a lack of self-belief. Learning to play to their strengths and addressing their weaknesses develops MULs into self-aware high-performing employees. This level of awareness can for example be gained through reflection (eg keeping a reflective diary), enhancement of analytical and problem-solving skills, appraisals, 360 degree feedback (including psychometrics) and further education etc ...

(On Social Awareness) ... As the point of contact and the face of leadership for the unit managers, MULs have to be ever conscious of their perceived role. They provide stability in a fast paced, ever-changing environment – so it is essential that MULs act appropriately at all times but in particular that they show presence and maturity in the face of crisis or extenuating circumstances. Effective MULs understand their impact on others from the subtlety of not looking at their phones during a meeting to the content of their language (eg avoiding inflammatory statements) to accepting that it is natural that a unit manager might 'attack' when things aren't going well or their performance is being criticised. In other words, effective MULs know when it is appropriate to wade-in and when it is essential to stand back when dealing with the Centre or unit managers ... Social awareness is an extension of self-awareness. By understanding our own motivations and responses we can begin to look at those of others and begin to understand just as we sometimes feel excessively stressed or threatened there are times when others do too. This creates a level of empathy which allows MULs to consider the best way to interact with those around them to the advantage of all stakeholders. Through effective communication, observation and a keen sense of timing (developed through observation and experience) MULs can enhance their levels of social awareness ...

(On Relationship Management) ... Due to the MUL's position in the company he is usually in the firing line from his direct reports and those he reports to (the Centre). Effectively managing the requests, motivations and political agenda

of these perceived adversarial organisational levels means relationship management is a critical skill in any MUL's arsenal … Effective MULs leverage this ability with great efficiency and authenticity creating buy-in and support through articulation of the win-win proposition in such a compelling way that each party forgoes the need to press their own agenda as absolute. The resulting positive outcome strengthens these relationships further and boosts level of confidence and trust in the MUL …Taking the time to understand the needs and motivations of others allows the MUL to see things from others' perspectives. Putting time and effort into relationship 'foundation-laying' pays dividends when change is being implemented as resistance can be headed off long before it escalates into conflict and becomes destabilising. Appreciative inquiry (focussing on the positives), active listening (actually hearing what's been said) and actively building social networks are some of the key methods of honing the relationship management skill …'

Case Study 22 – An Academic's Reflections on MULs and Emotional Intelligence

Paul Turner is Professor of Management Practice at Birmingham City Business School and the joint author of 'The Admirable Company', an analysis of UK's most admired companies. A former Vice President of the CIPD, he has also held senior executive positions at multi-unit enterprises Convergys, Lloyds-TSB and British Telecom.

… Given the devolved and dynamic nature of modern businesses, leadership in the middle of organisations (particularly multi-unit enterprises) has never been more important. But what do effective leaders need to be successful? I would categorise needs as centring around 'technical' abilities to do the job and the ability to connect with a wide range of people. 'Technical' ability is what gets leaders to 'where they are' but the ability to connect is what 'gets them further'. But how does the leader balance both requirements in such an unpredictable business environment and how can the leader help his/her team to cope? What the effective leader requires is a high level of self-awareness and a knowledge concerning how his/her style connects with followers. Put simply they have to understand their customers and environment and what is required, know themselves, appreciate the impact they have upon others and adapt their style accordingly …In my experience in multi-unit contexts, leaders can be developed. One-to-one coaching can be extremely effective in developing leadership styles especially when it is backed up with psychometrics which provide a backdrop to personality traits. Even better are coaching discussions that are grounded in 360 degree feedback data; although I would caveat that with the proviso that the guidelines for this data need to be robust to ensure validity and reliability …

7.3 Energy

Expertise and EI are critical components in the makeup of the effective MUL but they will be diluted, potentially rendered irrelevant, unless individuals have high energy levels. Given the aforementioned challenges and stresses of the role – derived from geographical, span of control and positional pressures – effective MULs require significant reserves of energy to overcome 'interference' in order to get the job done. But what is energy? In the academic literature one useful definition of energy as a multi-dimensional construct is provided by Schwartz (2007):

> *Defined in physics as the capacity to work, energy comes from four main wellsprings in human beings; the body, emotions, mind and spirit. In each energy can be systematically expanded and regularly renewed by establishing specific rituals – behaviours that are intentionally practiced and precisely scheduled, with the goal of making them unconscious and automatic as quickly as possible ... (Schwartz 2007: 64).*

There is an increasing view amongst some commentators that 'well being' – the physical and spiritual fitness of managers – correlates to performance outcomes, as it enables them to discharge their jobs more effectively. It was a notable feature of this research that during the analysis of critical incidents and triangulation of respondent data that effective MULs demonstrated high reserves of energy or capacity to work, the principal dimensions of which were *stamina* coupled with *pace* and *passion*. These will be considered in turn.

7.3.1 STAMINA

The 24/7 nature of the MUL role dictates that they must have high levels of stamina and resilience to cope with the demands of the role. In academic terms stamina or physical energy is typically defined as the ability to sustain a prolonged physical or mental effort. Rituals such as nutrition, exercise, sleep and rest have a positive correlation with increased work capacity, engagement and motivation. Such habits are regarded by some commentators as the one of the most effective manners of controlling and reducing stressors. The reality, however, is that given the demands and intractable conundrums faced by most middle-managers on a day-to-day basis, few have the time or space to achieve physical or spiritual balance (Mintzberg 2009). Whilst a limited amount of stress is seen as a useful performance enhancer in certain circumstances, constant burdensome demands can sap stamina, eventually leading to declining levels of discretionary effort, high 'intention to quit' rates and, in extreme cases absence, sickness and burn out (Maslach et al 2001).

How do effective MULs build and replenish their stamina in order to maintain and increase their work capacity and effort?

- exercise regularly and eat nutritiously

- take regular holidays

- conserve energy through saying no to certain demands

- turning off iPhones and laptops at a pre-set times.

There is little doubt that the MUL role can, with its large amount of sedentary travel between units and unusual working hours, promote an exceptionally unhealthy lifestyle. Whilst some of the remedies above are adopted by some in order to maintain stamina and focus, analysis of the broad MUL population suggests that very few seem able to follow such routines. Why? In part the answer lies in the addictive nature of the job, the fact that MULs become, in the words of one respondent, 'e-mail junkies and iPhone addicts'. Observing MUL behaviour in one area meeting the author saw MULs constantly scrutinising their iPhones for new messages and texts, sending instant responses even while colleagues were speaking. To a certain extent the job with all of its demands provides constant affirmation of their identity; that they are needed and important.

How can organisations help MULs increase their levels of stamina? Many multi-unit organisations have policies that prescribe hours of work, grant regular health checks and counselling services, reasonable holiday allowances and (in some cases) detail methods by which MULs can recharge themselves (suggested ways of work with regards to laptop, iPhone and social/commercial media use etc). The reality is that these prescriptive methods have little effect unless MULs discipline themselves to work more efficiently and smarter through means detailed elsewhere in this book such as distributed delegation and Pareto prioritisation.

7.3.2 EXECUTIONAL EDGE

Another feature of effective MULs is their levels of pace and urgency. Given the service orientation of multi-unit enterprises where front-line staff are expected to respond immediately to customer demands, effective MULs set the dynamic tone by dispatching tasks and requests quickly and efficiently. In the industrial engineering literature, beloved of time and motion specialists in the 1960s and 1970s, it was postulated that measuring and understanding movement could lead to greater efficiency gains. Also in the field of psychology, academics such as Belbin (2000 a,b) argue that teams require 'completer finishers' alongside other actors such as 'shapers', in order to ensure that tasks were implemented on time, to specification. Jack Welch (Welch and Welch 2005) refers to 'executional edge' as being a prime requirement of leadership; ideas, concepts and innovation being irrelevant unless a cadre of leaders exists within organisations with real executional abilities.

With regard to MULs the view that, as one HRD respondent put it, 'we need people who land things', was pervasive among the line management population. The very nature of the role dictates that the MUL spends an inordinate amount of time ensuring that central policies and initiatives are enforced swiftly. In addition, remedying performance issues within the portfolio requires quick action with regular follow up checks. Examples of executional edge demonstrated by effective MULs include:

- anticipating and acting upon issues swiftly

- quick responses to requests

- progress chasing

- answering e-mails and iPhone messages regularly

- following up on promises

- turning around work swiftly and efficiently.

To a degree the MUL role requires a high degree of multi-tasking, therefore it is easy to see why some tasks and initiatives fall into abeyance. What is striking about effective MULs, however, is the degree to which their quick resolution and despatching of various problems and tasks allows them to move quickly on to deal with new challenges. Effective MULs, as another respondent remarked, 'close down things pretty fast and move onto the next thing with a vengeance'.

How do effective MULs generate pace? Many are formidably well-organised using personal organisers and checklists to chase down tasks. They are well prepared, leveraging every interaction with their staff and units to pursue defined objectives. They use their planning time (usually at the beginning and ends of weeks) to define and scope what they are aiming to achieve over the next week in a systematic, orderly fashion. This minimises time wasting and enhances concentration on the key variables within the portfolio. Thus, executional edge can be deconstructed as not only a state of mind but also learned attributes such as good organisational skills and effective prioritisation.

7.3.3 PASSION

The final dimension of energy displayed by effective MULs is passion. Multi-unit enterprises are people businesses where MULs need to convey infectious enthusiasm that engages and motivates people to deliver outstanding service. As one MUL respondent put it, 'if I show that I care about my staff, then my staff will care about the customer'. Within the academic literature passion is typically conceived as *personal commitment* or *positive energy*. With regard to the former, high levels of personal commitment are thought to be achieved through job role 'fit', goal alignment and HRM practice interventions such as development, reward, communication and involvement (Guest 1997). With regard to the latter, positive energy is conceptualised as helping people to perform at their best through techniques such as 'expressing appreciation to others' thereby fuelling 'positive emotions' (Schwartz 2007). In multi-unit contexts however, passion denotes a deep seated interest, concern and belief amongst MULs in what their people are doing or, as one respondent stated, 'the transmission of electric enthusiasm in the job and the people'.

Effective MULs are passionate about their role, believing that what they do really matters. How did effective MULs typically convey passion?

- humour, fun and enjoyment

- cheerleading success

- visibility and positivity.

Intriguingly, passionate behaviour had a positive effect on both receiver and giver, as energy flowed both ways. Many MULs stated that much of their inspiration and energy was derived from the passion of their people and that, in their view, site visits often served a re-energising need for themselves. Given the somewhat isolated home-working environment of their role and stifling demands of the Centre, MULs often found site visits refreshing and motivational. Seeing the positive outcomes of appointments that they had made and the successes of their people reinforced their sense of passion for the job.

How do effective MULs develop and sustain passion? From an attitudinal point of view the correctly profiled MUL will theoretically be highly engaged and motivated in their role. The reality is that this state of mind will fluctuate according to the demands and vicissitudes of the role. More likely, effective MULs will sustain a high level of passion through regular interaction with their staff and units, celebrating success and positively reinforcing good performance with a high degree of fun, enjoyment and humour.

Case Study 23 – MUL Energy in Retail

Sara Weller was Managing Director of the UK's largest multi-channel variety retailer Argos (750 stores), owned by the Home Retail Group, for seven years. From 2009 the company experienced extreme turbulence from channel shifts in categories such as consumer electronics and reductions in consumer discretionary spend. Previously Sara was Joint Managing Director of Sainsbury's and Marketing Director of Abbey National. Under her leadership Argos was a three time winner of Retail Week's 'Multi-Channel Retailer' of the year award.

… There is little doubt in my mind, having operated large multi-unit enterprises over a long period of time – and at this critical juncture in particular – that what effective MULs need most is a shared vision backed up by energy and drive for results. The best performers are those that are positive, proactive and have the capacity to bounce back through character and tenacity. But they also require a desire and understanding to *work through people* to get results. As face-to-face meeting are infrequent, they need to find a way to build relationships quickly and ensure they make an impact – even when they're not there! They achieve this by devolving responsibilities and might create cluster groupings around the four or five key KPIs (each group focusing on one KPI) or geography clusters (such as Scotland for instance). They then use the four or five key trusted people heading these groups to get the message out and become best practice champions … A major coaching programme that we put in that ran from the top to bottom of the organisation also proved successful in enabling MULs to generate 'emotional commitment' from their managers. It allowed MULs *'to share their loads'* by moving their people on a capability journey, increasing their capacity to grow and learn – increasing Area and unit effectiveness at the same time ... I have seen individuals display huge amounts of passion and energy in taking their Districts with them, although I have worked in different cultures where the MUL job is made easier (or harder!) according to the prevailing culture.

A great example of MUL energy at Argos could be seen around catalogue launch time. This was a critical period where back of house 'bins' had to be reconfigured for new and discontinued product lines and frontline colleagues had to become conversant with the new offer. The change in catalogue could have an adverse effect on service standards if units were not set up right. At Argos, like other retailers, we had in house measures such as speed of service (displayed in the back of the unit on screens), stock accuracy measures and home delivery targets. External measures came through online data, in house feedback pads and visual mystery shopper. Incentives were designed through quality (standards), service speed and experience (service). But really effective MULs would lead by example around catalogue launch time, passionately demonstrating the standards and service they expected. One of my MULs made it his objective to get around all of his 35 stores in 2 days to energise and enthuse his colleagues saying to his people 'I won't leave until I see a fantastic piece of service!' These quick, sharp visits were obviously balanced against longer, more strategic meetings where the full unit performance was discussed. The point is that there is a time for high energy and passion (which might be at different times of the trading calendar) – the best way to communicate that is to be visible, touching as many people as possible during the process to energise and mobilise people.

Although energy is down to individuals; some organisations create the conditions for it to flourish more successfully than others. In many senses Argos was a quite young organisation (only 30 years old) and had quite an innovative culture. Our colleagues at Argos didn't really see change as change and were generally willing to try anything that might improve the business. This helped in the DGCS (Delivering Great Customer Service) and Operational Excellence programmes we launched over my time there ... Also, from an executional point of view there weren't layers of hierarchy and when people said 'yes' they meant 'yes'. In many ways it had a small business feeling which was useful given the amount of part-time colleagues we had. Shared beliefs, a strong sense of team and executional simplicity is the key in order to generate emotional engagement from this cohort ... In this environment MULs could operate more effectively because the behaviours conducive to the successful expedition of their roles were already embedded within the organisation. Certainly, this was not the case in other organisations that have suffered more drastically or gone out of business during the recent recession ...

Case Study 24 – MUL Energy in Leisure and Hospitality

Simon Longbottom is the Managing Director of Greene King Pub Partnerships (1,500 units). Since 2010 innovations have included the introduction of a new franchise (Eat and Meet), new product and standards guidelines and a comprehensive customer satisfaction system 'Retail Eyes'. An experienced senior leisure operator, Simon was previously Managing Director of the Gala Gaming Group (170 Bingo and 27 Casino sites).

… Effective MULs need high levels of stamina because of the nature of the job. In both retail and leisure the long opening hours means that the most effective MULs tend to be out there all the time – and when they're not, they're answering e-mails, taking calls or just thinking about it. It really is a 24/7 job. Some of this stems from the psychology of the situation. There is a feeling that 'if the Unit Managers are doing it, I've got to demonstrate rapport and empathy by being out there to support them'. In a sense what effective MULs are trying to do is 'match' their unit managers' effort and output. I remember when I started off in leisure as an Area Manager I used to take my girlfriend around my sites on a Friday night to observe peak trading periods – I used to get a lot of kudos from that (although not from my girlfriend!). There are two issues with the levels of effort required, however – lack of balance and a kind of addictive behaviour that can lead to burn out. In terms of lack of balance the very fact that effective MULs are out there all the time means that they have less time to keep fit and renew their levels of energy; the physical and mental health of MULs can suffer as a result. Also the relentless nature of the job can lead to addictive behaviours – the job itself presents never ending challenges – MULs can work too hard, too long … a position that is unsustainable in terms of well-being.

An important question for me is how do effective MULs sustain high levels of output and effort without suffering burn-out or, ultimately, developing a cynical attitude? What I have observed is that those who survive and prosper have a great love of the job, have great 'bouncebackability', relentless focus and are invariably well organised. Fundamentally, they have a positive attitude which they maintain through staying away from 'dementor' types who have negative force fields. They know it is a tough job but are able to ride its complexity and ambiguity. They rarely engage in game play and genuinely seek to just get on with the job to the best of their ability. Why are they like this? I think that they tend to have extremely resilient, positive personality traits and they deploy very effective coping strategies with good mates and networks within the organisation. You tend to find that 'like attracts like' and the more resilient, long-term MULs forming small informal networks where they support one another.

Effective MULs need to have high energy levels generally because they will be tested by their Unit Managers. There is a kind of 'what would you do if I put the keys on the counter – could you run it?' challenge. In order to gain credibility MULs have to expend a lot of effort (especially when they take over a new patch) to be taken seriously – especially if they've come from the Centre or from outside the sector. What you tend to find that in order to gain respect MULs will 'over-index' in the areas that they know a lot about in order to gain credibility. For instance a restaurant retailer going into Bingo might drive F&B or a person out of finance might know the numbers inside out. But by being humble, being willing to learn and doing things like going 'back to the floor' in order to earn your stripes and understand the operation MULs can gain good followership. Also the best MULs overcome resistance by delivering on their promises; this really is the foundation stone for building rapport. But again it takes a lot of get up and go, chasing down things, getting back to people – showing real effort and determination to close things down with people (say at the Centre) for whom you might not be the only priority … What they are really saying to their GMs is 'if I show this level of energy and passion to sort things out for you, I expect the same level of executional effort in return!'…

7.4 Summary

This Chapter has reflected upon the personal characteristics that MULs require for operational effectiveness. There are, however, two points that need to be made about the ordering and sequencing of these characteristics. First, effective MULs require some degree of explicit and tacit technical knowledge in order to apply sound judgement and act with a high degree of confidence and adaptability; particularly with regard to *exchange processes*. Cognitive faculties are a mediator; the ability to interpret the complex and ambiguous terrain in which they operate, linking inputs to outputs in order to solve non-trivial problems and, through EI faculties, to understand self and others in order to apply appropriate practice-based behaviours and/or *exchange currencies*. Second, MULs might have expertise and EI, but will be rendered ineffective unless they have high levels of energy. Given the aforementioned stresses and demands of the role, MULs need to have high levels of stamina to generate the levels of pace and executional edge required in order to keep abreast of the job. In addition, given the people-centric nature of the role, high levels of passion and personal commitment – 'electric enthusiasm' – are necessary to 'energise their people' to delight customers. All of these characteristics can be developed within MULs by organisations through a range of developmental interventions, although it is easier if they have as one HRD put it elegantly the 'neurological capacity for emotional, intellectual and cognitive development'.

8

Conclusions

This book was prompted by the insight that within multi-unit enterprises there is a key cohort of employees – multi-unit leaders – whose core activities, practices and personal characteristics are under-researched and, as a consequence, are not well understood. Its pertinence and relevance is heightened by the major issues currently facing land-based multi-unit enterprises, which, with their vast levels of fixed costs, must seek to maximise the role and contributions of all their assets – both physical and human – in order to survive and prosper. It is the contention of this author that to date the contribution and impact of effective MULs has been under-recognised by practitioners and academics. By looking at MULs within a variety of organisational contexts the research for this book established that there was plenty of evidence first, that upper-quartile performers did things differently from their colleagues and second, that many of their practices and personal characteristics seemed to have a high degree of convergence.

This chapter will reprise the key themes and arguments of this book by revisiting first, the disruptive context which confronts contemporary multi-unit enterprises and then second, the degree to which such a context has prompted firms to adopt cost-led, compliance-based policies. Third, consideration will be given to the fact that this has posed a significant dilemma for multi-unit leaders; the so called 'commitment-control' paradox which causes MULs to wrestle with the seemingly intractable problem of how, on the one hand, they fulfil organisational cost and change agendas, while on the other, simultaneously motivating and engaging their staff to provide excellent sales-led service.

The way in which effective MULs solve this conundrum is then advanced, namely; *effective MULs optimise their portfolios through a deft application of vertical and horizontal social exchange.* This is to say, whatever the organisational context, *effective MULs formally and informally transact with unit staff, colleagues and central support in order to effect optimal outcomes.* Following consideration of the practices they deploy, this section will lastly elucidate the personal characteristics that are pre-requisites to operating in such a manner, arguing that, in particular, high levels of self-awareness and mental toughness are particularly important attributes. Further sections will then consider the contribution of the concepts advanced by this book, followed by an acknowledgement of the further research required to establish the dynamics of the effective MUL.

8.1 Key Themes and Arguments

8.1.1 KEY CHALLENGES; CUSTOMERS AND SERVICE QUALITY

The Introduction outlined the pressures faced by multi-unit enterprises in developed economies. These were classified as, first, the 'macro' threats of the disruptive 'trinity'; on-line threat, changing consumer expectations and straitened economic conditions. The on-line revolution that allows consumers to make instant price comparisons, 'fish' for coupons, speed up payment (bypassing traditional cash transaction processes) and resort to order and collect mechanisms has shifted power and choice to the consumer. They are, in turn, making use of this channel due to the economic crisis that has resulted in inflationary pressures on living costs, contracting job markets, higher taxes, declines in real wages and pensions and an easing of 'free' credit. Of these, however, it is *changing consumer expectations*, partly as a result of the aforementioned factors, that are of greatest significance.

Addressing and satisfying consumer expectations in a changing technological and economic environment are absolutely crucial to organisational success. This means that firms have had to consider how they offer a combination of price, quality and service in order to attract customers. In itself this is a conundrum, given that the provision of excellent service and high quality product and environment is resource intensive in multi-unit enterprises, given the high levels of fixed costs; something that has, in the past, been supported by higher rather than lower pricing. Companies can offset decreased margins through driving volume to compensate, but this in itself becomes a zero sum game. Alternatively companies can see other ways to become more efficient through increasing process effectiveness and cutting costs out of the value chain. Problems arise, however, when these cuts alight upon areas such as service-providing labour, which proves deleterious to the major challenge of the multi-unit enterprise; that of optimising unit-based human capital.

Five specific multi-unit-related challenges were outlined in the introduction; optimising unit-based human capital, consistency of standards, standardisation versus customisation, format and channel proliferation and centre versus local tensions. Some of these factors, such as a drive towards greater customisation and channel proliferation, have been in part a reaction to changing customer expectations and technological innovation, yet they introduce a higher degree of complexity into the standardised multi-unit offer. These factors, coupled with a need to improve service and quality, would imply that firms would seek to optimise their service-providing human capital in order to adapt and prosper. For many firms, however, this represents a major paradigm shift. Service-led multi-unit enterprises (particularly in retail, leisure and hospitality) have a high level of part-timers and transient workers who suffer from low rates of pay and job status. Increased investment in quality HRM systems and practices (ie pay, selection, training and succession etc) is both expensive and time consuming. Indeed, the default reaction of many multi-unit firms to the challenges they have faced has been to reduce labour costs and at the same time to increase operating compliance and conformance.

8.1.2 GENERIC RESPONSES; COST-LEADERSHIP AND COMPLIANCE

The way in which multi-unit organisations have responded to disruptive forces was outlined in Chapter 2. Their strategic responses were mediated by their degree of corporate agility, with contingent factors including ownership structure, service firm life cycle maturity and adaptive leadership capacity. Whilst some firms chose paths of differentiation and value-focus, one common theme – in contrast to the key challenges outlined above – was their adoption of cost reduction strategies (often wrapped in 'growth rhetoric') in order to survive, stabilise and/or prosper. They focused upon removing cost from the end-to-end value chain through initiatives such as supply chain improvements, capital spend reductions and an increase in promotions and sales effectiveness. In addition, companies universally increased their focus upon front-line labour efficiency and operational and process improvement. In turn, as Chapter 3 elucidated, this meant that the 'implementers' of organisational policies, the MULs, were directed by policy-makers to supervise and monitor labour reductions and the introduction of compliance-led systems. As a result of being expected to enforce the will of the Centre, sometimes with inaccurate data and badly conceived procedures and initiatives – through means of punishment if necessary – a majority of MULs interviewed and surveyed for this book described their anxiety and frustration. Being closer to the customer than the policy-makers at the Centre they could witness for themselves the impact that reducing the amount and quality of labour had on customer experiences. This presented them with a major conundrum; how could they generate commitment amongst their service providers to meet customer expectations within this surrounding control and compliance culture?!

8.1.3 MUL DILEMMA; COMMITMENT-CONTROL PARADOX!

At the heart of this book lies a major dilemma. At an organisational level there might be a concerted drive to reduce costs by reducing staff and/or hours and increase conformance (through the belief it will increase efficiency) by the introduction of a myriad of rules and procedures. As the raison d'etre for most service-based organisations is their ability to service and satisfy customer needs through engaged and motivated staff, such practices might run counter to what the organisation *should* exemplify or what they *say* their strategic rationale is, namely 'satisfied staff' and 'delighted customers'. At another level the organisational HRM infrastructure (incentives, communications, training etc) might be inadequate or unfit for purpose within a multi-unit environment. This raises an uncomfortable paradox for MULs; given their high level of interdependence with their followers (Garvin and Levesque 2008) *how do they fulfil the organisation's control and compliance agenda whilst (simultaneously) engaging and motivating their staff to increase performance*? How do they encourage self-expression, innovation and high levels of discretionary effort? As the chapters at the heart of the book demonstrate (Generating Commitment, Ensuring Control and Implementing Change), they (rather improbably) achieve this difficult task through adopting a *local leadership approach where they optimise their portfolio through social exchange-based practices.*

8.1.4 EFFECTIVE MUL SOLUTION; POSE

Social exchange theory states that organisational actors in a state of mutual interdependence will encourage reciprocity through socio-emotional transactions (Cropanzano and Mitchell 2005). It is through such means that – due to extant constraints of time, distance and, consequently, span of control issues – effective MULs seek to optimise their portfolios. The way they achieve this is through the application of vertical and horizontal exchange practices, designed to optimise effort, knowledge, skills and physical resources across their districts. In order to do this they first have to understand the characteristics, dimensions and gaps within their portfolios and second, gain an understanding of what formal and informal transactions are required either vertically or horizontally to achieve optimal performance.

8.1.4.1 Key MUL objective; portfolio optimisation

According to modern portfolio theory, investors can reduce risk by proportionately spreading their allocation and mix of investments (Markowitz 1959). By the same token effective MULs will review their portfolios with a view to establishing where and why underperformance lies (either on a site, cluster, family or team basis). How can it be addressed? What interventions are required to raise individual site or general performance? The effective MUL will recognise that the starting point is utilising knowledge and talent more efficiently (redeploying and promoting talent or 'moving underperformers on'), but also, in addition to getting the right people into the right sites there is a requirement given (potentially) a conformance and compliance agenda, to cajole, transact and negotiate with unit managers and key service providers to deliver exceptional service standards and performance. They achieve this through (as Chapters 4, 5 and 6 demonstrate) transacting both vertically and horizontally.

8.1.4.2 Vertical social exchange

What stands out from the narratives presented in the 24 Case Studies (and a vast body of research not presented in this book) is the usage of words and phrases such as 'informal contract', 'joint interest', 'part of the bargain', 'returns', 'backing', 'buy-in', 'indebtedness' and 'mutual benefit' – all expressions that imply forms of 'currency' exchange and transaction between MULs and their followers. However, the first question that the effective MUL asks is what will their unit managers and team value? That is to say, what formal and informal practices or *currencies* do they have at their disposal that will 'fit' individual/ team-based situational or behavioural requirements, stimulating engagement and performance? The chapters referring to the 3Cs outlined a range of practices that effective MULs deploy locally in order to encourage the required behaviours. These practices bear a close resemblance to resources of exchange, namely love, status, information, goods, money and services (Foa and Foa 1974, 1980) and/or currencies of exchange – inspiration, task, position, relational and personal (Cohen and Bradford 1989). More significantly, it can be argued that these transactional items can be recast and grouped under the generic process headings; *mutual goal attainment, free market exchange, compensated costs and uncovering hidden value.*

i) Mutual Goal Attainment

The concept of social exchange through goal attainment is based on the insight that engendering cooperation between different parties helps potential allies to achieve personal and/or organisational goals. In the case of MULs this relates to making the super ordinate goals of the organisation pertinent to their portfolio and individual units; albeit through gaining buy-in to the questions 'why?' and 'what's in it for me?'. To this end, as previous chapters on behavioural practices demonstrate, they do the following:

- Local direction setting and prioritisation – a major form of exchange is inspiration and/or clarity with regard to what the local priorities of the unit/team should be. Often there are innumerable goals and targets within multi-unit enterprises. By explaining the 'why', setting out their expectations, making organisational goals locally relevant and prioritising, the MUL provides guidance to those who need it and a platform for others to meld their 'local visions' and plans. The unit can seem a distant entity from the organisation – granting permission to apply local relevance is a key objective of any effective MUL. This is something that Ian Burke acknowledged in Case Study 1 when he highlighted the key questions that all MULs and General Managers should ask themselves:

  What sort of assessment do GMs make of a club when they assume local leadership responsibility? ... What is the GM's local vision? (eg "to be the leading community gaming based entertainment business in Dundee") and business plan for the club over the next three years? Ian Burke, Executive Chairman and CEO, Rank Plc.

  This position is endorsed by Nick Andrews in Case Study 7, when he considered how effective MULs ensured control:

  ... The way in which successful Area Directors operated was to, first, understand how the scorecard was weighted, second, communicate out key priorities and, third, put a plan together with their branch managers to align resources accordingly ... Nick Andrews, Operations Director, Lloyds Bank.

- Ability to influence – in addition, effective MULs can also trade with their unit managers on the amount of influence and input they have into nascent change initiatives and emergent policy implementation. By appointing 'champions' and 'lead managers' they not only engage in the 'distributed delegation' of key tasks but signal to appointees that their expertise and views are valued and can determine outcomes. As Kelly Grimes in Case Study 9 and Alfie Molinaro in Case Study 4 reflected:

Not only did this improve the system but also increased [the GM's] levels of confidence and made her feel that she was making a valuable contribution to influencing and improving our estate through the use of her skills and knowledge ... Kelly Grimes, Operations Director, Ramada Encore.

In terms of developing technical skills on my area I use my "leads", "champions" and "houses of excellence" extensively. Although they are not formally rewarded for these positions it grants them a level of status and influence within my district and puts them on a potential development track for RBM. It benefits both me and them! Alfie Molinaro, RBM, Harvester Restaurants.

ii) Free market exchange

In attempting to generate commitment, ensure control and implement change, effective MULs are adept at offering something of high transactional value in return for behaviours and actions they valued. They do this in the following fashion:

- Positional patronage – the pivotal role of the MUL is to appoint unit managers, ensuring efficient 'talent matching' within the portfolio. This key decision-making role gives them considerable patronage-based exchange given that larger unit appointments command higher salaries (which are usually contingent on sales). Also they are the main arbiters of unit performance; falling out favour with the MUL could lead to being placed on a 'performance plan' or being demoted/moved on. As one unit manager stated, his MUL was his 'judge, jury, saviour or executioner!' This ability to determine the future of underperforming managers was highlighted, in particular, by Tim Elliot in Case Study 3:

So what I did was bring [the unit manager's] personal development review forwards and was completely honest with him; "this is how the previous ROM viewed you, but I think you are in the 'underachieving' box". I also followed up with lots of one-to-ones and "visits with a purpose" to put him on the right track. The upshot was that he decided to leave the Company and work for one of our competitors ... Tim Elliot, Regional Operations Manager, Sainsbury's.

- Protection from punishment – on the other hand effective MULs act as guardians or shields with regard to their followers. Punishment and retribution is the constant fear of unit managers working in multi-unit enterprises, given the number of conformance standards and measures (operational/business, customers and staff). The effective MUL transacts socio-emotionally by either protecting unit managers from sanctions when they are non-compliant with central policies (due to a lack of time and resources and/or focusing on other more important priorities) or making allowances for under-performance due to extenuating circumstances (such as unbridgeable stretch budget targets set by the Centre). This ability to, as one unit manager put it, 'extend a helping hand when people are down', by acting contrary to the way in which compliance-driven organisations expect (or demand) gains the effective MUL huge claims for a high degree of reciprocity in the form of commitment and effort. Such an approach, however, requires a high degree of judgement, confidence and adaptability on behalf of the MUL:

  It is quite clear to us (Regional Operations Managers) that some of the rules and procedures fall into the "business prevention" category but the Audit Team hammer the Units if they don't comply when they come in and do their quarterly checks. What I do is tell my people to ignore some of the trivial box ticking and focus on what really matters – the customer. Anything that relates to selling more ... creating a good customer experience in a safe environment will do for me ... There have been times when I have gone to quite senior personnel to get some of these "process jockeys" off my case ... My team know I stick up for them and am trying to so the right thing so (as a consequence) I think they trust me and therefore "put more out" for me ... I really do ... Regional Operations Manager, Retail.

- Promissory speed – the speed with which effective MULs 'turn things around' are also an important form of informal exchange; the same behaviour will be expected of unit managers in return. This is not to say that MULs will have all the answers or, when they do, they will be in the affirmative. Indeed, the ability to say no is a prime requirement of an effective MUL. It is the fulfilment of a promise made to get back to people with an answer or solution, quickly, which is the most important requirement. An example of the potential payoff of promissory speed was provided by Bill Stevens in Case Study 6a:

I then asked the team "where are we?" and how are" we are we going to get there?" on standards and service. I compiled a site per site list of the priority areas and said to the guys "ok, I'll give you the resources in this order but in return … your part of the bargain … is to deliver better brand standards, superior customer interaction and sales". I think some of them thought "bollocks, he'll never do it!" but I was as good as my word and chased down a lot of the items for them, such as maintenance requests. What happened was that over a six months period my net promoter score went up by 14 per cent… Bill Stevens, District Manager, Vacation Inns.

- Permission to innovate – the granting of licence to deviate from accepted norms in a 'value added' way (applying 'patch ups' and workarounds) and act in a semi-autonomous manner is designed to encourage imagination, innovation and (ultimately) improvement. Another way of viewing it is as a sophisticated form of exchange, where the effective MUL allows self-expression in return for conformance in other ways (ie acceptance of his/her authority, meeting non-negotiable targets on service and customers etc) However, bound up with this informal contract is the implicit understanding that the effective MUL will tolerate failure, as long as it is a basis for learning and, ultimately, improved performance in the future. A prime example was provided by David Thompson in Case Study 11:

…if they see that I am pushing the boundaries they know that I am striving for us to get better and they imitate my behaviour. They just don't accept that "nothing can be done"… David Thompson, Area Manager, Spar.

- Scarce resource access – from a practical point of view the effective MUL will act as a conduit for improving their unit manager and team's access to scarce valuable resources that are either being limited by the organisation (say labour and other managerial costs) and where the district is in direct competition with others (capital, talent systems, maintenance, delivery slots etc). To this extent effective MULs are able to mobilise their 'enabling networks' more efficiently than their peers due to their understanding where boundaries and resource 'gates' within the organisation lie. As Clive Clinton in Case Study 13 observed, giving his unit managers more access to labour had a very positive effect:

In order to make sure the initiative succeeded on my District I made sure that I gave my managers the staffing hours to do it properly from the start. I also reacted quickly to requests from managers for more staff hours in stores that were doing exceptionally well. I understood that in order for this to be a success managers had to have the right amount of staff to do it well. I think my managers appreciated this and reacted in a very positive committed manner … Clive Clinton, Area Manager, Greggs.

iii) Compensated costs

Given the issues that beset many multi-unit enterprises – not least its demanding service-based nature (involving multiple transactions, long hours and repetitive tasks) and the cost-leadership and compliance practices applied by the Centre – effective MULs acknowledge that high personal costs are endured by unit managers which require compensation through a number of formal and informal means. As previous chapters have highlighted, they do this through a number of means, including:

- Public recognition – exchange will also occur around visible recognition through awards, team-briefings and round-robin e-mails. The effective MUL will use such mechanisms to act as public positive reinforcement of desired behaviours, but also as a subtle form of trading; recognition for past effort, but also an encouragement for continued output! In particular they are judicious in their use of league tables that, rather than being used to castigate 'offenders' for poor absolute performance, acknowledge good relative performance:

Unlike some of the managers I've had before this one does send out sinister district e-mails praising a few and then dumping on the rest by highlighting people at the bottom of league tables in red!

... actually what he does is recognises how far some people have come on certain measures and praises improvement as well as top performance ... Unit Manager, Retail.

- Granting of autonomy – given that the rules and strictures of most multi-unit enterprises, combined with low wages (for most front-line service providers) and repetitive task-based roles, can create feelings of alienation, dissatisfaction and disengagement, the granting of some level of discretion and autonomy can serve as a highly motivational tool. The returns for allowing unit managers and staff some leeway for self-expression and determination (within certain boundaries) can be disproportionate, with more engagement potentially leading to better customer service scores, for instance – as Jeremy Hyde explained in Case Study 10:

... we were trying to release people, "engendering the spirit of worthwhile work" ... This was not only designed for improvement purposes but as way of us saying "you are important, your views count" – a position that we believe leads to even more effort and commitment ... demarcations were broken down ... What is the net result of allowing Area Managers to encourage autonomous behaviours within certain boundaries ... sales have been significantly above core business growth, net promoter scores are up 10 per cent + and "guest complaints per cheque" are down 35 per cent ... Jeremy Hyde, Director of Service Development, Pasta House.

- Emotional capital – in addition to formal exchanges such as coaching and recognition, the 'expenditure' of emotional capital such as remembering names, enquiring after family and health, unsolicited phone calls which focus on things other than business and displays of empathy for the relentless demands placed upon unit managers by many multi-unit enterprises, provides engagement 'dividends' to the MUL, if not the organisation. This approach is not dictated by sentimentality, or conducted in a 'gossipy' way; MULs who use their unit managers as emotional crutches are more like as not to be secretly despised, ridiculed and open to compromise. However, by showing a genuine interest in the feelings of their people, effective MULs are likely to promote a genuine response in their aims and interests in return. As one unit manager remarked in Case Study 5:

My Retail Business Manager is good at remembering our birthdays and always delivers a present … a few bottles of wine or a tin of sweets at Xmas. It's a personal touch and we really appreciate it … Actually, we would walk over hot coals for him! … Unit Manager, Leisure.

- Treats – MULS have limited room to manoeuvre with regard to cash incentives and performance related pay (frameworks and budgets being generally designed at the Centre). There are, however, some valuable transactional treats that are within their gift such as extra time off, items that can be charged against expenses (ie flowers, meals, short-breaks etc) or free stock that can be written off against the Unit P&L. While there is no formal procedure for their usage and application, the informal exchange of such things in return for exceptional effort can result in returns that are disproportionate to actual costs:

Our Area Director held a competition for the most new Accounts opened in a quarter … what he did as a reward was to run the store for a day with some of the other store managers and gave me and my team a day out at the races which he wrote off against the District P&L … You should have seen the amount of engagement and buy-in that created! Unit Manager, Merchanting.

- Portable skills – granting unit managers and their wider teams access to further training and development either on company-driven or 'tailored' local courses, can be seen as a form of exchange where the MUL signals their commitment to improvement and (possibly) progression. Another message conveyed by supporting training and development is that the MUL does not feel threatened by giving their people additional portable skills that might, at some point, lead to the recipient moving out of the district or further on in the organisation. As Alfie Molinaro stated in Case Study 4:

I am passionate about demonstrating that I am absolutely committed to self-improvement and progression to the wider team. Most importantly, these development meetings show these key people that they are valued by me … I am interested in their progression and well-being and I get to know them. I think I get more back from them because if I am interested in them, they are likely to respond ... by returning that interest in spades! Alfie Molinaro, RBM, Harvester Restaurants.

- *Behavioural Coaching* – Another form of exchange includes the one-to-one coaching of unit managers to increase their self-awareness and effectiveness. This can either take the form of honest feedback during appraisal, based on close observation, or (where trained) specific coaching sessions based around tools such as TGROW. Through fostering a close connection of this nature the effective MUL is trading time, empathy and personal interest in the individual in return for higher levels of discretionary effort. This was another dimension reflected upon by Alfie Molinaro:

I take total ownership of the situation through one-to-one coaching ... The sense of accomplishment and achievement they feel in making real behavioural change has increased their levels of confidence, self-esteem and effort – I know they are grateful for this direct coaching and honesty ... I am also pleased with the returns...

iv) Uncovering hidden value

In addition, effective MULs operationalise the 3Cs through motivating their followers by means of uncovering and exchanging for value; either through making hidden costs eradicable or potential sales visible. In the case of effective MUL these include:

- Knowledge transfer – sharing technical expertise, know-how and best practice 'tips' which make the job of the unit manager easier (particularly in relation to administration, process improvement, capacity management and change implementation) is another form of exchange. Often this knowledge will have been garnered by their own experiences as ex-unit managers and/or observing and learning from similar situations in other units. It is often deployed as a form of exchange with new appointees that require a high degree of 'task management'. This form of exchange is highly dependent on the MUL's absorptive capacity and communication skills. As Nolan Spratt commented in Case Study 16:

The guys have really bought into this concept of continually trying to innovate and improve everything if they can see it unlocks value;

increasing sales improves their P&Ls – nice at bonus time! Nolan Spratt, RBM, Nicholsons.

- Valuable insights – effective MULs are also adept, due to their 'insight networks' and processing skills, to 'fill in the spaces' for their people with regard to the background reasons behind various initiatives, communications and policy changes. Through such means, the effective MUL displays their nous and grip upon the 'reality' of the organisation. Such intelligence is traded in a mature manner, with staff that is more willing to commit, once they have understood the real 'why'.

8.1.4.3 Horizontal social exchange

In addition to formal and informal means of vertical exchange, effective MULS practiced horizontal forms of exchange along three levels:

- Colleague level – effective MULs who operated within close geographical proximity or overlapped territories in multi-brand environments swapped hard tangible assets (equipment, machinery, technology and stock) and soft intangible assets (best practice knowledge, problem-solving techniques, competitive information and people). In particular, effective MULs traded people either to solve immediate gaps or deal with capacity issues, on the basis that such reciprocity mediated against significant operational issues down the line.

- Support staff level – with regard to support staff, making the job of important intermediaries easier by responding to requests, empathising with their problems, recognising excellent service all contributed to a high degree of exchange, as exemplified by Daniel Wilkinson in Case Study 8:

  … It is absolutely critical to create and sustain cross-functional relationships. Support functions that are respected will act for specific Regional Managers – politeness and a lack of "them and us" approach really does get me further. I suppose, in a way, it's about manipulating relationships to your own advantage … They will go the extra mile if they have confidence in you … In order to make it a two way process I give them the heads up on what

might be coming down the line and do my best to resolve any inaccuracies for them ... The two admin. people assigned to my area also cover other patches; what I aim to do is make my agenda their agenda. I create good relations by calling in and spending time at Head Office. It makes a huge difference in driving my profit and performance ... Daniel Wilkinson, Regional Manager, Greene King.

- Inter-unit level – effective MULs encouraged reciprocity between units by setting up appropriate enabling processes (meetings, forums and away days) and structures ('clusters' and geographical 'families') where hard and soft assets could be traded and/or shared. As Paul Benton reflected on joint problem-solving in Case 17:

...(we also hold) "can't crack it sessions" which enables people to "show off their dirty washing". What it allows GMs to do is talk about problems they might have encountered from an employee relations point of view or systems and standards implementation. It is another way of approaching best practice discussions, in my view, because sometimes best practice can perceived as bragging! If you can create an open, honest and trustful environment where people can speak up with confidence in a close knit environment, people can get a lot out of it ... Paul Benton, Area Director, Grosvenor Casinos.

Taking into account these vertical and horizontal exchange approaches, the leadership style that effective MULs could be described as deploying would fit into the aforementioned 'situational leadership' approach, where style (task or relationship) is adapted to follower readiness. The over-riding conclusion, though, is that is dualistic; featuring both leadership and management approaches, with an intuitive appreciation of psychology and sociology, through social exchange techniques that are grounded in both emotion and function.

8.1.5 KEY PERSONAL CHARACTERISTICS OF MULS

In terms of the personal characteristics of effective MULs, attributes attached to the overarching constructs of expertise, EI and energy were posited as a result of this research. The question then arises, which of the attributes are dominant, the absence of which will discriminate against optimal performance? From a 'cluster' perspective, expertise and EI will come to nought over the longer term without energy; particularly given the unrelenting demands of this role. Also, within each of the 3Es, there are characteristics that stand out as being particularly important such as 'tacit expertise', executional edge and mental toughness.

'Tacit expertise' accounts in part for the intuitive knowledge of how to transact and exchange effectively; what Kevin Todd (in Case Study 18) called 'informal contracting':

> *Informal contracting occurs when trust has been built up, where they gain commitment from their GMs from implicit understandings. Fundamentally they do not bully but contract on a trust-based level. This is learnt over quite a period of time ... It is perceptible the degree to which great MULs have a positive effect on unit operations through their local leadership and behaviour! Kevin Todd, President and CEO, Rosinter Restaurants, Russia.*

'Executional edge' is also a vitally important requirement of effective MULs, not only, as Simon Longbottom said in Case Study 24 to 'close things down' but also to 'match' their GMs and conduct an exchange for desired behaviours:

> *Also the best MULs overcome resistance by delivering on their promises; this really is the foundation stone for building rapport. But again it takes a lot of get up and go, chasing down things, getting back to people – showing real effort and determination to close things down with people (say at the Centre) for whom you might not be the only priority ... What they are really saying to their GMs is "if I show this level of energy and passion to sort things out for you, I expect the same level of executional effort in return!" Simon Longbottom, MD, Greene King.*

By demonstrating the service-led behaviours they wanted at store level by turning up the energy dial, as Sara Weller reflected in Case Study 23, it encouraged imitation and mobilisation:

> *The point is that there is a time for high energy and passion (which might be at different times of the trading calendar) – the best way to communicate that is to be visible, touching as many people as possible during the process to energise and mobilise people ... Sara Weller, MD, Argos.*

However, given the 'commitment-control dilemma' faced by many MULs, there is also a high requirement for mental toughness and resilience in order to pursue a commitment-based approach within a (potentially) command and control environment. In order to develop this level of hardiness, a sufficient level of self awareness was required, as Dr Nollaig Heffernan commented in Case Study 21:

> *The often excessively stressful nature of the MUL's job means it is essential that MULs understand their response to critical situations, their limitations and their overall well-being so that are resilient enough to optimise in their roles ... Dr Nollaig Heffernan, MUL Psychologist.*

Mental toughness and resilience is something which companies such as Sainsbury's acknowledged they have measured in the past, but perhaps underestimated in its overall effect upon effective levels of performance, as Helen Webb reflected in Case Study 20:

> *Given the stress and pressure of the role we also use a specific tool to measure psychological balance and ability to perform under pressure. We are currently looking at this resilience measure which we are coming to understand might have more importance in predicting future performance than we had thought before ... Helen Webb, Retail and Logistics HRD, Sainsbury's.*

In a statement of the obvious, it cannot be said that effective MULs possess all these personal characteristics. Some might (as Simon Longbottom commented in Case Study 24) over-index on certain dimensions to compensate for weaknesses; such as technical expertise rather than EI (particularly acute amongst ex-unit managers). However, as previously stated, there are appropriate development interventions that can improve the key competencies of MULs should organisations choose to do so, with the most important requirement being that these interventions 'fit' the right gaps and that the recipients are at an appropriate state of readiness to learn and develop.

8.2 Contributions

8.2.1 INTEGRATED MODEL OF MUL

As stated in the Introduction, this book has been constructed around an integrated model of effective MUL, something that has been hitherto lacking in the literature. Previous research on multi-unit managers in fast food and casual dining contexts (Umbreit and Tomlin 1986, Umbreit 1989, Mone and Umbreit 1989, Umbreit and Smith 1991, Ryan 1992, Muller and Campbell 1995, Di Pietro et al 2007) refer to critical 'job dimensions' or 'success factors' highlighting key focus areas for multi-unit managers such as operations, HRM, financial management, promotions and facilities and safety. One of the most important insights provided by this literature is its isolation of HRM (and leadership in Di Pietro et al 2007) by respondents as a key variable in multi-unit manager success, particularly during transition from unit manager. Lack of HRM skills are also cited as one of the main reasons for multi-unit manager turnover and failure. However, it is surprising that these commentators fail to make a connection between HRM as an *input* variable having a mediating effect on *outputs* and the degree to which local HRM is deployed as a 'currency' exchange mechanism in order to facilitate commitment, change and control behaviours. Also they fail to describe the personal characteristics that successful multi-unit managers require in order to be effective, which hypothetically – due to the importance of HRM and social exchange – must have a strong behavioural bias.

Hence this book advances an integrated conceptual model of MUL (Figure 8.1) based upon extensive research amongst a range of respondents situated within retail, leisure and hospitality organisations.

There are a number of critical dependencies in this model. First, personal characteristics of MULs (energy, expertise and EI) have a mediating effect on the behaviourally-based practices (commitment, control and change) that ultimately affect portfolio outcomes (systems, standards and service). Second, a spine runs through the model of key variables – energy, commitment and service – the absence of any of which (potentially) disables the effectiveness of MULs. Third, within each cluster, critical dependencies exist between the items. Within characteristics, expertise and EI are rendered redundant in the absence of energy. Commitment is the starting point in behavioural practices, easing the process of exerting control and implementing change. Finally, service is underpinned by the application of effective operating systems and brand standards.

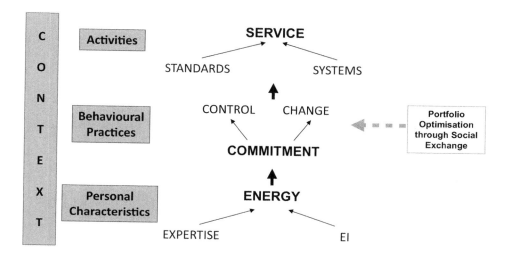

Figure 8.1   **Effective MUL Model**

8.2.2 GUIDING THEORY (POSE)

Another contribution of this work is its surfacing of a guiding theory; portfolio optimisation through social exchange. A key insight of the research was the fact that whatever the cyclic position of the multi-unit enterprise in question (dying, surviving, stabilising or growing) there was a cohort of MULs that outperformed its peers. Obviously their job would be greatly assisted through a clear strategy, focused balanced scorecard and aligned KPIs, excellent operational systems and 'good' HRM at an organisational level. However, what this research established was that whatever the organisational context, it was the capacity of the MUL to optimise their portfolio through vertical and horizontal exchange mechanisms (as outlined above) that was deemed by respondents to be a major variable in their success – in *relative terms* – in comparison with their peers.

In every context, effective MULs transacted socio-emotionally with their subordinates to effect optimal outcomes due to demands placed upon the units by the Centre (particularly during disruptive macro-economic circumstances) and the structural form of the multi-unit organisation that creates in itself a unique management challenge of 'managing at a distance'. This insight and its supporting empirical data is a contribution, partially addressing a gap acknowledged by Cropozano and Mitchell (2005):

> *By and large, organizational researchers have focused on the social relationships that develop between employees and their employing organization. Exchange orientation provides an interesting avenue for future research (e.g., relations with supervisors, co-workers, outsiders, and among groups) ... As noted by Liden and colleagues (1997), very few studies directly examine exchange processes – or the "black box" of social exchange. As a result, we really know little about the processes of social exchange... Cropanzano and Mitchell (2006: 878-880).*

Two points need to be made about the application of this theoretical perspective to the subject in question. First, POSE is not a manifestation of either transformational or transactional leadership (Burns 1978); it is a judicious combination of both. The fact that social exchange theory involves 'dealing', generating 'reciprocity' and 'indebtedness' would suggest it fits into the transactional style, however it's socio-emotional – rather than punishment – perspective, means that it also has transformational elements. To this extent, it exhibits both management and leadership-type approaches, as portrayed in the literatures outlined in Chapters 4 and 5. This was found to be the case with effective MULs – at a local level they had to organise and inspire, but also, given the constraints of the role (scarce resources and spatial impediments,) bargain, contract and exchange for optimal outcomes within their portfolio. Second, whilst effective MULs sought to ensure that the vertical and horizontal transactions they made ensured that costs to individuals were outweighed by *perceived* benefits (fitting their needs, desires and expectations), they made sure (for their own self-interested purposes) that the benefits to the portfolio outweighed *actual* costs.

8.3 Further Research

This book has made a bold attempt to present an integrated model of MUL. Its original draughts and scripts have been greatly assisted by comments from practitioners, many of whom, having 'sense tested' its research findings and central arguments, have expressed great support for its central thesis of *portfolio optimisation through social exchange*. Further research would include further testing of the constructs and dependencies of the conceptual model not only within the service contexts chosen for this book but also on a broader multi-site plane. It is arguable that the principles of this book also apply to other organisations which are not standardised through branded chain formats, but are multi-site forms bound together by common rules, procedures and practices (such as privately-owned hospital and dentistry chains, schools, water, utilities and telecoms etc) There are also some specific questions relating first to the prioritisation and contingent situational 'fit' of exchange-based behavioural practices; second, diversity issues relating to MULs (why are there proportionately fewer female MULs than male?) and third; cross-national comparative analysis of MUL practice and effectiveness (to what extent is there convergence or divergence with some of the observations and propositions of this book?) As previously stated, this under-researched area provides much fertile ground for further research!

8.4 Summary

This book does not make the claim that effective MULs are the sole contingent factor upon multi-unit enterprise success. The firm's product positioning and business model (ie its coalescence around a distinctive 'big idea'), ownership, senior leadership, service life cycle, structure and – most pertinently with regard to land-based multi-unit enterprises – site selection, provide the context for overall firm performance. What this book argues, however, is that within any multi-unit organisation there is a cohort of MULs that outperforms its peers on a comparative basis, taking into account other district-related contingent factors such as investment cycle, site and regional economics (ie London versus the rest of the UK). Additionally, there is a high degree of convergence relating to what distinguishes these higher performers from their colleagues, not least their personal characteristics of expertise, EI and energy that enable them to generate commitment, ensure control and implement change to assure appropriate systems, standards and sales-led service outcomes.

The central insight provided by this work, however, is an explanation of how they optimise their own individual portfolio of sites. It is the strong contention of this book that it is the effective MUL's understanding and, consequently, their application of *social exchange in pursuance of portfolio optimisation* that is their main differentiating factor from their peers. Given the distance of the MUL from their sites, their high level of interdependency with their followers and the ambiguities and complexities of operating in an (often) chaotic and disorderly multi-unit context, it is the effective MUL's ability to *exchange social, emotional and practical currencies* both horizontally and vertically – encouraging *value-added reciprocation* from his/her followers, peers and other providers – that marks them out as outstanding *local leaders*.

Bibliography

ACNielson. 2007. Good Value is the Top Influencer of Grocery Store Choice. *The Neilson Company News Release* 17 December, nielson.com, [accessed: 21 May 2009].

Aguilera, R. and Dencker, J. 2004. 'The Role of Human Resource Management in Cross-Border Mergers and Acquisitions'. *International Journal of HRM* 15(8), 1355–70.

Albrecht, K. 1992. *The Only Thing that Matters: Bringing the Power of the Customer into the Center of Your Business*. NY: Warner Books.

Albrecht, K. and Zemke, R. 1995. *Service America! Doing Business in the New Economy*. NY: Warner Books.

Angwin, D. 2000. *Implementing Successful Post-Acquisition Management*. London: Prentice Hall.

Applebaum, E. and Batt, R. 1994. *The New American Workplace*. Ithaca: ILR Press.

Aram, J.D. 1976. *Dilemmas of Administrative Behavior*. Englewood Cliffs, NJ: Prentice Hall.

Argyris, C. 1964. *Integrating the Individual and the Organization*. NY: Wiley.

Armstrong, P. 1987a. 'The Personnel Profession in the Age of Management Accountancy'. *Personnel Review* 17, 1–9.

Armstrong, P. 1987b. 'The Rise of Accounting Controls in British Capitalist Enterprises'. *Organisations and Society* 12(5), 415–36.

Arthur, J. 1994. 'Effects of Human Resource Systems on Manufacturing Performance and Turnover'. *Academy of Management Journal* 37, 670–87.

Arvey, R.D., Rotundo, M., Johnson, W., Zhang, Z, and McGue, M. 2006. 'The Determinants of Leadership Role Occupancy: Genetic and Personality Factors'. *Leadership Quarterly* 17, 1–20.

Autry, J. 2001. *The Servant Leader*. NY: Three Rivers Press.

Bach, S. and Sisson, K. 2000. *Personnel Management*. Oxford: Blackwell.

Baird, L. and Meshoulam, I. 1988. 'Managing the Two Fits of Strategic Human Resource Management'. *Academy of Management Review* 13(1), 116–28.

Barnard, C.I. 1968. *Functions of the Executive*. Boston, MA: Harvard University Press.

Bartlett, C. and Ghoshal, S. 1989. *Managing Across Borders*. London: Hutchinson.

Bass, B.M. and Bass, R. 2008. *The Bass Handbook of Leadership: Theory, Research, and Managerial Applications* 4th edn. NY: Free Press.

Batrus Hollweg International [BHI]. 2005a. (April 7). Tackling the multi-unit manager challenge, Part 1. *Peak Performance Update.* http:/www.batrushollweg.com/files/4-7-05.newsletter.MUM1.pdf.

Batrus Hollweg International [BHI]. 2005b. (April 7). Tackling the multi-unit manager challenge, Part 2. *Peak Performance Update.* http:/www.batrushollweg.com/files/4-24-05.newsletter.MUM_2.pdf.

Batt, R. 2000. 'Strategic Segmentation in Front-Line Services: Matching Customers, Employees and Human Resource Systems'. *International Journal of Human Resource Management* 11(3), 540–61.

Beck, A.P. 1981. 'A Study of Group Phase Development and Emergent Leadership'. *Group Dynamics* 5, 48–54.

Becker, B. and Gerhart, B. 1996. 'The Impact of Human Resource Management on Organisational Performance: Progress and Practice'. *Academy of Management Journal* 39(4), 779–801.

Becker, B., Huselid, M., Pickus, P. and Spratt, M.F. 1997. 'HR as a Source of Shareholder Value: Research and Recommendations'. *Human Resource Management* 36, 39–47.

Beer, M., Spector, B., Lawrence, P., Mills, D. and Walton, R.E. 1984. *Managing Human Assets*. New York: Free Press.

Belbin, R.M. 2000a. *Team Roles at Work*. NY: Butterworth-Heinemann.

Belbin, R.M. 2000b. *Beyond the Team*. NY: Butterworth-Heinemann.

Benne, K.D. and Sheats, P. 1948. 'Functional Roles of Group Members'. *Journal of Social Issues* 4, 41–49.

Bennett, N., Wise, C., Woods, P.A. and Harvey, J.A. 2003. *Distributed Leadership*. Nottingham: National College of School Leadership.

Bennis, W. 2001. 'The New Leadership.' In *Financial Times Handbook of Management* (2nd edition), eds S. Crainer and D. Dearlove. London: Prentice Hall.

Benson, J. and Ugolini, L. 2003. *A Nation of Shopkeepers*. NY: Tauris.

Berger, P. and Luckmann, T. 1971. *The Social Construction of Reality*. Harmondsworth: Penguin University Books.

Berman, B. 2011. *Competing in Tough Times*. NJ: Pearson.

Berman, B. and Evans, J.R. 2010. *Retail Management* 11th edn. NJ: Prentice Hall.

Berry, J. 1983. 'Acculturation: A Comparative Analysis of Alternative Forms.' In *Perspectives in Immigrant and Minority Education*, eds J. Samuda and P. Woods. Lanham: University Press of America.

Bird, A. and Beechler, S. 1995. 'Links Between Business Strategy and Human Resource Management Strategy in US-based Japanese Subsidiaries: An Empirical Investigation'. *Journal of International Business Studies* 26(1), 23–46.

Blackden, R. 2012. 'Best Buy's Problems Should Act as a Cautionary Tale for UK Retailers'. *Sunday Telegraph*, 15 (April), B6.

Blake, R.R. and Mouton, J.S. 1964. *The Managerial Grid: The Key to Leadership Excellence*. Houston: Gulf Publishing.

Blake, R.R. and Mouton, J.S. 1985. *The Managerial Grid III*. Houston: Gulf Publishing.

Blau, P.M. 1963. *The Dynamics of Bureaucracy* 2nd edn. Chicago: University of Chicago Press.

Blau, P.M. 1964. *Exchange and Power in Social Life*. London: Wiley.

Braverman, H. 1974. *Labour and Monopoly Capital: The Degradation of Work in the Twentieth Century*. London: Monthly Review Press.

Boselie, P., Dietz, G. and Boon, C. 2005. 'Commonalities and Contradictions in HRM and Performance Research'. *Human Resource Management Journal* 15(3), 67–94.

Boak, G. and Coolican, D. 2001. 'Competencies for Retail Leadership: Accurate, Acceptable, Affordable'. *Leadership and Organization Development Journal* 22(5/6), 212–20.

Bower, J. 2001. 'Not all M&As are Alike and that Matters'. *Harvard Business Review* 79(3), 93–101.

Boxall, P. and Purcell, J. 2003. *Strategy and Human Resource Management*. Basingstoke: Macmillan.

BRC. 2011a. *BRC/Springboard-ATCM Footfall and Vacancies Monitor Aug/Oct 2011: Worst Footfall Drop This Year* [Online: British Retail Consortium 02/09/11]. Available at www.brc.org.uk [accessed 19 September 2011].

BRC. 2011b. *BRC-Google On-Line Retail Monitor Q3 2011: 1 in 10 Retail Searches on Mobile* [Online: British Retail Consortium 17/10/11]. Available at www.brc.org.uk [accessed 29 October 2011].

BRC. 2012a. *BRC Sales Monitor December 2011: Stronger December Reflects One-Off Factors* [Online: British Retail Consortium 06/01/12]. Available at www.brc.org.uk [accessed 08 January 2012].

BRC. 2012b. *BRC Warns of More Retail Administrations* [Online: British Retail Consortium 09/01/12]. Available at www.brc.org.uk [accessed 20 January 2012].

Brezicki, M. 2008. *Examining the competencies required to be a successful multi-unit manager*. Unpublished PhD dissertation defense, North Central University.

Budhwar, P. 2000. 'Strategic Integration and Devolvement of HRM in the UK Manufacturing Sector'. *British Journal of Management* 11, 285–302.

Buono, A. and Bowditch, J. 1989. *The Human Side of Mergers and Acquisitions*. San Francisco: Jossey-Bass.

Burns, J.M. 1978. *Leadership*. NY: Harper & Row.

Burns, T. and Stalker, G.M. 1961. *The Management of Innovation*. London: Tavistock.

Burnes, B. 2004. *Managing Change*. 4th Edn. Harlow: Prentice Hall.

Butler, S. 2011. 'Stores in Scramble for Smartphone Salvation'. *Times (London, England)* 31(May), 38.

Carlson, S. 1951. *Executive Behaviour: A Study of the Work Load and the Working Methods of Managing Directors, Stockholm: Strombergs. Reprinted by Uppsala University in 1991 with comments by H. Mintzberg and R. Stewart*. Uppsala: Uppsala University.

Carlton, J. 1997. 'Cultural Due Diligence'. *Training (New York, N.Y.)* (November): 67–75.

Carlyle, T. 1841. *On Heroes, Hero-Worship and the Heroic History*. Boston, MA: Houghton Mifflin.

Carnall, C. 2007. *Managing Change in Organisations*. Harlow: Prentice Hall.

Cartwright, S. and Cooper, C. 1996. *Managing Mergers, Acquisitions and Strategic Alliances: Integrating People and Cultures*. Oxford: Butterworth-Heinemann.

Cave, A. 2011. 'A Whole New Way of Shopping'. *Sunday Telegraph* 11(December), B5.

Chandler, A.D. 1962. *Strategy and Structure*. Boston, MA: MIT Press.

Chase, W.E. and Simon, H.A. 1973. 'Perception in Chess'. *Cognitive Psychology* 4, 55–81.

Chatterjee, S., Lubatkin, M., Schweiger, D. and Weber, J. 1992. 'Cultural Differences and Shareholder Value in Related Mergers: Linking Equity and Human Capital'. *Strategic Management Journal* 13, 319–34.

Cheetham, G. and Chivers, G. 1998. 'The Reflective (and Competent) Practitioner: A Model of Professional Competence Which Seeks to Harmonise the Reflective Practitioner and Competence Based Approaches'. *Journal of European Industrial Training* 22(7), 267–76.

Child, J. 1988. *Organization: A Guide to Problems and Practice*. 2nd edn. London: Paul Chapman.

Christensen, C.M. and Overdorf, M. 2000. 'Meeting the Challenge of Disruptive Change'. *Harvard Business Review* 78(2), 67–76.

Cloke, D. and Goldsmith, J. 2002. *The End of Management and the Rise of Organizational Democracy*. San Francisco: Jossey-Bass.

Clough, P.J. and Strycharczyk, D. 2008. 'Developing Resilience through Coaching – MTQ48.' In *Psychometrics in Coaching: Using Psychological and Psychometric Tools for Development*, ed. J. Passmore. London: Kogan.

Cohen, A.R. and Bradford, D.L. 1989. *Influence without Authority*. USA: Wiley.

Cohen, Y. and Pfeffer, J. 1984. 'Employment Practices in the Dual Economy'. *Industrial Relations* 23(1), 58–72.

Collins, J. 2001. *Good to Great: Why Some Companies Make the Leap....and Others Don't*. London: Random House.

Crainer, S. 1998. *Key Management Ideas: Thinkers that Changed the Management World* 3rd edn. London: Prentice Hall.

Craven, N. 2011. 'Pioneering Wickes Turns Back the Clock'. *Mail on Sunday* 11(December), 63.

Craven, N. 2012a. 'Our Stores are in Fantastic Shape – We are Doing the Right Things'. *Mail on Sunday* 15(January), 79.

Craven, N. 2012b. 'High Street Carnage Fear Over Rates Rise'. *Mail on Sunday* 22(January), 71.

Craven, N. and Bridge, S. 2012. 'How Private Equity Debt sank the Peacocks Chain'. *Mail on Sunday* 22(January), 73.

Cropanzano, R. and Mitchell, M.S. 2005. 'Social Exchange Theory: an Interdisciplinary Review'. *Journal of Management* 31, 874–900.

Cully, M., Woodland, S. and O'Reilly, A. 1999. *Britain at Work: As Depicted by the 1998 Workplace Employee Relations Survey*. London: Routledge.

Dahl, R.A. 1961. *Who Governs? Democracy and Power in an American City*. New Haven, CT: Yale University Press.

de Vries, M.F., Korotov, K.R. and Florent-Treacy, E. 2007. *Coach or Couch: The Psychology of Making Better Leaders*. Paris: INSEAD Business Press.

Delery, J. and Doty, D. 1996. 'Modes of Theorising in Strategic Human Resource Management: Tests of Universalistic, Contingency and Configurational Performance Predictions'. *Academy of Management Journal* 39(4), 802–35.

Denis, J.L., Lamothe, L. and Langley, A. 2001. 'The Dynamics of Collective Leadership and Strategic Change in Pluralistic Organizations'. *Academy of Management Journal* 44, 809–37.

Denzin, N. 1970. *Sociological Methods: A Source Book*. NY: McGraw Hill.

DiPietro, R.B., Murphy, K.S., Rivera, M. and Muller, C.C. 2007. 'Multi-unit Management Key Success Factors in the Casual Dining Restaurant Industry: A Case Study'. *International Journal of Contemporary Hospitality Management* 19(7), 524–36.

Drucker, P.F. 1955. *The Practice of Management*. London: Pan Books.

Drucker, P.F. 1989. *The Practice of Management* 9th edn. London: Heinemann Professional.

Dumez, H. and Jeunemaître, A. 2006. 'Reviving Narratives in Economics and Management: Towards an Integrated Perspective of Modelling, Statistical Inference and Narratives'. *European Management Review* 3, 32–43.

Dunford, R.W. 1992. *Organizational Behaviour: An Organisational Analysis Perspective*. Addison Wesley: Sydney.

Eisenhardt, K. 1989. 'Building Theories from Case Study Research'. *Academy of Management Review* 14(4), 532–50.

Emerson, R.M. 1976. 'Social Exchange Theory'. *Annual Review of Sociology* 2, 335–62.

Ericsson, K.A. 2000. *Expert Performance and Deliberate Practice*. Available at http://www.psy.fsu.edu/faculty/ericsson/ericsson.exp.perf.html [accessed 21 June 2001].

Evans, P. 1986. 'The Strategic Outcomes of Human Resource Management'. *Human Resource Management* 25(2), 149–62.

Fayol, H. 1916. 'Administration industrielle et generale'. *Bulletin de la Societe de l'Industrie Minerale* 10, 5–164.

Federal Trade Commission. 1975. *Statistical Report on Mergers and Acquisitions*. Washington, DC: US Government Printing Office.

Felsted, A. 2011. 'Data Shows a Patchy Picture for Shopping Malls.' *Financial Times*, 28 (September), 4.

Felsted, A. 2012a. 'Food Retailing Analysis – All Lined Up.' *Financial Times*, 6 (January), 9.

Felsted, A. 2012b. 'Credit Insurer Will Not Raise its Cover for UK Retailers.' *Financial Times*, 23 (January), 18.

Felsted, A. and Jopson, B. 2011. 'Tesco Highlights Retailers' US Travails.' *Financial Times*, 6 (September), 19.

Fiedler, F.E. 1967. *A Theory of Leadership Effectiveness*. NY: McGraw-Hill.

Fitzsimmons, J.A. and Fitzsimmons, M.J. 2006. *Service Management* 5th edn. NY: McGraw-Hill.

Fleishman, E.A. 1953. 'The Description of Supervisory Behavior'. *Journal of Applied Psychology* 37(1), 1–6.

Fleishman, E.A., Mumford, M.D., Zaccaro, S.J., Levin, K.Y., Korothin, A.L. and Hein, M.B. 1991. 'Taxonomic Efforts in the Description of Leader Behavior: A Synthesis and Functional Interpretation'. *Leadership Quarterly* 2(4), 245–87.

Foa, U.G. and Foa, E.B. 1974. *Societal Structures of the Mind*. Springfield ILL: Charles C Thomas.

Foa, U.G. and Foa, E.B. 1980. 'Resource Theory: Interpersonal Behavior as Exchange.' In *Social Exchange: Advances in Theory and Research*, eds K. Gergen, M. Greenberg and R. Willis. NY: Plenum.

Fombrun, C., Tichy, N. and Devanna, M. 1984. *Strategic Human Resource Management*. NY: Wiley.

Fortson, D. and Marlow, B. 2012. 'Day of the Zombies'. *Sunday Times*, 27 (May), 5.

Foti, R.J. and Hauenstein, N.M. 2007. 'Pattern and Variable Approaches in Leadership Emergence and Effectiveness'. *Journal of Applied Psychology* 92, 347–55.

Fox, A. 1974. *Beyond Contract: Work, Power and Trust Relations*. London: Faber and Faber.

Fox, E.J. and Sethuraman, R. 2006. 'Retail Competition.' In *Retailing in the 21st Century: Current and Emerging Trends*, eds M. Krafft and M. Mantrala. Berlin: Springer.

Frean, A. 2011. '"Hourglass" America is Squeezing Middle Class.' *The Times*, 16 September, 48.

Freeman, L. 2006. *The Development of Social Network Analysis*. Vancouver: Empirical Press.

French, J.R. and Raven, B. 1968. 'The Bases of Social Power.' In *Group Dynamics: Research and Theory* 3rd edn., eds D. Cartwright and A. Zander. NY: Harper and Row.

Fuller, R. 1975. *Synergistics*. NY: Macmillan.

Gardner, H. 2004. *Changing Minds*. Boston, MA: Harvard Business School Press.

Garvin, D.A. and Levesque, L.C. 2008. 'The Multi-Unit Enterprise'. *Harvard Business Review* (June): 1–11.

Galbraith, J.W. 1977. *Organizational Design*. Reading, MA: Addison-Wesley.

George, B., Sims, P., McLean, A.N. and Mayer, D. 2007. 'Discovering Your Authentic Leadership'. *Harvard Business Review* (February): 129–38.

Gibb, C.A. 1954. 'Leadership.' In *Handbook of Social Psychology* Vol. 2., ed. G. Lindzey. MA: Addison-Wesley.

Gladwell, M. 2008. *Outliers: The Story of Success*. NY: Little, Brown and Co.

Goffee, R. and Jones, G. 2006. *Why Should Anyone Be Led By You? What It Takes To Be An Authentic Leader*. Boston, MA: Harvard Business School Press.

Golden, K. and Ramanujam, V. 1985. 'Between a Dream and a Nightmare: On the Integration of the Human Resource Management and Strategic Planning Processes'. *Human Resource Management* 24, 429–52.

Goldman, A.I. 1999. *Knowledge in a Social World*. Oxford: Oxford University Press.

Goldsmith, W. and Clutterbuck, D. 1998. *The Winning Streak Mark II*. London: Orion Business Books.

Goleman, D. 1996. *Emotional Intelligence*. NY: Bloomsbury.

Goleman, D. 1998. *Working with Emotional Intelligence*. NY: Bantam Books.

Goodman, M. 2011. 'Road to Recovery – Leisure Industries; Back in Shape.' *Sunday Times*, 29 May, B9–11.

Goss-Turner, S. 1999. 'The Role of the Multi-unit Manager in Branded Hospitality Chains'. *Human Resource Management Journal* 9(4), 39–58.

Goss-Turner, S. 2002. 'Multi-site Management: HRM Implications.' In *Human Resource Management International Perspectives in Hospitality and Tourism*, eds N. D'Annunizo-Green, G. Maxwell and S. Watson. London: Thomson Learning.

Goss-Turner, S. and Jones, P. 2000. 'Multi-unit Management in Service Operations: Alternative Approaches in the UK Hospitality Industry'. *Tourism and Hospitality Research* 2(1), 51–66.

Gouldner, A. 1960. 'The Norm of Reciprocity: A Preliminary Statement'. *American Sociological Review* 25, 1–16.

Gratton, L., Hope-Hailey, V., Stiles, P. and Truss, C. 1999. *Strategic Human Resource Management: Corporate Rhetoric and Human Reality*. Oxford: Oxford University Press.

Greenwood, J.E. 1977. *A Cap for Boots: An Autobiography*. London: Self Published.

Gronn, P. 2002. 'Distributed Leadership as a Unit of Analysis'. *Leadership Quarterly* 13, 423–51.

Grugulis, I. and Bozkurt, O. (2011). *Retail Work*. Basingstoke: Palgrave Macmillan.

Guest, D. 1987. 'Human Resource Management and Industrial Relations'. *Journal of Management Studies* 24(5), 503–21.

Guest, D. 1997. 'Human Resource Management and Performance: A Review and Research Agenda'. *International Journal of HRM* 8, 263–76.

Guest, D. 1999. 'Human Resource Management: The Workers' Verdict'. *Human Resource Management Journal* 9(3), 5–25.

Guest, D. 2000. 'HR and the Bottom Line: Piece by Piece'. People Management, January, 26–31.

Guest, D. 2001. 'Human Resource Management: When Reality Confronts Theory'. *Human Resource Management Journal* 12, 1092–106.

Guest, D. and Conway, N. 1997. *Employee Motivation and the Psychological Contract. Issues in People Management, 21*. London: IPD.

Guest, D. and Peccei, R. 1994. 'The Nature and Causes of Effective Human Resource Management'. *British Journal of Industrial Relations* 32, 219–41.

Guthrie, J., Spell, C. and Nyamori, R. 2002. 'Correlates and Consequences of High-Involvement Work Practices: The Role of Competitive Strategy'. *International Journal of Human Resource Management* 13(1), 183–97.

HBR (Harvard Business Review). 2008. *On Retailing and Merchandising*. Boston, MA: Harvard Business School Publishing Corporation.

Hackman, J.R. and Wageman, R. 2005. 'A Theory of Team Coaching'. *Academy of Management Review* 30(2), 269–87.

Hackman, J.R. and Walton, R.E. 1986. 'Leading groups in organizations.' In *Designing Effective Work Groups*, ed. P. Goodman. San Francisco: Jossey-Bass.

Haeckel, S.H. and Nolan, R.L. 1993. 'Managing by Wire'. *Harvard Business Review* 71(September–October), 122–32.

Hall, J. 2011a. 'Vive la Difference, says Tesco's New Supremo.' *Daily Telegraph*, 23 April, 35.

Hall, J. 2011b. 'Starbucks CEO Attacks Coffee Speculators.' *Daily Telegraph*, 11 (May), B1.

Hall, J. 2011c. 'The Sunday Interview; Kate Bostock M&S.' *Sunday Telegraph*, 22 (May), B9.

Hamel, G. 2000. 'Waking Up IBM: How a Gang of Unlikely Rebels Transformed Big Blue'. *Harvard Business Review* (July-August): 137–44.

Handy, C. 1994. *The Age of Paradox*. Boston, MA: Harvard Business School Press.

Harley, B. and Hardy, C. 2004. 'Firing Blanks? An Analysis of Discursive Struggle in HRM'. *Journal of Management Studies* 41(3), 377–400.

Harrison, R. 1972. 'How to Describe Your Organization's Culture'. *Harvard Business Review* (May-June): 119–28.

Haspeslagh, P. and Jemison, D. 1991. *Managing Acquisitions: Creating Value through Corporate Renewal*. NY: Free Press.

Hayes, R. 1979. 'The Human Side of Acquisitions'. *Management Review* 11, 41–46.

Heinicke, C.M. and Bales, R.F. 1953. 'Developmental Trends in the Structure of Small Groups'. *Sociometry* 16, 7–38.

Hemphill, J.K. 1949. *Situational Factors in Leadership*. Columbus: Ohio State University Bureau of Educational Research.

Hemphill, J.K. 1950. 'Relations between the Size of the Group and the Behavior of "Superior" Leaders'. *Journal of Social Psychology* 32, 11–22.

Hendry, C. and Pettigrew, A. 1990. 'Human Resource Management: An Agenda for the 1990s'. *International Journal of HRM* 1(1), 17–43.

Hersey, P. and Blanchard, K.H. 1993. *Management of Organizational Behavior: Utilizing Human Resources* 6th edn. NY: Prentice-Hall.

Heskett, J.L., Sasser, W.E. and Schlesinger, L.A. 2003. *The Value Profit Chain*. NY: The Free Press.

Higgs, M. and Rowland, D. (2001). 'Developing Change Leaders'. *Journal of Change Management* 2(1), 47–66.

Higgs, M. and Rowland, D. (2005) 'All Changes Great and Small: Exploring Approaches to Change and its Leadership'. *Journal of Change Management* 5(2), 121–152.

Hitt, M., Harrison, J. and Ireland, R. 2001. *Mergers and Acquisitions: A Guide for Creating Value for Shareholders*. NY: Oxford University Press.

Hooper, A. and Potter, J. 1999. 'Take it from the Top'. *People Management* 5(16), 46–49.

House, R.J. 1971. 'A Path-Goal Theory of Leadership Effectiveness'. *Administrative Science Quarterly* 16, 321–38.

Huczynski, A.A. and Buchanan, D.A. 2004. *Organisational Behaviour*. 5th Edn. Hemel Hempstead: Prentice Hall.

Hume, M. 2011. 'The Secrets of Zara's Success.' *Daily Telegraph*, 22 June, 23.

Huselid, M. 1995. 'The Impact of HRM Policies on Turnover, Productivity and Corporate Financial Performance'. *Academy of Management Journal* 38, 635–72.

Huselid, M. 1998. 'The Impact of HRM Policies on Turnover, Productivity and Corporate Financial Performance.' In *Strategic Human Resource Management*, eds C. Mabey, G. Salaman and J. Storey. NY: Sage.

Janis, I. 1972. *Victims of Groupthink*. Boston: Houghton Mifflin.

Jeffreys, J.B. 1954. *Retail Trading in Britain 1850–1950*. Cambridge: Cambridge University Press.

Jemison, D. and Sitkin, S. 1986. 'Corporate Acquisitions: A Process Perspective'. *Academy of Management Review* 11, 145–63.

Johnson, M. and Felsted, A. 2011. 'Inditex Keeps its Finger on the Pulse.' *Financial Times*, 23 (May), 13.

Johnston, R. 2001. *Service Excellence = Reputation = Profit*. Colchester: Institute of Customer Service Publications.

Johnston, R. and Clark, G. 2008. *Services Operations Management – Improving Service Delivery*. London: Pearson.

Jones, P. 1999. 'Multi-unit Management in the Hospitality Industry: A Late Twentieth Century Phenomenon'. *International Journal of Contemporary Hospitality Management* 11(4), 155–64.

Jones, P. and Inkinci, Y. 2001. *An analysis of multi-unit management in UK restaurant chains*. Proceedings from the 2001 CAUTHE National Research Conference, Queensland, Australia: Council for Australian University Tourism & Hospitality Education.

Jopson, B. 2012a. 'US Retailers Cut Forecasts Despite Gains.' *Financial Times*, 6 (January), 21.

Jopson, B. 2012b. 'New Look May Close 100 Stores.' *Financial Times*, 23 January, 18.

Judge, T.A., Bono, J.E., Ilies, R. and Gerhardt, M.W. 2002. 'Personality and Leadership: A Qualitative and Quantitative Review'. *Journal of Applied Psychology* 87(4), 765–80.

Kant, I. 1985. *Foundations of the Metaphysics of Morals* (L.W. Beck, trans.). London: Macmillan.

Keeley, G. 2012. 'How 50 Ideas a Day Help Keep the Customer Satisfied'. *Times*, 14 (April), 48.

Kelly, J. 1999. 'Social Partnership in Britain: Good for Profits, Bad for Jobs and Unions'. *Communication Review* 30, 3–10.

Kersley, B., Alpin, C., Forth, J., Bryson, A., Bewley, H., Dix, G. and Oxenbridge, S. (2006). *Inside the Workplace: Findings from the 2004 Workplace Employment Relations Survey*. London: Routledge.

Kickul, J. and Neuman, G. 2000. 'Emergence Leadership Behaviors: The Function of Personality and Cognitive Ability in Determining Teamwork Performance and KSAs'. *Journal of Business and Psychology* 15, 27–51.

Kirkpatrick, S.A. and Locke, E.A. 1991. 'Leadership: Do Traits Really Matter?' *Academy of Management Executive* (May): 48–60.

Kitching, J. 1967. 'Why do Mergers Miscarry?' *Harvard Business Review* (November): 84–101.

Klein, K.J., Ziegert, J.C., Knight, A.P. and Xiao, Y. 2006. 'Dynamic Delegation: Shared, Hierarchical, and Deindividualized Leadership in Extreme Action Teams'. *Administrative Science Quarterly* 51(4), 590–621.

Klemp, G.O. 1980. The assessment of occupational competence. Report to the National Institute of Education, Washington, DC, cited in R.E. Boyatzis (1982), *The Competent Manager: A Model for Effective Performance*. NY: Wiley.

Kobasa, S.C. 1979. 'Stressful Life-events, Personality and Health: An Inquiry into Hardiness'. *Journal of Personality and Social Psychology* 37(1), 1–11.

Kochan, T. and Barocci, T. 1985. *Human Resource Management and Industrial Relations: Texts, Readings and Cases*. Boston: Little, Brown.

Kotter, J.P. 1982. 'What Effective General Managers Really Do'. *Harvard Business Review* 60(6), 156–62.

Kotter, J.P. and Cohen, D.S. 2002. *The Heart of Change*. MA: Harvard Business School Press.

Kozlowski, S.W., Gully, S.M., Salas, E. and Cannon-Bowers, J.A. 1996. 'Team Leadership and Development: Theory, Principles, and Guidelines for Training Leaders and Teams.' In *Advances in Interdisciplinary Studies of Work Teams: Team leadership* Vol. 3. Elsevier Science/JAI Press.

Ladd, D. and Henry, R.A. 2000. 'Helping Co-workers and Helping the Organization: The Role of Support Perceptions, Exchange Ideology, and Conscientiousness'. *Journal of Applied Social Psychology* 30, 2028–49.

LaNuez, D. and Jermier, J.M. 1994. 'Sabotage by Managers and Technocrats: Neglected Patterns of Resistance at Work'. In *Resistance and Power in Organisations,* eds. J.M. Jermier, D. Knights and W.R. Nord. London: Routledge.

Larsson, R. 1989. *Organizational Integration of Mergers and Acquisitions.* Lund: Lund University Press.

Lashley, C. 1995a. 'Towards an Understanding of Employee Empowerment in Hospitality Services'. *International Journal of Contemporary Hospitality Management* 7(1), 27–32.

Lashley, C. 1995b. 'Empowerment Through Delayering: A Pilot Study at McDonald's Restaurants'. *International Journal of Contemporary Hospitality Management* 7(2/3), 29–35.

Lashley, C. 1997. *Empowering Service Excellence: Beyond the Quick Fix.* London: Cassell.

Lashley, C. 1999. 'Employee Empowerment in Services: A Framework for Analysis'. *Personnel Review* 28(3), 169–91.

Lashley, C. and Taylor, S. (1998) 'Hospitality retail operations types and styles in the management of human resources'. *Journal of Retailing and Consumer Services,* 5(3), 153–165.

Lawler, E.E. 1976. 'Control Systems in Organizations.' In *Handbook of Industrial and Organizational Psychology,* ed. M.D. Dunnette. NY: Rand McNally.

Lechner, C. and Kreutzer, M. 2010. 'Coordinating Growth Initiatives in Multi-Unit Firms'. *Long Range Planning* 43, 6–32.

Lee, R. and Lawrence, P. 1985. *Organizational Behaviour Politics at Work.* London: Hutchinson.

Lees, S. 2003. *Global Acquisitions: Strategic Integration and the Human Factor.* Basingstoke: Palgrave.

Legge, K. 1995a. *Human Resource Management: Rhetorics and Realities.* Basingstoke: Macmillan.

Legge, K. 1995b. 'HRM: Rhetoric, Reality and Hidden Agendas.' In *New Perspectives on Human Resource Management,* ed. J. Storey. London: International Thomson Business Press.

Legge, K. 1998. 'The Morality of HRM.' In *Experiencing Human Resource Management,* eds C. Mabey, D. Skinner and T. Clark. London: Sage.

Legge, K. 2001. 'Silver Bullet or Spent Round? Assessing the Meaning of the 'High Commitment Management'/Performance Relationship.' In *Human Resource Management: A Critical Text,* ed. J. Storey. London: Thomson Learning.

Legge, K. 2005. *Human Resource Management: Rhetorics and Realities (Anniversary Edition)*. Basingstoke: Palgrave Macmillan.

Leithwood, K., Day, C., Sammons, P., Harris, A. and Hopkins, D. 2006. *Successful School Leadership: What It Is and How It Influences Pupil Learning*. Nottingham: DfES Publications.

Leithwood, K., Steinbach, R. and Ryan, S. 1997. 'Leadership and Team Learning in Secondary Schools'. *School Leadership & Management* 17, 303–26.

Lengnick-Hall, C. and Lengnick-Hall, M. 1988. 'Strategic Human Resources Management: A Review of the Literature and a Proposed Typology'. *Academy of Management Review* 13, 454–70.

Levitt, T. 1972. 'Production-lining Service'. *Harvard Business Review* (June): 22–31.

Lewin, K. 1951. *Field Theory in Social Science*. NY: Harper and Row.

Lewin, K., Lippitt, R. and White, R. 1939. 'Patterns of Aggressive Behavior in Experimentally Created Social Climates'. *Journal of Social Psychology* 10, 271–301.

Liden, R.C., Sparrowe, R.T. and Wayne, S.J. 1997. 'Leader-member Exchange Theory: The Past and Potential for the Future.' In *Research in Personnel and Human Resources Management*, ed G.R. Ferris. Greenwich, CT: JAI.

Lindblom, C. 1959. 'The Science of Muddling Through'. *Public Administration Review* 19, 79–88.

Lord, R.G., De Vader, C.L. and Alliger, G.M. 1986. 'A Meta-analysis of the Relation between Personality Traits and Leadership Perceptions: An Application of Validity Generalization Procedures'. *Journal of Applied Psychology* 71(3), 402–10.

Lowe, J., Delbridge, R. and Oliver, N. 1997. 'High Performance Manufacturing: Evidence from the Automotive Components Industry'. *Organization Studies* 18(5), 783–98.

Lubatkin, M. 1983. 'Merger and the Performance of the Acquiring Firm'. *Academy of Management Review* 8, 218–25.

Lubatkin, M. 1987. 'Merger Strategies and Stockholder Value'. *Strategic Management Journal* 8, 39–53.

Lublin, J. and O'Brien, B. 1997. 'When Disparate Firms Merge, Cultures Often Collide.' *Wall Street Journal*, 11/09/07, 18.

McCartney, W.M. and Campbell, C.J. 2006. 'Leadership, Management and Derailment'. *Leadership and Organization Development Journal* 27(3), 190–202.

McClelland, D. 1973. 'Testing for Competence Rather than for Intelligence'. *American Psychologist* 28(1), 1–40.

McGrath, J.E. 1962. *Leadership behavior: Some requirements for leadership training*. Washington, D.C.: U.S. Civil Service Commission.

MacBeath, J., Oduro, G.K. and Waterhouse, J. 2004. *Distributed Leadership in Action: A Study of Current Practice in Schools*. Nottingham: National College for School Leadership.

MacDuffie, J. 1995. 'Human Resource Bundles and Manufacturing Performance: Organisational Logic and Flexible Production Systems in the World Automobile Industry'. *Industrial & Labor Relations Review* 48, 197–221.

Marchant, D.C., Polman, C.J., Clough, P.J., Jackson, J.G., Levy, AR. and Nicholls, A.R..2009. 'Mental Toughness: Managerial and Age Differences'. *Journal of Managerial Psychology* 24(5), 428–37.

Marginson, P., Armstrong, P., Edwards, P. and Purcell, J. 1995. 'Managing Labour in the Global Corporation: A Survey-Based Analysis of Multinationals Operating in the UK'. *International Journal of HRM* 6(3), 702–19.

Markowitz, H.M. 1959. *Portfolio Selection: Efficient Diversification of Investments*. NY: Wiley.

Marks, M. 1982. 'Merging Human Resources, A Review of Current Research'. *Mergers and Acquisitions* 17, 38–44.

Maslach, C., Schaufelli, W.B. and Leiter, M.P. 2001. 'Job Burnout'. *Annual Review of Psychology* 52, 397–422.

Mathias, P. 1967. *Retailing Revolution: A History of Multiple Retailing in the Food Trades Based upon the Allied Suppliers Group of Companies*. London: Europa Publications.

Mayer, J.D., Salovey, P., Caruso, D.R. and Sitarenious, G. 2001. 'Emotional Intelligence as Standard Intelligence'. *Emotion (Washington, D.C.)* 1, 232–42.

Mayer, J.D., Salovey, P., Caruso, D.R. and Sitarenious, G. 2003. 'Measuring Emotional Intelligence with the MSCEIT V2.0 Edition'. *Emotion (Washington, D.C.)* 3, 97–105.

Meeker, B.F. 1971. 'Decisions and Exchange'. *American Sociological Review* 36, 485–95.

Meyer, J.P. and Allen, N.J. 1991. 'A Three-component Conceptualization of Organizational Commitment: Some Methodological Considerations'. *Human Resource Management Review* 1, 61–98.

Miles, M. and Huberman, A. 1994. *Qualitative Data Analysis*. Thousand Oaks, CA: Sage.

Miles, R. and Snow, C. 1994. 'Designing Strategic Human Resources Systems'. *Organizational Dynamics* (Summer): 36–52.

Mintzberg, H. 1973. *The Nature of Managerial Work*. NY: Harper Row.

Mintzberg, H. 1979. *The Structuring of Organisations*. NY: Prentice Hall.

Mintzberg, H. 2009. *Managing*. London: Pearson.

Mintzberg, H., Ahlstrand, B. and Lampel, J. 1998. *Strategy Safari*. NY: Free Press.

Mirvis, P. and Marks, M. 1992. *Managing the Merger: Making it Work*. Englewood Cliffs, NJ: Prentice Hall.

Molm, L.D. 1994. 'Dependence and Risk: Transforming the Structure of Social Exchange'. *Social Psychology Quarterly* 57, 163–76.

Monaghan, A. 2012. 'UK economy picks up despite slower service growth'. *Daily Telegraph*, 5 (March), www.telegraph.co.uk [accessed: 6 March 2012].

Mone, M.A. and Umbreit, W.T. 1989. 'Making the Transition from Single-unit to Multi-unit Fast-service Management: What are the Requisite Skills and Educational Needs?'. *Journal of Hospitality & Tourism Research (Washington, D.C.)* 13(3), 319–31.

Morgeson, F.P. 2005. 'The External Leadership of Self-Managing Teams: Intervening in the Context of Novel and Disruptive Events'. *Journal of Applied Psychology* 90(3), 497–508.

Morris, S. and McDonald, R. 1995. 'The Role of Moral Intensity in Moral Judgements: An Empirical Investigation'. *Journal of Business Ethics* 14(9), 715–26.

Muller, C.C. and Campbell, D.F. 1995. 'The Attributes and Attitudes of Multi-unit Managers in a National Quick-service Restaurant Firm'. *Journal of Hospitality & Tourism Research (Washington, D.C.)* 19(2), 3–18.

Muller, C.C. and DiPietro, R.B. 2006. 'A Theoretical Framework for Multi-unit Management Development in the 21st Century'. *Journal of Foodservice Business Research* 9(2/3), 7–25.

Mutch, A. 2006. Allied Brewers and the Development of the Area Manager in British Brewing 1950–1984. *OUP: Business History Conference proceedings*, 15/02/06, 353–379.

Navandi, A. and Malekzadeh, A. 1988. 'Acculturation in Mergers and Acquisitions'. *Academy of Management Review* 13(1), 79–90.

Newman, J.E., Holti, R. and Standing, H. 1995. *Changing Everything at Once*. London: Tavistock Institute.

Nicholls, A.R., Polman, R.C., Levy, A. and Backhouse, S.H. 2008. 'Mental Toughness, Optimism, Pessimism and Coping Among Athletes'. *Personality and Individual Differences* 44(5), 1182–92.

Nonaka, I. and Takeuchi, H. 1995. *The Knowledge-Creating Company*. NY: Oxford University Press.

Nonaka, I. and Takeuchi, H. 2011. 'The Wise Leader'. *Harvard Business Review* (May): 58–67.

NSBA – National School's Board Association. 2006. *Ten characteristics of well functioning teams*, www.nsba.org/sbot/toolkit/LeadTeams.html [accessed 15 January 2011].

OECD. 2005. 'Growth in Services. Fostering Employment, Productivity and Innovation'. www.oecd.org/dataoecd/58/52/34749412.pdf [accessed 29 October 2011].

Olsen, M.D., Tse, E.C. and West, J.J. 1992. *Strategic Management in the Hospitality Industry*. NY: Van Nostrand Reinhold.

Orgland, M.Y. 1997. *Initiating, Managing and Sustaining Strategic Change*. London: Macmillan.

Paauwe, J. and Boselie, P. 2005. 'HRM and Performance: What Next?'. *Human Resource Management Journal* 15(4), 68–83.

Paauwe, J. and Richardson, R. 1997. 'Introduction to Special Issue on HRM and Performance'. *International Journal of HRM* 8, 257–62.

Pagano, M. 2011a. 'Business Interview; Andy Street, MD John Lewis.' *Independent on Sunday*, 11 (December), 86–87.

Pagano, M. 2011b. 'Death of the High Street? No, it's the Birth of the i-Street.' *Independent on Sunday*, 11 (December), 89.

Pagano, M. 2012. 'Tesco Must Decide: Price or Quality – or Both?' *Independent on Sunday*, 15 (January), 87.

Peach Report. 2011. *Trends: BrandTrack*. 8, 6–10.

Pearce, C. and Conger, J.A. 2003. *Shared Leadership: Reframing the Hows and Whys of Leadership*. London: Sage.

Peck, S. 1994. 'Exploring the Link Between Organisational Strategy and the Employment Relationship: the Role of Human Resource Policies'. *Journal of Management Studies* 31(5), 715–36.

Perlmutter, H. 1969. 'The Tortuous Evolution of the Multinational Firm'. *Columbia Journal of World Business* (January): 9–18.

Peters, T. and Waterman, R. 1982. *In Search of Excellence: Lessons from America's Best-Run Companies*. New York: Harper & Row.

Peters, T.J. 1980. 'A Style for All Seasons'. *Executive* 6(3), 12–16.

Pfeffer, J. 1994. *Competitive Advantage through People*. Boston, MA: Harvard Business School Press.

Pfeffer, J. 1998. *The Human Equation: Building Profits by Putting People First*. Boston, MA: Harvard Business School Press.

Polanyi, M. 1962. *Personal Knowledge*. NY: Harper.

Portas, M. 2011. Portas Report: Key Recommendations. www.guardian.co.uk [accessed: 13 December 2011].

Porter, M. 1980. *Competitive Strategy*. NY: Free Press.

Porter, M.E. 1987. 'Corporate Strategy: The State of Strategic Thinking'. *The Economist*, 23 May, 17–22.

Pugh, D. 1984. *Organisation Theory*. London: Penguin.

Purcell, J. 1999. 'Best Practice and Best Fit: Chimera or Cul-de-sac?'. *Human Resource Management* 9, 26–42.

Purcell, J. and Ahlstrand, B. 1994. *Human Resource Management in the Multidivisional Company*. Oxford: Oxford University Press.

Quinn, J.B. 1980. *Strategies for Change: Logical Incrementalism*. Homewood ILL. Irwin.

Quinn, R.E., Faerman, S.R., Thompson, M.P. and McGrath, M. 1990. *Becoming a Master Manager: A Competency Framework*. NY: Wiley.

Rankine, D. 1998. *A Practical Guide to Acquisitions*. Chichester: Wiley.

Reichheld, F. and Markey, R. (2011) *The Ultimate Question 2.0: How Net Promoter Companies Thrive in a Customer Driven World*. Boston, Mass: HBR Press.

Reynolds, D. 2000. 'An Exploratory Investigation into Behaviorally Based Success Characteristics of Foodservice Managers'. *Journal of Hospitality & Tourism Research (Washington, D.C.)* 24(1), 92–103.

Reynolds, J., Howard, E., Cuthbertson, C. and Hristov, L. 2007. 'Perspectives on Retail Format Innovation: Relating Theory and Practice'. *International Journal of Retail and Distribution Management* 35(8), 647–60.

Ritzer, G. 1993. *The McDonaldization of Society*. Thousand Oaks, CA: Sage.

Rivera, M., Di Pietro, R.B., Murphy, K.S. and Muller, C.C. 2008. 'Multi-unit Managers: Training Needs and Competencies for Casual Dining Restaurants'. *International Journal of Contemporary Hospitality Management* 20(6), 616–30.

Rugman, A.M. 1981. *Inside the Multinationals: The Economics of Internal Markets*. NY: Columbia Press.

Rugman, A.M. and Hodgetts, R.M. 2003. *International Busines*. London: Pearson.

Ryan, W.E. 1992. *Identification and comparison of management skills required for single and multi-unit management in independently operated college and university food services*, unpublished doctoral dissertation, Oklahoma State University, Stillwater.

Saks, A.M. 2006. 'Antecedents and Consequences of Employee Engagement'. *Journal of Managerial Psychology* 21(7), 600–12.

Sales, A. and Mirvis, P. 1984. 'When Cultures Collide: Issues in Acquisition.' In *The Challenge of Managing Corporate Transition*, eds J. Kimberly and R. Quinn. Homewood ILL.: Irwin.

Sanz-Valle, R., Sabater-Sánchez, R. and Aragón-Sánchez, A. 1999. 'Human Resource Management and Business Strategy Links: An Empirical Study'. *International Journal of HRM* 10(4), 655–71.

Sasser, W.E., Olsen, R.P. and Wyckoff, D.D. 1978. *Management of service operations: Text, cases and readings*. Boston, MA: Allyn and Bacon.

Schein, E. 1985. *Organizational Culture and Leadership: A Dynamic Review*. San Francisco: Josey-Bass.

Schmenner, R. 1986. 'How are Service Businesses to Survive and Prosper?'. *Sloan Management Review* (Spring): 21–32.

Schuler, R. and Jackson, S. 1987. 'Linking Competitive Strategies and Human Resource Management Practices'. *Academy of Management Executive* 1(3), 207–19.

Schwartz, I. 2007. 'Manage Your Energy, Not Your Time'. *Harvard Business Review* (October): 63–73.

Schweiger, D. 2002. *M&A Integration: A Framework for Executives and Managers*. New York: McGraw-Hill.

Schweiger, D. and Goulet, P. 2000. 'Integrating Acquisitions: An International Research Review.' In *Advances in Mergers and Acquisitions*, eds C. Cooper and A. Gregory. Greenwich, CT: Elsevier Press.

Schweiger, D. and Walsh, J. 1990. 'Mergers and Acquisitions: An Interdisciplinary View.' In *Research in Personnel and Human Resource Management*, eds K. Rowland and G. Ferris. Greenwich, CT: JAI Press.

Schweiger, D., Ivancevich, J. and Power, F. 1987. 'Executive Action for Managing Human Resources Before and After Acquisition'. *Academy of Management Executive* 1, 127–38.

Seligman, M. 2011. *Flourish*. Australia: William Heinemann.

Selznick, P. 1957. *Leadership in Administration. A Sociological Interpretation*. Evanston ILL: Peterson.

Seth, A. and Randall, G. 1999. *The Grocers: The Rise and Rise of the Supermarket Chains*. London: Kogan Page.

Sibun, J. 2011. 'Swann out to Prove There's Life After Penny Pinching'. *Daily Telegraph* 25(April), B4.

Simon, H.A. 1969. *The Sciences of the Artificial*. Cambridge, MA: MIT Press.

Sims, R. 1991. 'The Institutionalization of Organizational Ethics'. *Journal of Business Ethics* 10(7), 493–506.

Sirower, M. 1997. *The Synergy Trap*. NY: The Free Press.

Skinner, B.F. 1976. *About Behaviorism*. NY: Vintage Bodis.

Slack, N., Chambers, S., Johnston, R. and Betts, A. 2009. *Operations and Process Management – Principles and Practice for Strategic Intent*. London: Pearson.

Sorenson, H. 2010. *Inside the Mind of the Shopper* 4th edn. NJ: Pearson.

Spillane, J.P. 2006. *Distributed Leadership*. San Francisco, CA: Jossey-Bass.

Steiner, R. 2011. 'Room at the Top in Corporate UK.' *Daily Mail*, 23 November, 73.

Steiner, R. 2012a. 'Retail Chains Squeezed by Wary Lenders.' *Daily Mail*, 20 (January), 69.

Steiner, R. 2012b. 'McDonald's Profits from the Late Shift.' *Daily Mail*, 25 (January), 57.

Steiner, R. 2012c. 'Cheap own labels overtake branded goods at the shops'. *Daily Mail*, 23 (May), 11.

Storey, J. 1992. *Developments in the Management of Human Resources: An Analytical Review*. Oxford: Blackwell.

Suboleski, S. 2006. *Multi-unit restaurant management training: An exploratory study*. Unpublished Master's thesis, University of Nevada, Las Vegas.

Subramony, M. 2006. 'Why Organisations Adopt Some Human Resource Management Practices and Reject Others: An Exploration of Rationales'. *Human Resource Management* 45(2), 195–210.

Tannenbaum, A.S. 1968. *Control in Organizations*. NY: McGraw-Hill.

Taylor, F.A. 1916. *The Principles of Scientific Management*. NY: Harper.

Terazano, E. 2011. Screwfix Leads Web Order Race. *Financial Times*, 23 April, 6.

Tichy, N. 1983. *Managing Strategic Change*. NY: Wiley.

Tichy, N.M. and Bennis, W.G. 2007. 'Making Judgement Calls'. *Harvard Business Review* (October): 94–102.

Tily, G. (2006) 'Improvements to timely measures of service sector output'. *Economic Trends* 630, London: Office of National Statistics.

Toffler, A. 1970. *Future Shock*. NY: Pan Books.

Townley, B. 1994. *Reframing Human Resource Management: Power, Ethics and the Subject at Work*. London: Sage.

Truss, C. 2001. 'Complexities and Controversies in Linking HRM with Organisational Outcomes'. *Journal of Management Studies* 38(8), 1121–49.

Uhu-Bien, M. 2006. 'Relational Leadership Theory: Exploring the Social Processes of Leadership and Organizing'. *Leadership Quarterly* 17, 654–76.

Ulrich, D. 1997. *Human Resource Champions: The Next Agenda for Adding Value and Delivering Results*. Boston: Harvard Business School Press.

Umbreit, W.T. 1989. 'Multi-unit Management: Managing at a Distance'. *Cornell Hotel and Restaurant Administration Quarterly* 30(1), 53–59.

Umbreit, W.T. and Smith, D.I. 1991. 'A Study of the Opinions and Practices of Successful Multi-unit Fast Service Restaurant Managers'. *Hospitality Research Journal* 14, 451–58.

Umbreit, W.T. and Tomlin, J.W. 1986. Identifying and validating the job dimensions and task activities of multi-unit foodservice managers, *Proceedings of the 40th Annual Conference on Hotel, Restaurant, and Institutional Education*, August, 66–72.

Van Looy, B., Gemmel, P. and Van Dierdonck, R. 2003. *Services Management: An Integrated Approach*. London: Prentice Hall.

Van Velsor, E. and Leslie, J.B. 1995. 'Why Executives Derail: Perspectives Across Time and Cultures'. *Academy of Management Executive* 9(4), 62–72.

Vroom, V.H. and Yetton, P.W. 1973. *Leadership and Decision-Making*. Pittsburgh: University of Pittsburgh Press.

Wall, T. and Wood, S. 2005. 'The Romance of Human Resource Management and Business Performance, and the Case for Big Science'. *Human Relations* 58(4), 429–62.

Wallop, H. 2011. 'Its Buy Before You Try as the Fashion for Online Clothes Shopping Doubles.' *Daily Telegraph*, 15 (April), 13.

Wallop, H. 2012. 'Tesco to scale back hypermarkets to focus on web and small stores'. *Daily Telegraph*, 14 (April), 29.

Wallop, H. and Ruddick, G. 2012. 'End of the Race for Space.' *Sunday Telegraph*, 29 (January), B7.

Walsh, K. 2012. 'Tesco's Blueprint for Change.' *Sunday Times*, 15 (January), B7.

Walsh, K. and Goodman, M. 2011. 'Boots Strides Out Across the Globe.' *Sunday Times*, 30 (October), B7.

Walter, G. 1985. 'Culture Collisions in Mergers and Acquisitions.' In *Organizational Culture*, eds P. Frost, L. Moore, M. Reis. and C. Lundberg Beverly Hills, CA: Sage.

Watson, T.J. 1994. *In Search of Management: Culture, Chaos, and Control in Managerial Work*. London: Routledge.

Watson, T.J. 2002. *Organising and Managing Work: Organisational, Managerial and Strategic Behaviour in Theory and Practice*. London: Prentice Hall.

Welch, J. and Welch, S. 2005. *Winning*. NY: Harper Collins.

Weston, J., Chung, K. and Siu, J. 2001. *Takeovers, Restructuring and Corporate Governance*. New Jersey: Prentice Hall.

Weyer, M.V. 2012. 'Say Goodbye to the Folding Stuff'. *Daily Telegraph*, 20 (April), 21.

Whittington, R. 1993. *What is Strategy – And Does it Matter?* London: Routledge.

Wood, S. 1999. 'Human Resource Management and Performance'. *International Journal of Management Reviews* 1(4), 367–413.

Wood, Z. 2012. 'McJobs Aplenty as Fast-Food Outlets Push On with Expansion.' *The Observer*, 29 (January), B47.

Wright, P. and Gardner, T. 2003. 'Theoretical and Empirical Challenges in Studying the HR Practice–Firm Performance Relationship.' In *The New Workplace: People, Technology and Organisation*, eds D. Holman, T. Wall, C. Clegg et al. Chichester: Wiley.

Wright, P. and Heggerty, J. 2005. Missing Variables in Theories of Strategic Human Resource Management: Time, Cause and Individuals, *Working Paper Series 03–05, CAHRS, Cornell University*.

Wright, P. and McMahon, G. 1992. 'Theoretical Perspectives for Strategic Human Resource Management'. *Journal of Management* 18(2), 295–320.

Wright, P. and Snell, S. 1991. 'Toward an Integrative View of Strategic Human Resource Management'. *Human Resource Management Review* 1, 203–25.

Yin, R. 2003. *Case Study Research: Design and Methods*. Beverly Hills, CA: Sage.

Yukl, G. 2006. *Leadership in Organizations*. 6th edn. Upper Saddle River, NJ: Prentice Hall.

Zaccaro, S.J., Gulick, L.M. and Khare, V.P. 2008. 'Personality and Leadership.' In *Leadership at the Crossroads*, eds C. Hoyt, G. Goethals and D. Forsyth. Westport, CT: Praeger.

Zaccaro, S.J., Rittman, A.L. and Marks, M.A. 2001. 'Team Leadership'. *Leadership Quarterly* 12(4), 451–83.

Zaleznik, A. 1977. 'Managers and Leaders: Are They Different?'. *Harvard Business Review* (May–June): 67–78.

Index

Note: page numbers in *italics* refer to Figures.

Printed in Great Britain
by Amazon